DISCARD

A PROMISE
FOR BREANNA

OTHER BOOKS BY AL LACY

Angel of Mercy series:
A Promise for Breanna (Book One)
Faithful Heart (Book Two)

Journeys of the Stranger series:
Legacy (Book One)
Silent Abduction (Book Two)
Blizzard (Book Three)
Tears of the Sun (Book Four)

Battles of Destiny (Civil War series):
Beloved Enemy (Battle of First Bull Run)
A Heart Divided (Battle of Mobile Bay)
A Promise Unbroken (Battle of Rich Mountain)
Shadowed Memories (Battle of Shiloh)
Joy From Ashes (Battle of Fredericksburg)

THE ANGEL OF MERCY SERIES

A PROMISE FOR BREANNA

BOOK ONE

AL LACY

MULTNOMAH BOOKS

This book is a work of fiction. With the exception of recognized historical figures, the characters in this novel are fictional. Any resemblance to actual persons, living or dead, is purely coincidental.

A PROMISE FOR BREANNA
© 1995 by Lew A. Lacy

published by Multnomah Books
a part of the Questar publishing family

Edited by Rodney L. Morris
Cover design by David Carlson
Cover illustration by Ed Martinez

International Standard Book Number: 0-88070-797-6

Printed in the United States of America.

For information:
Questar Publishers, Inc.
Post Office Box 1720
Sisters, Oregon 97759

96 97 98 99 00 01 02 03 — 10 9 8 7 6 5 4 3

To Judi Young

My sweet little sister.
What a bright spot you are in my life!
I love you more than you will ever know.

PROLOGUE

I was born and raised in the Rocky Mountain West, and developed an interest in the history of my part of America at an early age. History books that told the romantic stories of the great migration westward seized and held my attention...and still do today.

In 1803 President Thomas Jefferson purchased what was known as the Louisiana Territory from France. Some Americans saw this as a gross extension of his authority as president, and though there was a great deal of controversy over the purchase amongst politicians in Washington, D. C., it did serve to turn America's eyes westward.

In 1804 Meriwether Lewis and William Clark set out on their expedition to explore the newly purchased land. They made maps and recorded information about the trees, plants, and animals of the vast territory. Returning to the East in 1807, they told of the many Indian tribes they had met and of bountiful plains, mountains, lakes, and rivers in what had been named "Oregon Territory."

Their stories aroused the interest of fur trappers, hunters, dreamers, and adventurers alike, and in the minds of government leaders, strengthened America's claim to the land.

In 1818 a treaty was signed between the United States and Great Britain fixing the northern border of the vast Oregon Territory at the 49th parallel from Lake of the Woods in Minnesota to the Rocky Mountains. The treaty provided for the joint occupation of the Territory and allowed for settlement and existence of fur trading companies of both nations.

In 1819 the Adams-Onis Treaty was signed between the United States and Spain setting the 42nd parallel as the southern boundary between the Oregon Territory and Mexico. Spain thus gave up her claim to any part of the region.

In 1824 the northern boundary was set when Russia agreed to the 54-40 parallel as Alaska's southern border, thus giving up her claim to the Oregon Territory. Only the United States and Great Britain still held claim to the area. Then in 1846 the British bowed out, and the vast region was left to the United States. Two years later the borders that today make up Oregon proper were set, and Oregon became an official United States Territory.

The Oregon Territory story was in all the Eastern newspapers, sparking interest in what kind of land lay at the other end of the continent. However, only fur traders and explorers ventured that direction. The now-famous mountain men such as Tom Fitzpatrick, Bill Sublette, Jed Smith, and Jim Bridger headed west in 1824. They blazed a trail toward Oregon, traversed South Pass in the rugged Rocky Mountains of southwestern Wyoming Territory, and made their way to Oregon, marking out a trail for others to follow.

In 1827, many easterners who wanted to go west and start new lives decided to aim for something closer than Oregon. They would go to New Mexico Territory. Independence, Missouri, became the jumping off place for those who would venture westward on what became known as the Santa Fe Trail.

Word began to spread about the trail blazed by Jim Bridger and his companions, kindling more interest in Oregon and California. By 1830 supply wagons were using Independence as their jumping off place to carry goods to the fur trappers and explorers. The wagons followed the Santa Fe Trail for a few days, then split northwestward toward the Platte River. In 1832, Captain Ben Bonneville led a small wagon train of men, using the same trail as the supply wagons, and headed toward Oregon.

Thus along with the Santa Fe Trail, the Oregon Trail had its roots at Independence, Missouri.

In 1836 two preachers, Dr. Marcus Whitman and Henry Spalding, headed west with their wives to take the gospel to the Cayuse and Nez Perce Indians in Oregon. Narcissa Whitman and Eliza Spalding became the first white women to cross the South Pass in Wyoming. During the next four years, other missionaries followed the Whitmans and Spaldings to Oregon.

In 1841 the first bona fide emigrant wagon train pulled out of Independence with people who planned to settle and make their homes in the West. They followed the Oregon Trail across Nebraska and Wyoming into Idaho, then at the base of Bear Mountain, the company split. Half of the wagons veered off toward California, while the other half proceeded on to Oregon. Thus was born the "California Trail" in Idaho's southeastern corner.

In 1842 Kit Carson led Lieutenant John C. Fremont's expedition toward Oregon. In 1845, Fremont went to Washington, D. C., and provided Congress a wealth of geographic information and presented them a topographical map of the trail from Missouri to Oregon.

In the mid 1840s, emigrants began moving westward. There was only a trickle of wagons at first, then the trickle turned into a steady stream. By the mid-1850s, it became a torrent. From that time through the 1870s, between 350,000 and 400,000 hardy pioneers followed the Oregon and California Trails to the "promised land."

As early as 1842, an Eastern newspaper columnist named Horace Greeley wrote, "Go West, young man, and grow up with the country." The Oregon and California Trails drew easterners like some giant magnet toward adventure, romance, excitement, and an opportunity to start a new life on their own land.

In 1849 came the California Gold Rush, which offered another opportunity—sudden riches. The California Trail led directly over the high Sierras into the Sacramento-San Francisco area, and in those rugged mountains were abundant gold veins.

Though the number of wagon trains dwindled in the 1880s and 1890s, thousands of people migrated westward, populating Colorado, Arizona, Nevada, Washington, Idaho, Montana, Wyoming, Nebraska, Kansas, the Dakotas, and Utah.

One reason the emigrants banded together in wagon trains was the Indian threat. Though a few tribes showed themselves friendly to the white intruders, most did not. By traveling together, the pioneers found relative safety in numbers. Indians were more hesitant to attack large trains than when they found only three or four wagons in a group.

Surprisingly, during the first five years of emigration (1840-1844), no deaths due to Indians were reported on the overland routes. Things changed in 1845. From that year through 1853, there were 227 reported deaths due to Indian attacks on the Oregon and California Trails. In the next six years (1854-1859), somewhere between 150 and 200 emigrants were killed by hostile tribes.

With the Indian Wars of the 1860s came more bloodshed for people who ventured west. The Indian threat remained severe in the early 1870s, and eased somewhat in the late 1870s and 1880s because of the forts that were built and occupied by cavalry units along the trails.

An even greater threat than the hostile Indians were accidents and disease. Many children died when they fell from wagons and were run over by the wheels or trampled by the draft animals. There were many reports of people killed by accidental gunshots and by drownings. Many women lost their lives giving birth. But the greatest killers were cholera, typhoid, dysentery, small pox, and a variety of unnamed fevers.

Unless there happened to be a medically trained person in a wagon train, little was known about sanitation. Opportunities for bathing and laundering were severely limited. Water supplies were often in close proximity to human and animal wastes, spoiled food and garbage, and putrefied animal carcasses. In some long stretches between water holes or streams, pure drinking water grew scarce, and people drank whatever water was available. Often, typhoid broke out in the trains shortly thereafter.

Historians estimate that from the early 1840s through the mid-1880s, some twenty-five thousand people died on the trails.

The ink of history, while faded some, is still legible along the Oregon, California, and Santa Fe Trails. Some of the grave markers are still there today.

Though fewer men than women kept diaries on the journeys, their diaries are different in simple and subtle ways. When women wrote of the decision to leave their homes in the East, it was almost always with anguish—a note conspicuously absent from the diaries of men.

Men wrote of excitement and adventure. They wrote in explicit detail of fighting Indians, hunting game, and of the challenge of the journey. The westward move became a test of manhood. Traveling the overland passages was a breaking away from the old life in the East, a chance to improve themselves and the status of their families in the West.

The women saw no adventure to their long, hard journeys. One in five women was in some stage of pregnancy when she rode away from the banks of the Missouri River. The majority of women who traveled the trails were under thirty-five, and most of those traveled with small children.

Their diaries are filled with the distress and heartache of

having to bury their children and husbands alongside the trails. It was especially hard when a woman was widowed on the trail. She wanted to go back east to family and friends, but was forced to keep moving west. The only wagons traveling east were supply wagons going back to fill up and return, and the drivers were reluctant to take on passengers, especially women and children.

Women's diaries are filled with the heartbreak of disease, accidents, deaths, and burials. As wives and mothers, their job was to care for the sick and the dying along the way. They were the actuaries of the trail, noting the cost of the westward movement in human life, tallying the miles with the lives that were lost. They recounted the mishaps, recording every accident, illness, and Indian atrocity that befell them on the journey. They wrote of the rainstorms, hailstorms, and duststorms. They wrote of the weariness, the sleepless nights, the poisonous snakes, the pesky mosquitoes, the mud, the heat, and the cold—and they recorded the births and deaths.

However bravely those gallant women started their westward journeys, however they mustered the courage and strength to meet the demands of each day, however they reached deep within themselves to appreciate the splendors of the scenery, they were intimately affected by the journey's dreadful toll.

I want to tell you the story of one such journey.

If you have read any or all of the first three books in my Journeys of the Stranger series, you are acquainted with the compassionate but plucky young nurse, Breanna Baylor. Blond, blue-eyed Breanna has captured the hearts of readers all across America, and even in foreign countries where the Stranger books have gone.

I have received letters and phone calls and have had face-to-face conversations with readers—male and female, young and old—who not only are intrigued by John Stranger, but have fallen in love with Breanna. So great has been the response that my publisher and I now give you Breanna in a new series of her own, the Angel of Mercy series.

1

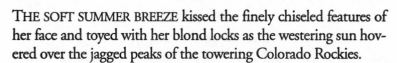

THE SOFT SUMMER BREEZE kissed the finely chiseled features of her face and toyed with her blond locks as the westering sun hovered over the jagged peaks of the towering Colorado Rockies.

Centuries before, the mighty hand of God had smoothed out the plains and rounded off the hills. He had compressed and arched the rock mantle of the earth, thrusting great masses of stone upward to altitudes twelve, thirteen, fourteen thousand feet above the level of the sea.

The sun shone into the thick forest of Ponderosa pine, blue spruce, and white-barked aspen, slanting lengthy shadows across the porch of the cabin where Breanna Baylor stood, looking toward the east. The hills that lined the open meadows to the east were dotted with clumps of small pines that thinned out as they touched the gentler slopes and hollows that made up the grassy meadow. Daisies and other wild flowers of various colors grew in the grass that carpeted the open fields.

The day Breanna had prayed for had finally come. After many long months of agony of soul, she was going to meet with John face to face and tell him how much she loved him. Her eyes searched the low, rolling hills, yearning to see horse and rider coming toward her.

Breanna had tried to form the exact words she would say, but the harder she tried to put them together, the more difficult it became. Practicing would not help. She would just have to let the words flow on their own. The main thing was to tell this man what a horrible mistake she had made in sending him out of her life...and to impress upon him that she loved him with every fiber of her being.

Because John had proven his love for her over and over again, she had no fear of rejection. He had agreed to meet her at the cabin, and she knew he would forgive her for that awful day in Wichita when she so foolishly sent him away.

Breanna reached into the pocket of her printed cotton dress and took out the note. She had probably read it a dozen times, but she wanted to read it again.

Dearest Breanna,

As you well know, whenever I have come to Denver, I have made contact with Dr. Goodwin to learn your whereabouts. When I arrived in town today, I was told by Chief U. S. Marshal Solomon Duvall that he had seen you earlier at the doctor's office. He told me that you had left a written message for Dr. Goodwin to give me next time I contacted him.

I waited until you had left the office for the day, then went in with my heart thundering, hoping that the message was that you had changed your mind since that day in Wichita, and wanted me back in your life.

Oh, how I have prayed that our Lord would give you back to me. I love you, Breanna, more than mortal words can ever express. Just give this stranger from a far land the opportunity, and I will shower you with so much love you'll be hunting for someplace to put it!

I will meet you tomorrow, as you requested, at Dr. Goodwin's cabin in the foothills an hour before sundown.

With abounding and unending love,

John

Breanna's lips quivered as she returned the note to her pocket. She took a hanky from the other pocket and dabbed the tears from her cheeks.

"Thank You, Lord," she breathed. "Thank You for giving me a man like John. The way he came into my life, there is no way I could doubt that You purposely crossed our paths."

Breanna's mind drifted back to the day it all started. Almost since the day she had earned her certificate as a Certified Medical Nurse, she had been doing the work of a "visiting nurse," moving about wherever assigned by her sponsoring physician, Wichita's Dr. Myron Hunter. After nursing Kansas farmer Will Scott back to health from a bad fall, she bid him and his wife Althea good-bye, then climbed into her buggy. She was about to leave when she heard the rumble of distant thunder. Across the Kansas plains to the northwest, dark thunderheads were gathering.

"Maybe you shouldn't go till the storm passes," Althea said.

"I'll be all right," she smiled. "If I put Nellie to a trot, we should beat the storm to Wichita."

"Well, on your way, then," Althea said. "If the storm catches you, pull into a farm house and wait it out."

"I will. Good-bye."

Breanna had been on the narrow, rutted road for an hour

when she topped a gentle rise and spotted a huge herd of cattle about a mile ahead of her. The herd was being driven south to the railhead at Wichita by a crew of shouting, whistling drovers.

The angry storm was closing in behind her. The sun had vanished moments before behind dark, rolling clouds, and lightning crackled in the north, followed by the rumble of thunder.

Breanna looked for a ranch or farm where she could go for shelter, but there was nothing in sight. She remembered a small community maybe three or four miles ahead. If she could get the drovers to clear a path for her through the herd, she could probably beat the heavy part of the storm to shelter.

Breanna put Nellie to a gallop and shortly drew up to the rear of the noisy herd. A pair of young cowpokes saw the buggy and rode up. "Howdy, ma'am," one of them said. "Were you needin' to get through?"

"Yes! That storm looks plenty mean. I need to get through as fast as possible."

"All right, follow us!"

Nellie showed nervousness as she pulled the buggy amid the milling, bawling cattle. Breanna noted the long, pointed horns that clattered as the steers jostled each other. She couldn't get past them fast enough. It took some ten minutes to bring the buggy out in front of the herd, but it seemed more like ten hours to Breanna. She thanked the drovers and put Nellie into a steady trot.

The entire sky was now black, and the wind was getting stronger. Breanna had gone another mile or so when lightning split the sky above her. Nellie whinnied and tossed her head, slowing down.

"No, Nellie!" shouted Breanna, snapping the reins. "Go, girl, go!"

Thunder clapped like a thousand cannons all around, and the frightened horse bolted, heading straight south on the road. The buggy bounced and fishtailed. Breanna screamed at Nellie to slow down and pulled back on the reins with all her might. Suddenly the crazed animal veered off the road and plunged down a grassy slope. There was a two-foot-deep ditch some eight-feet wide at the bottom of the slope. Breanna saw the ditch yawning at her and braced herself for the impact.

The buggy hit the ditch full-force and came to a sudden stop against the far bank, sending Breanna headlong into a patch of long, thick grass. Nellie bounded across the field dragging reins, harness, and singletree behind. The buggy was dug into the bank, with both front wheels broken.

Breanna scrambled to her feet, her heart pounding and her breath coming in short gasps. She was a bit dizzy and bruised, but the soft bed of grass had saved her from serious injury.

Breanna made her way back to the road. Rain began to fall, driven by the fierce wind. All she could do was keep going south and hope to find shelter.

As Breanna stumbled along the road, the rain pelting her face, she heard something different than wind, lightning, and thunder. It took her a few seconds to place its source, but when she looked behind her, she found it. It was the sound of rushing hooves. The lightning had frightened the cattle, and they were stampeding straight toward her. There was nowhere to run. An overpowering helplessness took possession of her, a foreboding of death.

The herd was no more than two hundred yards away. Breanna thought of the ditch at the side of the road, but the solid wall of wild-eyed cattle told her it could offer no protection.

Frozen with terror, Breanna steeled herself for what was

coming. Then something out of the corner of her eye caught her attention. It looked at first like some kind of apparition speeding toward her, but it quickly crystallized into a horse and rider. The horse was jet-black, and the man in the saddle was dressed in black.

The cattle and the rider were closing in fast. The front line of steers was so close, Breanna could see the whites of their bulging eyes. Horror and panic stabbed her heart. She could scarcely breathe.

The herd was no more than fifty yards away when the horse drew near. The rider leaned from the saddle and snatched her off the ground, holding her tight against him as they veered to the right and headed south.

The black gelding quickly put space between itself and the deathly horns and hooves. The space widened the more as the gallant horse carried its master and Breanna Baylor on a beeline south, outrunning the danger. When the horse settled into a smooth lope, the rider shouted above the sounds of the storm and herd, "Get a good hold around my neck, ma'am! I'll swing you up behind me!"

Breanna had been clutching the arm that held her. Letting go one hand at a time, she reached up and wrapped her arms around the man's neck. He twisted in the saddle and swung her up behind him. Breanna clung to him with one hand and used the other to adjust her skirt, then wrapped both arms around his waist. Breanna looked behind to see the herd losing ground. The big black was pulling farther and farther ahead.

"You all right, ma'am?"

"Yes, thanks to you!"

Rain continued to pour down from the heavy sky. Horse,

rider, and passenger were soaked. Water from his hatbrim sprayed Breanna in the face, but she didn't care. The Lord had sent this man from out of nowhere to save her. Silently she thanked Him.

"We're safe, now," the rider told her over his shoulder.

"Yes, thank the Lord!"

"That's right! Thank the Lord!"

"And thank you!"

"No need to thank me. I was just doing my job. We'll be in Wichita shortly. Ebony can run like this for hours."

"How do you know I want to go to Wichita?" Breanna asked, blinking against the spray in her eyes.

"That's where you live, isn't it?"

"So you're from Wichita, too?"

"No, ma'am."

"Then how do you know I live there?"

The man in black did not reply.

They passed through the small community where Breanna had intended to seek shelter. Everyone was inside, out of the storm.

"So your horse's name is Ebony?"

"Yes. Fits him, don't you think?"

"Perfectly! He's as black as any ebony wood I've ever seen." She paused a moment, then asked, "Could he really run like this for hours with my extra weight on board?"

The stranger laughed. "You're lighter than a feather, ma'am. He doesn't even notice you!"

Some time later Wichita came into view. Lightning bolts

were still chasing each other across the sky, and the deep-throated thunder continued to rumble. When they reached the edge of town, the rider slowed his horse and trotted him onto Broadway. There was little traffic on Broadway or any of the side streets.

"I live on Kellogg Street, west of Broadway a block and a half," Breanna said, freeing a hand to wipe rain from her eyes.

Breanna cast a glance at the Arkansas River off to her right. It was swollen and muddy. Her mind went to Nellie. She loved the horse and hoped Nellie was all right. Her heart felt heavy at losing her. There was no way of knowing how far she had run, or which direction she might have gone after Breanna last saw her.

And then there was her medical bag. It might still be intact, unless the steers had slammed into the wagon. She was sure Dr. Hunter would understand and replenish her supplies without charge, but it would be up to her to purchase a new bag. She was thankful that the Scotts had paid her generously.

Breanna had not noticed when they turned onto Kellogg Street, but she did notice when the man who had saved her life hauled up in front of the boarding house where she lived, and dismounted. "Well, here you are, ma'am. Safe and sound. Wet...but safe and sound."

Breanna had not realized how tall he was until he eased her down beside him. She was four inches over five feet, and it was evident that he stood more than a foot taller. She noticed twin jagged scars on his right cheek. His eyes were silver-gray and seemed to penetrate to the center of her soul. He had coal-black hair and wore his sideburns to the middle of his ears. His dark temples showed a few flecks of gray, and he was clean-shaven except for a well-trimmed mustache. She estimated him to be somewhere around forty, maybe even a little younger...some nine or ten years older than she. The stranger's craggy, angular features were handsome in their own way.

Breanna wanted to ask him how he knew where she lived, but could not work up the courage. Instead, she thanked him for saving her life, then told him her name and that she was a visiting nurse. But something inside told her he already knew all that. She had never met a man like him.

There was still no movement on the rolling hills east of the cabin. Breanna turned and looked at the sun. It would touch the tips of the tallest peaks in another twenty minutes or so.

She let her mind return to that day in Wichita when the strange man accepted her invitation to come back the next evening for supper. When she mentioned that he had not told her his name, he said in his deep, soft voice, "You can call me John."

John did not volunteer his last name to her at all that day, nor did he reveal what it was as they spent more and more time together. It was some time later when she learned that people who knew him called him John Stranger.

She smiled to herself as she recalled how John showed up for supper that next night with Nellie, a new buggy, and her medical bag.

Breanna thought of all the times she and John had spent together in the next few months, and of how his presence was both comforting and disconcerting. There was a gentleness in him she had never seen in a man, yet a mysterious aura kept her off balance. That, however, began to fade as they became better acquainted, and she recalled the expression in his iron-gray eyes that drew her like a magnet.

The more time they spent together, the weaker she found her resistance to him. John was making his feelings known to her, and it was apparent that he was falling in love.

Breanna began to struggle with her own feelings. Her heart had been deeply wounded by a man named Frank Miller, and the scars were still there. After a sweet courtship of many months, Frank had proposed marriage, and Breanna had invested her love and all her hopes for the future on him. Shortly after the engagement, she had heard the gospel of Jesus Christ and opened her heart to Him. As a new Christian, she desired Frank to be saved also, but her Christian friends advised her to be "wise as a serpent and harmless as a dove" in her approach to him. Coming on too strong too soon could drive him away.

Breanna prayed daily that God would give her wisdom, and she dropped "a word fitly spoken" now and then, relating to Frank the joy and peace she knew since opening her heart to Jesus. He listened as if he were interested, and Breanna had hopes of seeing Frank become a Christian before the wedding.

And then her whole world fell apart. Out of the blue, Frank sat Breanna down and calmly announced that he was going to marry another woman. He gave no reason, only that he had fallen in love with someone else. Frank Miller walked out of her life, never to return.

After the pain eased and Breanna picked up the pieces of her life, she vowed to never again let such a thing happen to her. No man would ever hurt her again. She would bury herself in her medical work and never be involved romantically with another man.

John Stranger was a wonderful man, she knew, but he was still a man. If she let herself, she would fall in love with him. *But she would never let it happen.*

As time passed, Breanna realized she was letting her guard down a little at a time. Each time she and John were together, she found it harder to let him go. Finally, she told herself the only thing to do was to break it off. It wasn't fair to him to string him along in a relationship that would lead nowhere.

Breanna let her mind return to that cold, bleak November day just four months after John Stranger had saved her from the stampede.

The sky was heavy and the wind brisk when John Stranger came to the boarding house to see Breanna after being gone for a couple of weeks. She steeled herself for what she must do and explained that she would have to be at Dr. Hunter's office in about an hour. They could walk down by the river, but from there she would have to head for the doctor's office. John understood and decided to take Ebony along.

They chatted about Breanna's latest nursing jobs while John led his horse along the streets. When they reached the east bank of the river, Breanna's stomach was in knots. She swallowed hard, knowing this was the moment she would do what she had to do. She cleared her throat nervously, then looked John in the eye. "John, I…I have to tell you something."

"All right," he nodded.

"I…John, this is very difficult for me, but…I've come to a decision."

"About what?"

"John, you saved my life, and I'll always be grateful. You've been so kind and good to me, and I could never thank you enough. But…I'm asking you not to come and see me anymore."

"You mean...never?"

"Never, John. I...I find myself growing more attracted to you than I should. I can never trust my heart to another man. Please try to understand."

"I'm not sure I will ever understand, Breanna," John said with obvious hurt in his eyes.

"Please try," she said in a choked, half-whisper. "This is the way it has to be. Please don't make it any more difficult for me than it already is."

She had told him of Frank Miller, but Stranger had hoped she would not let the scars from that wound keep her from falling in love with him. His words came out in a solemn monotone. "All right, Breanna. If that's the way you want it, I'll move on. I'm sorry for what Frank did, but his jilting you for that other woman doesn't mean all men are like him."

He turned to his horse and swung into the saddle, then looked down at her through misty eyes. "Good-bye, lovely lady. I will be out of your life, but you will never be out of my heart. From time to time, I may be looking at you, but you'll never know I'm near. I'll respect your request."

With that, John Stranger wheeled Ebony about and trotted toward the center of town.

Tears welled up in Breanna's eyes as she watched horse and rider diminish in size. They were not yet out of sight when she realized she had made a horrible mistake. She was not on the verge of falling in love with John, she already had! His name was on her lips over and over again as she reached toward him. Then he vanished from her sight.

Breanna wept as she walked toward town. "Oh, dear God," she sobbed, "what a fool I am. John loves me. I know he does.

And I love him, with all my heart! And now I've sent him out of my life forever!"

She struggled to control her emotions as she walked slowly toward the doctor's office. She would not want Dr. Hunter or his staff to know she had been crying. Arriving at the office, Breanna approached the receptionist's desk.

"Hello, Breanna," Rachel Franklin said cheerfully. "You're just in time. I have the list made up for you."

"Johnny-on-the-spot, aren't you?" Breanna smiled as Rachel placed an envelope in her hand.

"I try to be. From that list, it looks like you'll be plenty busy."

"Good. I need to keep busy."

Rachel cocked her head and squinted. "Breanna, are you all right?"

"Why, yes. Why do you ask?"

"Well, you just seem a bit melancholy or something."

"I'm fine. Thanks for asking, though."

"Oh! Wait a minute," Rachel exclaimed, pushing aside a stack of papers on her desk. "This is for you."

Rachel picked up a white handkerchief that was folded around something about the size of a silver dollar. Extending it to Breanna, she said, "A tall, dark-haired man came in here a few minutes ago and asked me to give you this."

"Oh. Thank you."

When she was back on the street, Breanna paused and unfolded the handkerchief. The object was exactly the size of a silver dollar and was made of pure silver. It was a medallion. Emblazoned in its center was a five-point star, and around the edge were the words: *THE STRANGER THAT SHALL COME*

FROM A FAR LAND—Deuteronomy 29:22.

Breanna was crying again. People stared as they passed by her on the street, but no one stopped.

"John, what does this mean?" she said, voice quivering. "Where are you from? Oh, I've made such a horrible mistake! I love you, John! I love you!"

Movement on the rolling hills to the east captured Breanna Baylor's attention. The sun was halfway behind the Rockies, throwing its golden hue on the land. She kept her eyes on the tiny speck in the distance while pulling a silver medallion from one of her dress pockets. She read its inscription for the thousandth time.

Breanna had more than a half-dozen of the medallions. John Stranger had kept his promise to look in on her while keeping himself from her sight. Twice he had saved her from certain death, and several other times he had rescued her from danger. On each occasion, he had left behind one of the silver medallions, just to let her know he had been there.

Breanna raised her eyes and focused on the object moving fast toward her. A few more seconds and she could tell it was a rider on a huge black horse.

It was John. He was coming as fast as Ebony could carry him!

Breanna's heart drummed her ribs. A sweet warmth welled up within her. The long-awaited moment had finally arrived. "Thank You, Lord," she whispered, thumbing away tears. "Thank You for bringing John back to me. Please...help me to say just the right words."

Horse and rider were now less than a hundred yards from the cabin. John was dressed in his black flat-crowned hat, white shirt with string tie, black pants, and shiny black boots. She knew his Bible would be in a saddlebag and the Colt .45 would still ride his hip in a tied-down holster.

Suddenly Breanna could hear the birds singing in the trees overhead. The smell of the pine on the warm breeze was sweeter than it had ever been before. The whole world seemed brighter. The man she loved was coming to her. Soon she would be in his arms.

Ebony nickered as he carried the tall man closer. The horse's hoofbeats seemed to pound in rhythm with Breanna's heart. Stranger smiled as he reined in. Breanna smiled back and stepped off the porch. For a brief moment, Stranger looked down at her from the saddle, his expressive gray eyes conveying the love that was in his heart for the woman who stood below him, tears spilling down her cheeks.

John slowly dismounted and looked into her eyes. She took three faltering steps, and they were within arm's reach of each other.

John reached a hand toward her. "Breanna..." He said her name softly, waiting for her to meet his hand.

She reached out to him. Their fingers touched. They stood there for a moment, hands touching, looking into each other's eyes. It seemed to be happening in a silent, far-away world out of the realm of time.

John squeezed her hand and pulled her close. She relinquished herself to his arms, and the dam within her burst. Her words came in sobs.

"Oh, John, my darling John! I love you! I made such a horrible mistake that day I sent you out of my life. Please forgive me, John! I've been so—"

John's forefinger was on her lips. "Shh," he said. "You don't have to do this. All that matters is that I know you love me as I love you...that we can have each other. There's nothing to forgive."

Breanna pushed back gently so as to look into his eyes. "Oh, but there is! I did you wrong! I hurt you deeply! I knew it by the look in your eyes. Oh, John...you weren't even out of sight yet when I realized what a fool I was. I called to you, but you didn't hear me. Then when I went to the office and Rachel gave me the medallion—"

"Don't punish yourself, Breanna," John said softly. "You don't have to think about it anymore, and you don't have to say anymore."

"Oh, but I do! You've been so good to me...over and over again. Nobody could blame you if you just up and washed your hands of me."

"But I couldn't do that, Breanna. I love you with everything that's in me. When I told you that even though I would be out of your life, you would never be out of my heart, I meant it."

"Yes, John, and you have proven it repeatedly." Breanna reached up and touched his cheek, then said in a half-whisper, "And I love you, my darling. If you gave me what I deserve and sent me away forever, I would still love you. I will always love you."

John leaned down, and Breanna closed her eyes as his arms tightened around her once again. Tenderly, he kissed her eyelids, then her lips.

Suddenly there was a loud banging noise behind her. It sounded as if someone was pounding on the cabin door.

Breanna sat bolt upright in bed. There was darkness all around her. The pounding continued, this time punctuated by a male voice.

"Miss Breanna! Miss Breanna! It's Deputy Wally Frye, ma'am! Marshal Stone sent me to get you! We have an emergency!"

"All right!" she called toward the hotel room door. "I'll be with you in a moment!"

"Thank you," came the deputy's relieved voice. "I'll wait right here!"

"Fine!" Breanna called.

She threw back the covers and sat up, rubbing her eyes. She fumbled for a match on the bedstand, scratched it into life, and lit the kerosene lantern. The ticking clock next to the lantern told her it was two-thirty in the morning.

Five minutes later, Breanna was dressed, heading for the door, medical bag in hand. Her dream still haunted her. She could almost smell John's masculine scent, feel his arms around her, taste the sweetness of his lips on her own.

She turned the skeleton key and opened the door. "What's the emergency, Wally?"

"A wagon train pulled into town a few minutes ago, Miss Breanna. There's a woman in the train about to give birth to a baby, but she's having some problems. Her husband is beside himself with worry."

"Where is she?"

"They're carryin' her to your office right now."

2

✧

BREANNA BAYLOR and Deputy Marshal Wally Frye hastened along the dimly lit main street of South Pass, Wyoming. Kerosene lanterns were positioned at intervals sixty feet apart along the boardwalk. It was two blocks from the Sweetwater Hotel to the clinic. Breanna's skirt made a swishing sound as they hurried down the street.

South Pass City was the halfway point between the Missouri River and the West Coast. Wagon trains that launched their westward treks from Independence or St. Joseph, Missouri, depended heavily on the merchants of South Pass City to replenish their food and supplies. This was no problem, for gold had been discovered near the town, and along with several saloons and gambling casinos, there were plenty of merchants to meet the needs of the wagon trains.

From South Pass City, the pioneers would travel southwest a hundred and twenty miles to Fort Bridger. From there, they would veer on a northwesterly course a hundred and forty miles to the north tip of Bear Lake in Idaho Territory's extreme southeast corner. At that point, the Oregon Trail split in two. The southern trail became the California Trail, and the Oregon Trail continued northwest to Oregon.

Breanna Baylor had moved to Denver from Wichita shortly after sending John Stranger out of her life. She attached herself to Dr. Lyle Goodwin's office there, and received her assignments from him. All Certified Medical Nurses who worked as "visiting nurses" were required to work under the sponsorship of a practicing physician.

Breanna had enjoyed working under Dr. Goodwin's sponsorship and was held in his highest regard, both as a nurse and as an intelligent, compassionate human being.

She had been sent to South Pass City the last week of June to fill in for elderly Dr. Allen Rudd, who had taken sick and died. It was now the third week of July. A new young doctor named Everett Wall was on his way from back East to take over Dr. Rudd's practice, and was to arrive soon.

To qualify as a Certified Medical Nurse, Breanna had worked for twenty-eight months with one or more physicians. She had helped them perform many kinds of surgery and had worked side by side with them, setting broken bones, treating various diseases, patching up gunshot wounds, and delivering babies. In addition, the experience gained in her work since receiving her certificate had placed her in Dr. Goodwin's mind as the best-qualified nurse to fill in at the South Pass City clinic until Dr. Wall could get there.

A single Conestoga wagon stood in front of the clinic, its canvas top yellowed by the soft glow of a nearby street lamp. The ox team looked on as nurse and deputy moved swiftly to the door, where South Pass's town marshal, Bill Stone, stood waiting for them in the warm night air.

"Sorry to get you out of bed, Miss Breanna," Stone said, "but we've got a little gal in here who's about to have a baby, and there seems to be some complications."

"No need to apologize, Marshal," Breanna smiled, moving past him into the office. "It's to be expected in my profession."

Both lawmen followed Breanna through the waiting room and into the clinic. A large man stood beside the examining table with his back toward the door. On the table lay a small woman, gripping his hand so hard her knuckles were white. Her face was twisted in a mask of pain.

The man turned to look as Breanna entered the room. Worry was evident in his eyes. On the opposite side of the table stood a young woman, whose features were also lined with concern.

Marshal Stone hurried ahead of Breanna and said to the man, "Larry, this is Nurse Baylor. I'm sure she'll be able to take care of your wife."

Breanna set her medical bag on a nearby counter which was built around a long-handled water pump. Next to the pump was a water bucket, and nearby were metal pans and other medical items. Beside the counter stood a tall cabinet with glass doors, revealing medicines, antiseptics, bandages, and the like.

"How far along is she?" Breanna asked as she drew up beside the young woman.

"She's in her ninth month, ma'am," the worried husband said.

"This is her first child, I assume."

"Yes, ma'am."

"What's her name?"

"Lawanda Hughes, and this here's Carolyne Fulford. She's been the midwife in our wagon train ever since we crossed the Missouri in April."

"Hello, Carolyne," Breanna smiled. "You're awfully young to be delivering babies."

"I'm twenty-three, Miss Baylor," Carolyne said. "My father is a physician in St. Louis, and I've assisted him with somewhere between sixty and seventy childbirths. There are older women in the wagon train who've acted as midwives, but none with my experience, so I was elected before we ever crossed the river into Kansas. I've delivered four babies since we started this journey to California."

Lawanda drew her legs up, sucked air through her teeth, and wailed.

"You've brought Lawanda here because there are complications?" Breanna asked Carolyne.

"Yes, ma'am. She's been in labor for about an hour, but I think she's going to have a real problem delivering. The cervix..." She looked up at Larry, then at the marshal and deputy. "Wouldn't it be best if the men sat out in the waiting room?"

"I was about to suggest that," Breanna nodded, smiling.

Larry held onto Lawanda's hand and set worried eyes on the nurse. "Ma'am, I'd really rather not leave her."

"I understand how you feel," Breanna said, "but I can do my work better if you'll wait with Marshal Stone and Deputy Frye in the outer office. Once I've made an assessment, I'll come and talk to you."

"Okay," he said reluctantly. "But if she calls for me, you come and get me."

"Will do," Carolyne smiled.

The three men entered the outer office and closed the door. Breanna took hold of the expectant mother's hand and said, "You're as pretty as your name, Lawanda."

Lawanda's face was pale, but she managed a "thank you" through clenched teeth.

Breanna felt Lawanda's abdomen with experienced, probing fingers. "How far are you into your ninth month?"

"If we had it figured right, I'm within a week of the time the baby is due."

Breanna nodded, moved to the end of the table, and took hold of the hem of Lawanda's dress. "I assume, Carolyn, you were about to tell me her cervix is not dilating properly."

"Yes. I'm really worried. We pulled the wagon train to a halt just east of town at sundown. Lawanda was having some noticeable discomfort then, but it only got worse as night fell. The water came, and her real labor began, as I said, just over an hour ago. When I saw that the cervix was not dilating normally, I told Larry we should bring her into town to the doctor."

Carolyne stood by quietly while Breanna made her examination. When she was finished, she said, "Lawanda, Carolyne's assessment was right on target. Your cervix is not dilating as it should. I won't beat around the bush with you. Unless your baby is brought by Cesarean section, your life and the baby's are in peril. Do you understand?"

Breanna's hands were once again on Lawanda's midsection, and she could feel the rigid tension take over. The sound that came from Lawanda's throat was something between a sob and a cry of fear.

Breanna pulled Lawanda's skirt down to her ankles and said to Carolyne, "Would you bring Larry in?"

Carolyne went to get Larry Hughes, and Breanna looped a white apron over her head and tied it around her waist.

Larry bolted into the room with Carolyne following. Eyes wide, he looked at Lawanda, then at Breanna. "Carolyne said you wanted to talk to me."

"Yes. We have a serious situation here, and I'm going to have to perform a Cesarean section to try to save the lives of your wife and child. Do you know what a Cesarean section is, Larry?"

"I've heard of it, but I don't really know what it is."

"It's the surgical removal of the baby from the uterus through an abdominal incision," Breanna said. "I'll have to cut through Lawanda's abdomen and remove the baby that way. Her cervix is just not opening enough for a normal birth."

"Oh."

"I want you and Lawanda to understand that I am only a nurse. No medical school has given me a doctor's degree and pronounced me qualified to do this. I have aided doctors on five occasions when they have performed Cesarean sections, but I've never done one myself. I haven't asked Carolyne yet, but since she's a midwife, I'm sure she'll be glad to help me. I won't do it, however, unless I have permission from both you and Lawanda."

Larry stepped close to the table and took hold of Lawanda's hand.

"I don't know a lot about it, Larry," spoke up Carolyne, "but I know Miss Baylor is telling you the truth. This procedure is the only earthly hope you've got, and it's important that she get started right away."

Larry looked down at Lawanda. "Okay, sweetheart?"

Lawanda's pain kept her mouth in a tight line. "Yes," she nodded.

"All right," said Breanna. "Larry, please wait in the outer office. You'll hear the baby cry, but please don't come in until we call for you. I'll have to stitch Lawanda up after the baby's born, and I want to keep it as sterile as possible in here."

"Will you put her out so she doesn't feel the surgery?" he asked.

"Of course. I'll use chloroform. She's not as liable to get sick to her stomach as she would if I used ether."

Larry looked down at Lawanda and said, "I'll be praying, honey."

Breanna smiled. "How about if we stop and pray together right now?"

"I'd like that, ma'am," Larry said.

Breanna took hold of Lawanda's other hand and led in prayer, asking the Lord to give her wisdom and to guide her hands as she performed the operation. When she finished, Larry quickly left the room.

"Now I know why I have such a good feeling about you," Carolyne said. "You're a Christian."

"That's right. The born-again, blood-washed kind."

"I am too," Carolyne said.

"So am I," Lawanda said. "I'm only a few months old in the Lord, but I know He can see the baby and me through this. Larry's not saved yet, but he's thinking strong on it. I was so glad to hear him say he would be praying for the baby and me."

"Maybe the Lord will use this situation to work on Larry's heart," Breanna said.

Lawanda went into another spasm of pain, and Breanna turned to the cupboard and pulled out the proper instruments for performing the operation. She quickly built a fire in a small stove that stood in the corner and put the instruments in a pan of water to boil. While the water was heating, she began preparing the chloroform.

"What can I do to help?" Carolyne asked.

"As soon as I have this chloroform ready, I'll want you to work the water pump while I wash my hands."

"*While* you wash your hands? You aren't going to just pump water into a basin and wash them?"

"No. I learned something about germs from my sponsoring doctor in Denver—that is, from Dr. Lyle Goodwin *and* from God's Word."

"What's that?"

"I learned that to get my hands germ-free, I must wash them in running water. No time to explain right now, but you might want to take a look sometime at Numbers 19. Actually, the Bible has quite a lot to say about disease prevention. Maybe we can talk about it sometime."

"I'd like that."

When the instruments had been duly sterilized and everything else was ready, Carolyne worked the water pump while Breanna washed her hands with lye soap. The chloroform was administered, and whe Lawanda was sufficiently under, the surgery began.

Breanna's steady hands worked fast but accurately. Within a very few minutes, the baby girl was free of the uterus. Breanna tied a thin, sterilized length of rawhide to the umbilicus an inch and a half from the baby's fat belly. Nimble fingers picked up a sharp knife from the instrument pad and cut the umbilical cord just above the knotted rawhide. Breanna smiled and gave the little wet rump a quick slap. Baby Hughes sucked in her first breath of air and ejected a shrill cry.

Breanna handed the tiny girl to Carolyne, who was prepared with warm water to clean her up. The placenta was quickly discarded, and Breanna worked fast to suture up the incision.

When the mother had been cleaned up and covered and the baby was ready for display, Larry Hughes was called in.

He eyed the tiny one in Carolyne's arms, wrapped in a blanket, and shot a glance at Lawanda, who lay, eyes closed, on the table.

Breanna smiled and said, "Your wife and baby are fine, Larry. You have a little daughter. I estimate she'll weigh about six pounds."

Larry grinned from ear to ear. "A daughter, huh? Well, I said all along I didn't care whether it was a boy or a girl, as long as he or she was healthy."

"She's a healthy one," Breanna said. "Did you and Lawanda have a name picked out?"

"Yeah, but I think we'll want to change it. She was to be named after one of Lawanda's favorite school teachers, but I'd like to name her after you, ma'am."

"Me?" Breanna said, putting a hand to her chest.

"Yes, ma'am. If it weren't for you, Lawanda and little Breanna here wouldn't have made it. I'm sure Lawanda will agree to name her after you."

"Would you like to hold her?" Carolyne asked.

Larry's eyes widened. "Me?"

"Of course. You're her father."

He wiped a nervous hand across his mouth. "But...I haven't held a baby since I was a kid."

"Well, it's high time you get in practice then," Carolyne said, lifting the infant toward her father.

Larry Hughes took the tiny baby in his huge hands, looked

into the little face, and said, "Boy, she sure is pretty! Looks just like her mother!"

"She can be thankful for that!" laughed Breanna.

Larry laughed, too, then carried little Breanna Hughes out to the waiting room to show her to the marshal and his deputy. When the two men knew all was well, they excused themselves to return to their beds.

While they waited for Lawanda to come around, Breanna talked to Larry about the Lord. She said it was God answering prayer that brought his wife and daughter through the Cesarean section. The big man's heart was tender, and Breanna took advantage of it to press the gospel home to him. She took a Bible from a nearby drawer and went over God's salvation plan with him. Larry was soon under deep conviction, and in honest repentance, called on the Lord Jesus Christ to save him.

When Lawanda came out from under the chloroform, Larry told her that they had a beautiful little daughter, and that Lawanda had a brand new husband...brand new in the family of God. Such news quickly cleared the fog from Lawanda's brain, and she rejoiced in her husband's salvation as she held her new-born daughter...the daughter whom she agreed would be named Breanna.

"You should go back to your hotel room and get some sleep, ma'am," Larry said to Breanna.

"I appreciate that, Larry, but it's best that I stay with Lawanda in case she needs anything. She'll have to feed the baby soon, and I want to be here to make sure everything's okay."

"Why don't *you* go get some sleep, Larry?" Carolyne said. "I'll stay here with Miss Baylor in case she needs my help."

The big man grinned, shaking his head. "You two are something else, I'll tell you that much. Okay, since I'm the one least needed here, I'll go get a little shut-eye before the sun decides to come up."

When Larry was gone, Carolyne held the baby while Breanna helped Lawanda into a position to nurse her newborn. Then Carolyne handed the baby to her mother, and Breanna and Carolyne sat in chairs beside the table.

"Breanna," Carolyne said, "my father has done a few Cesarean sections, but never when I was with him. We have never discussed it, and I'm curious."

"About what?" asked Breanna, stifling a yawn.

"When did doctors figure out how to do it? By it's name, I assume it happened back during the time of the Caesars in Rome?"

"Well, the history of the Cesarean section is a little vague," Breanna said, "but you're right. It did start with the Caesars in Rome. According to historians, such an operation was conducted for the first time by a Roman physician in order to save a mother's life. If the procedure was ever done before that, it's not recorded. And there's nothing else said about it in the history books—to my knowledge at least—until the tenth century when it was done successfully by physicians in Persia. There's no question they knew of it being done in Rome, for they called it a Cesarean delivery. And in 1491—if memory serves me—a doctor in Switzerland performed the operation on his own wife to save her life and the child's. In the sixteenth and seventeenth centuries, some European doctors performed abdominal deliveries, but from what's recorded, most of the mother's died, either from sepsis or hemorrhage. As this century came, the operation was being done quite frequently."

"Was it only done when the mother's birth canal was too

small for normal delivery…like with Lawanda?"

"No. It was also done when a baby was positioned improperly or if the mother had diabetes…and quite often in cases of *placenta praevia.*"

"*Placenta praevia?* Oh, I know…when the placenta is positioned so that it will expel from the uterus ahead of the child."

"Yes. It's always best to do a Cesarean section when that's the case."

"I can understand that," said Carolyne, covering her mouth for a yawn.

This caused Breanna to yawn again. Finishing, she took her hand from her mouth and said, "As doctors learned more about Cesarean deliveries, the percentage of deaths from hemorrhage diminished sharply."

Carolyne's eyebrows arched. "But deaths from sepsis didn't?"

"Not until just over thirty years ago, when men in the medical profession decided that God knew what He was talking about in the Bible."

"You mean about washing in running water? I'd sure like to hear about it," Carolyne said.

"Some other time, honey," Breanna said, rubbing her eyes. "Right now it looks like baby Breanna has gone to sleep. Must've gotten her little tummy full."

Carolyne bedded the baby down in a small crib nearby, and Breanna checked Lawanda's incision. The three women decided sleep was the best thing for all of them. Lawanda slept on the examining table and the other two slept on cots, in spite of the gray light of dawn coming through the windows.

3

THE FOUR HORSEMEN rode into Cheyenne City, Wyoming, heads bent against the slanting, swirling rain. It was high noon, but the heavy sky made it look more like dusk.

The wind whipped at the trees along Main Street, making the branches creak and groan. Lightning flashed periodically, splitting the dark sky. Thunder rumbled across the prairie, all the way to the Rocky Mountains several miles to the west.

The rain had driven most of the town's citizens off the streets. As the four riders swung up in front of the Broken Spur Saloon, Chet Lavery said, "You guys go on in. I gotta get some smokes over at the general store."

Ace Benson, Irv Sands, and J. D. Ratliff nodded as they dismounted, and paid their partner no more mind as he moved off toward Walton's General Mercantile, four doors farther down the street on the same side.

A bolt of lightning assaulted the heavy sky overhead as Chet made his way along the plank walk. Rain pelted his unshaven face, and thunder answered the lightning like a cannonade.

Two men, obviously ranchers by the cut of their clothes, were coming out the door as Lavery made his approach. One of them held the door open for him.

"Thanks," Lavery nodded, and the rancher nodded back with a slight smile.

Several other customers were in the store, both men and women. Most had already made their purchases and were idly moving about, scanning the shelves and waiting for the rain to ease up.

Lavery ran his gaze over the place. In one corner was a lattice-wire cage, which served as the local post office. Apparently the Walton who owned the store was also postmaster. On one side of the large room were shelves lined with all kinds of canned goods and staples. Next to a big potbellied stove—which hadn't been used since May—was a dill pickle barrel, and beyond the barrel were chest-high shelves bearing various toilet articles, hair tonics, straight-edged razors, and shaving mugs.

Cookie jars and glass containers of beef jerky and horehound candy were at the end of the long counter where the proprietor stood waiting on customers.

Across the room were shelves crammed with shiny boots, women's high lace-up shoes, tables loaded with bolts of cloth, and all manner of sewing supplies. In one corner was a rack of ladies' ready-to-wear dresses, and next to it was a table loaded with plumed hats and sunbonnets. In another corner were shelves of wide-brimmed Stetsons.

Chet Lavery spotted the tobacco and picked out what he wanted, then carried his purchase to the counter.

The proprietor was a short, stocky man in his midfifties with a gray fringe of hair above his ears and a shiny pate. He smiled and said, "Howdy, friend. I'm Oscar Walton, owner of this establishment." As he spoke, he extended his hand.

Lavery met it and grinned. "Name's Chet Lavery."

"New in town or just passin' through?" Walton asked.

"Just passin' through."

Walton nodded, noting Lavery's wet hat and slicker. "You ridin' on in this storm?"

"Well, me and my partners—they're wettin' their whistles at the Broken Spur—have about decided if the rain don't stop pretty soon, we'll hole up till it does."

"Been in Cheyenne City before?"

"Coupla times."

"Well, if you want a recommendation for a hotel, I'd say you want to stay at the Frontier. Wyoming Hotel is better, but a lot more expensive."

Lavery thanked the man, paid for his tobacco, and headed for the door. The wind had eased up, but a cold, misty rain was still coming down. The street was nothing but mud. Two wagons went by, rain dripping from the hatbrims of the drivers. The wheels left deep ruts in the street.

Street lanterns had been lit since Lavery entered the store, and patches of fog lurked between the buildings.

Lightning splintered out of the black clouds, turning Cheyenne City momentarily white, followed by an ear-splitting clap of thunder.

Lavery turned to head for the saloon when lightning lit up Main Street again. In the white light, he saw a lone rider, and the sight of him on his huge black gelding caused Lavery to freeze in his tracks. The man moved in the dripping grayness as though he were a ghost rider.

Lavery backed into the shadows of the store's overhang and watched the man dismount at the hitch rail almost directly in front of him.

It was him, all right.

Lavery would never forget how the man dressed himself in black, except for a white shirt with a black string tie. This time he wore a black slicker. When the man wrapped the reins around the hitch rail, the slicker came open enough for Lavery to spot the bone-handled Colt .45 on his hip—the same .45 that had killed Ace Benson's younger brother, Bobby.

Lavery began inching his way toward the saloon. He watched until the man-in-black entered Walton's, then ran to the Broken Spur and plunged through the batwings.

The saloon was dimly lit, but it took Lavery only a few seconds to locate his partners at a table near the back. A skinny little man with derby hat and arm garters on a striped shirt played the piano near the bar.

Because of the weather, the saloon was busier than usual for midday. A thick pall of smoke hovered near the ceiling amid wagon wheel chandeliers. Three or four card games were in progress. Most of the tables were occupied. A dozen or so men were bellied up to the bar, talking and laughing in the same hollow manner that was customary in such establishments.

Lavery hurried to the table where his friends sat and half-whispered, "Ace! He's here! I just saw 'im!"

Ace Benson swallowed a mouthful of warm beer, wiped a sleeve across his mouth, and said, *"Who's* in town, Chet? Ain't he got a name?"

"That dude who took out Bobby down in Santa Fe! You know...*John Stranger!*"

Benson's eyes widened, and his face settled into a rigid mask. "Stranger?"

Sands and Ratliff exchanged glances, then fixed their eyes on Benson.

"Yeah!" said Lavery. "You said if you ever got the chance, you'd brace him for killin' Bobby. Show him there was a Benson who could outdraw him and put him in his grave. Well, now's your chance!"

"Where'd you see him?"

"He's in the general store right now. He come ridin' up just as I came out."

"He's alone?"

"I sure didn't see nobody with him."

"You dead sure it's him?"

"I'll never forget the dude who took out Bobby."

Ace lifted his glass and downed the rest of the beer.

"Looks like fate just dealt you a good hand, Ace," Ratliff said.

Benson stood up and shoved back his chair, scraping it on the hard wooden floor. Sands and Ratliff followed suit.

"This is your day of revenge, Ace," Lavery chuckled. "You've waited over a year to get even."

Ace Benson's mind went back some fourteen months to that day in Santa Fe. His kid brother had spotted John Stranger coming out of a hotel and recognized him as the man who had outdrawn the infamous gunslick, Clint Meade, over in Durango, Colorado. Bobby had been in Durango the day it happened, and saw it all. From that moment on, his dream was to square off with John Stranger and kill him, making Bobby Benson a feared gunfighter.

Bobby had practiced his fast-draw every day for months, living for the moment he would run onto Stranger and challenge him. During those months, Bobby had taken out three well-known gunhawks, which increased his self-assurance and made him even more eager to brace Stranger.

Ace Benson, along with his drifter friends Chet Lavery, Irv Sands, and J. D. Ratliff, had been in a saloon in Santa Fe directly across the street from Stranger's hotel. Bobby had gone on an errand for Ace, and had been gone far too long. Chet volunteered to go look for the kid, and moved out onto the boardwalk just in time to see Bobby squared off in the middle of the street with John Stranger and going for his gun.

Stranger's Colt .45 was in his hand before Bobby could clear leather. When Lavery saw Bobby go down, he ran back into the saloon. By the time Ace Benson got outside, John Stranger was gone. As Ace knelt beside his dead brother, people on the street told him that the tall man-in-black had tried to talk Bobby out of going for his gun. But Bobby was so bent on taking him out that he said he would start shooting innocent people on the street if Stranger didn't give him a chance to outdraw him.

Ace was so filled with hatred for the man who had killed his little brother that he barely heard what the people were telling him. Moments after the gunfight was over, the hotel manager identified the tall man as John Stranger.

From that moment, a raw, burning hatred gnawed at Ace Benson's insides. Sooner or later, he would meet up with the man who called himself John Stranger, and when he did, Stranger would rue the day he let a greenhorn kid draw against him.

Benson reached the batwings and stepped out onto the boardwalk with his three cronies on his heels. He paused, looking toward Walton's store.

"See the big black at the hitch rail? That's his horse," Lavery said.

"Some animal. I think I'll claim him after I kill Stranger."

The rain was a misty wall now, without wind, and there was no more lightning. The sky was growing a bit lighter.

Ace Benson began a steady move down the boardwalk. He was within forty feet of Walton's door when it opened, and the man-in-black came out. Stranger was stuffing a small paper bag into the pocket of his slicker and pulling the door shut behind him when Benson stopped and bawled, "Stranger!"

John Stranger peered through the mist at Benson, noting the three men who stood at his heels. The street was virtually deserted. The only sound of any significance was that coming from the cheap piano in the Broken Spur.

Stranger could tell by the tone of the man's voice what he wanted. This was only one of dozens of such instances that had taken place in the past several years. He took three steps toward the four men, halted, and fixed Benson with gray eyes. "Do I know you?"

John Stranger was more than Ace Benson had expected. Benson had faced some of the West's toughest gunfighters and walked away, leaving them dead or dying...but he had never faced a man like this one. It felt like some kind of small animal was clawing at his stomach as he replied, "No, but I know you."

"And just what do you want?" Stranger asked.

"You killed my brother down in Santa Fe. He challenged you, but he was only a kid. Instead of trying to talk him out of it, you gunned him down."

"You talking about Bobby Benson?"

"Yeah. How'd you know his name?"

"He told me his name when he issued the challenge. And I did try to talk him out of it. He wouldn't listen. Threatened to start shooting people on the street if I didn't give him a chance at me. I had no choice but to take him out." He paused a moment, peering through the mist, then added, "Best thing for you is to realize your brother was a fool and forget what you've got in mind."

Ace Benson's good sense was overriding his hatred toward John Stranger. The man was almost more than human, the way he looked at Ace with a deadly calm in those icy gray eyes...eyes that seemed to probe into his very soul.

"You're gonna brace him, ain'tcha, Ace?" Lavery said. "Don't let this opportunity for revenge pass you by."

"That's right," Sands said. "He killed Bobby, Ace. Take 'im."

Ace Benson wanted revenge, all right, but his mind was screaming a warning. If he drew against John Stranger, it would be Stranger who walked away, and Ace Benson who would be buried.

"Well, what is it, Mr. Benson?" demanded Stranger.

The tension of the moment seemed to paralyze Benson. He stood immobile, eyes trained on the man-in-black. He took a deep, trembling breath and said shakily, "I...I guess I've been wrong about you, Mr. Stranger. I had it in my mind that you could've just walked away and left Bobby standing there. But he probably would've carried out his threat to shoot people if you refused to square off with him. It was important to Bobby to climb the big ladder, if you know what I mean."

Stranger nodded, keeping his steel-gray eyes riveted on Benson. "I know what you mean."

Ace sighed, slapped the sides of his slicker, and turned to his friends. "Well, boys, I guess we'd better ride. Seems the storm is about over."

Ratliff eyed Benson coolly. "I ain't ridin' with you no more."

"I ain't ridin' with no yella-bellied, big-mouthed coward," Lavery said. "All that big talk about how you was gonna brace this Stranger dude, and look at you. All you're doin' is lickin' his boots."

"Let's go," said Sands. "We don't need his company anymore."

Ace Benson stood in silence and watched the three men walk away. He stared at them until they mounted up and rode out of town westward, their horses' hooves tossing up mud behind them. When he turned back around, John Stranger was a half-block up the street, leading his big black gelding. Benson shrugged his shoulders, walked down the boardwalk, swung aboard his horse, and rode out of town due south. He took a deep breath of air and told himself it was good to be alive.

John Stranger led Ebony to the hitch rail in front of the Wyoming Overland Stagelines, wrapped the reins around the rail, and crossed the boardwalk. He paused at the door, scraping mud off his boots with the metal scraper built into the planks, then stepped inside.

There was no one behind the counter, and the waiting room was unoccupied. A blackboard on the wall behind the counter informed him that the stage to Laramie City was due in at four o'clock that afternoon and would leave at five. It was now just past one.

Stranger walked to the door of the inner office, hoping to find agent Dan Beemer doing paper work inside. Beemer was a solid Christian, an outstanding citizen of the town, and a dear friend. Stranger wanted to see him for a few minutes before moving on.

He started to knock, when suddenly there was an outburst inside. A male voice that was not Beemer's boomed, "I don't have to explain it, Dan! Just do as I say! Put us down as Mr. and Mrs. Kent Ballard, and when you wire your office in Laramie City, tell them to book us all the way to South Pass City by that name."

Dan Beemer's voice roared back, "Why, Frank? You running from the law or something?"

"No! I have my reasons, and I don't need to explain 'em to you!"

"Okay, okay," Dan said. "Hold on just a minute, though. I thought I heard the outer door open and close. May be a customer out there."

Heavy footsteps sounded, and Stranger took a step backward. The door came open, and the short, beefy man of fifty grinned from ear to ear. "Well, I'll be! John! I heard you come in. Why didn't you knock?"

Stranger could see a man in his mid-thirties sitting at the desk, looking at him through the open door. He was dressed sharply in a black suit with gold-threaded vest and a heavy gold watch chain strung from pocket to pocket. His hair was dark, and he wore a thin mustache.

"Well," Stranger replied softly, "I was about to, but then I heard what sounded like an argument. I...didn't want to butt in."

Beemer waved a hand. "Aw, it'd been all right. Frank and I were just having a little discussion. So where you been and where you goin', and how long you gonna be in Cheyenne City?"

"I've been in central Nebraska. I'm heading for Fort Boise up in Idaho...and I'm leaving Cheyenne City as soon as I walk out that door."

"Fort Boise, eh?"

"Yes. Colonel Gilman got a wire to me asking if I'd come and help him with a problem that's developed among his men."

Beemer grinned and shook his head. "Is there anything you can't do, John Stranger?"

"The list would be a long one," John grinned.

"You wouldn't be able to postpone moving on toward Fort Boise for a couple days, would you?"

"If circumstances warranted it. Why?"

"How about staying over till Sunday and preaching for us? We still don't have a pastor yet, but we meet at the town hall Sunday mornings and Sunday nights like when you were here before. Sure would be good to hear you preach again. And those folks who were here last time you preached still talk about your sermons. How about it? This is Friday. Only be a couple of days."

Stranger thumbed his flat-crowned hat off his forehead. "Well, since it's only a couple of days…"

"Good!" Beemer exclaimed, cuffing him on the shoulder. "I'll spread the word!"

Suddenly Beemer remembered the man sitting in his office. "Oh, c'mere, Frank. I want you to meet an old friend of mine."

Frank rose from the chair and walked slowly toward them. When he came through the door, Beemer said, "Frank Miller, I want you to meet an old friend of mine, John Stranger." Stranger recoiled when he heard the man's name, but he managed to conceal his astonishment.

Miller looked up at the taller man and, without offering his hand, said, "John Stranger? That really your name, preacher?"

"That's what they call me. Actually, I'm not a preacher in the sense that I pastor a church or do the work of an evangelist."

"Mighty good one when he preaches, though," Dan Beemer

said. "If you and Lorraine weren't heading out this afternoon, I'd invite you to come hear him preach."

Miller chuckled. "Sure. Can't you just see everybody welcoming a gambler into the services?"

"Church *is* for sinners," Stranger said.

"I ain't got time nor patience for religious people, pal," Miller said. "I was once engaged to a woman who got religion, and I dumped her."

"Her name didn't happen to be Breanna Baylor, did it?"

Miller's eyes widened and his features stiffened. "Well, yeah. You know her?"

"Quite well."

"So she told you about me, eh?"

"Yes, she did. You're quite the man, you are. Didn't even bother to tell her why you jilted her."

"I figured she'd know what it was."

"Well, let me explain something to you, Frank. Breanna didn't get religion. She came to know a Person. His name is Jesus Christ."

A look of disgust claimed Miller's eyes. He turned to the agent and said, "Dan, book us as Mr. and Mrs. Kent Ballard all the way to South Pass City. Got it?"

"Okay," Beemer nodded, watching Miller head for the door.

When the gambler reached the door, he opened it, holding the knob, and said, "And if anybody asks, you ain't seen me nor Lorraine for a long time. Got it?" Miller didn't wait for an answer. He gave Stranger an insolent look and disappeared through the door, slamming it hard behind him.

"Well, since I'll be staying through Sunday, I guess I best take

Ebony to the stable and get me a room at the hotel," Stranger said.

"That'd probably be a good idea," Beemer said. "Sure glad you let me talk you into staying."

The clouds were breaking up overhead and bold shafts of sunlight were shining through as Stranger left the stageline office. He went first to the stable, then headed for the hotel. Two covered wagons pulled to a halt in front of the general store, and a rider hauled up with them. Stranger recognized the rider and both drivers and hurried across the muddy street. "Hey, Rip! Curly! Jay!"

The three men looked at him and smiled when they saw who it was.

Stranger shook hands with Rip Clayson, Curly Wesson, and Jay Wyatt, whom he had met on the Nebraska plains some ten days previously. Clayson was wagon master of a train following the Oregon Trail westward to the California Trial in southeastern Idaho. Stranger had met up with them and had ridden along for two days before pulling away to go to Cheyenne City.

"I'm surprised to see you here," Stranger said. "The train parked outside of town?"

"Yep," Clayson nodded. "We pulled off the Oregon Trail three days ago and headed here. We're in need of supplies that we couldn't do without till we got to Fort Laramie, so we decided to stock up here. We'll head on north and join the trail again at Fort Laramie, then aim west for South Pass City."

"Well, it's good to see you guys again," smiled Stranger. "Elsie and Duane okay?" he asked, turning to Wyatt.

"Sure are," Jay said. "Duane's been a better shot with his rifle since you gave him those pointers."

"Glad to hear it. More meat now, eh?"

"I wouldn't say that," Wyatt said. "Just less ammunition spent gettin' it."

Curly Wesson spit a brown stream of tobacco into the street and asked, "You still aimin' fer Fort Boise, John?"

"Yes. I'm heading out Monday morning. Been asked to preach at the town hall Sunday morning and night. Maybe you should lag behind a little and come hear me."

Curly's face reddened. "Well, I...uh...there jist won't be any time fer it, John. We're runnin' close on our schedule, and—"

"I'd love to stay and hear you, John," Clayson said, "but we do have to keep moving." He winked at Stranger. "Of course, maybe I'd make an exception if I knew Curly would sit under your preaching."

Wyatt laughed. "That'll be the day when you get this old reprobate to sit in a church service!"

The men had a good laugh, then Stranger bid them good-bye and headed for the hotel.

4

↟

THE FULL MOON was sharp-edged and silver-pure against the blackness of the night as the Wyoming Overland Stage rocked its way on the muddy road westward toward Laramie City.

In the box at the reins was Zeke Halliday, and next to him was his youthful shotgunner Dwight Ward. Moonlight glinted off the double barrels of the weapon he held in his hands.

Driver and shotgunner were eager to get to Laramie City, where they would spend the night. They had made two trips that day between Laramie and Cheyenne City, and were ready for a good night's rest in their bunks at the way station. The forty-mile jaunt took about three hours. They would make Laramie City around nine o'clock, since a loose wheel had delayed their departure by an hour.

Inside the coach were four people. The two wealthy men who sat riding backwards were T. C. Nash and Warren Snider, both in their early sixties. They owned gold mines at South Pass City, which lay in South Pass, a natural break in Wyoming's Rocky Mountains between the towering peaks of the Wind River Range and the Sweetwater Range.

Across from them sat Frank and Lorraine Miller, traveling as Kent and Lorraine Ballard. There had been an obvious strain between the Ballards when they boarded the stage in Cheyenne City two hours previously, and they were not speaking. Lorraine sat with arms folded across her chest, staring absently out her window. The mine owners chatted briefly between themselves, then grew quiet and looked out at the moon-splashed scenery.

Frank Miller broke the silence. "So tell me, gentlemen, what mines do you own at South Pass City? All Mr. Beemer said was that you were mine owners there."

"I own the Northern Light Mine, Mr. Ballard, which is just a mile outside of town," Nash replied.

"And I own the King Solomon Mine," Snider said. "It's a mile farther out than the Northern Light."

"So, both of you have been in Cheyenne City on business, I presume."

"Correct," nodded Nash.

"Both mines still yielding a good amount of ore?"

"Yes, as are all seven mines in the area," Nash said.

"Pretty rich mountains around South Pass City, eh?" Miller said.

"One could say that," smiled Snider. "And what business are you in, Mr. Ballard?"

"I'm a gambler, and since there's plenty of gold floating around the town, I figured to see how I could do at the gaming tables. See if I can't get my hands on some of that gold."

T. C. Nash guffawed, "Well, sir, you'd better be good at your trade, because there are some sharp gamblers in South Pass City."

"I can handle myself," Miller said.

Lorraine bit her lip, gave her husband a sharp glance, and once again stared out the window.

While the men discussed gold and its rising market value around the world, Lorraine fought tears and thought back to the night before.

"Lorraine! Lorraine! Wake up!" Frank's voice sliced into her sound sleep.

She opened her eyes to see her husband standing over her in the dull light of the lantern on the dresser across the room. "What time is it?" she asked.

"It's ten minutes past midnight. We've got to talk."

Lorraine sat up and looked at her husband. "Do we have to talk right now? It's the middle of the night. Certainly it can wait till morning."

"No, it can't," Frank said, sitting down on the edge of the bed. "We've got to leave this town right away."

"Leave Cheyenne City? Why?"

"I was in a poker game tonight at the Blue Palace Saloon, and I caught a man—a well-known gambler named Billy Axtell— cheating on me. He pulled a Derringer, and I shot him. Put a bullet in his heart."

"It was self-defense, then, wasn't it?"

"Of course."

"Then why do we have to get out of town?"

"Axtell has some friends coming into town the day after tomorrow. On Saturday. They won't care anything about my acting in self-defense. All they'll care about is killing me."

"Where will we go?"

"South Pass City."

"Why there?"

"Because its surrounded by gold mines, honey. A good gambler can make plenty there. We'll take the afternoon stage tomorrow. We ought to take the morning stage, but that won't give us enough time to tie up our loose ends. We'll use fictitious names just in case Axtell's friends try to follow me."

"But Dan Beemer knows you, Frank," Lorraine said. "He's not going to go along with some made up name."

"I can convince him to go along with me on this, believe me."

"But won't Axtell's friends keep looking for you till they find you?"

"I don't think so. South Pass City's far enough away. When they've looked all over this town and checked to see if a Frank Miller left on a stage, they'll find better things to occupy them. We'll stay in South Pass City a couple of months, I'll pick up some good money, then I'll decide where we'll go next."

Lorraine continued to stare out her window at the moonlit landscape dotted with boulders and hills topped with ragged rock formations. Spruce and pine trees speckled the terrain.

Cheyenne City had been the Miller's home for nearly three years, and Lorraine had been happy there. Frank had done well at the gaming tables, and had made them a decent living. Sometimes he made short trips into Colorado or Nebraska to gamble, leaving her home, but he always came back after a week or so with his pockets full.

This was a different turn of events, and she disliked the thought of her husband being hunted by this Billy Axtell's friends. And though she dreaded having to stay in South Pass City for two months, she would have to go along with whatever Frank said. That was always the way it was. Frank didn't like it when she bowed her neck against any decision he made.

"Tell me about South Pass City, gentlemen," Lorraine heard her husband say. "I know it's a supply town for the wagon trains on the Oregon Trail, but I'd like to hear about its sudden growth and how it's doing now."

Nash and Snider spoke proudly of their town, explaining to Kent Ballard how the turn of the decade after the Civil War brought a boom to the South Pass area when gold was discovered there. The town was quickly established, and now had seven working mines around it.

"It's growing so fast," Nash said, "we can hardly keep up with it. The last census revealed that the population is somewhat over three thousand."

Miller smiled. "That's what I like to hear...a town on the grow."

"We have two sawmills in operation," Snider said, "and hundreds of houses have been built. There are eight saloons, all of which have gambling casinos. There are two fine hotels, several clothing stores, a huge general store, a bank, a pharmacy, a blacksmith shop, two meat markets, a schoolhouse, a town hall, a gun shop, and a marshal's office and jail."

Frank Miller chuckled, "What, no churches?"

"We have no organized church in South Pass City," Snider replied, "but preachers of several denominations have come there from time to time to hold services in the town hall."

"I don't want anything to do with preachers and church services."

"Me, either," Nash said.

The stage began to slow and veer off the road toward the Sweetwater River.

"What now?" Miller said.

"Horse watering time," Snider said.

The stage pulled to a stop at a spot where the bank was low and the crew could dip buckets conveniently to water the team.

Zeke Halliday called down, "We gotta water the animals, here, folks. If you want to stretch your legs, feel free to get out."

While Halliday and Ward watered the six-up team, the passengers stood in the moonlight, smelling the fresh, clean air.

"How much farther to South Pass City?" Lorraine asked the mine owners.

"About ten miles, ma'am."

"Mr. Snider, you mentioned a marshal's office and jail," Miller said. "Who's marshal in South Pass?"

"Name's Bill Stone. He's got a deputy, too—Wally Frye."

"Never heard of either," Miller said. "Must be a lot of lawlessness if the town needs two lawmen."

"Indeed," nodded Snider. "Gold draws outlaws of every description...and pardon me, but it also draws crooked gamblers."

"No offense taken," Miller grinned, "since I'm not the crooked kind."

"There's a shootout of some kind two or three times a week. Be a whole lot worse than that if we didn't have Stone and Frye. I forgot to mention that we also have a funeral parlor and undertaker. Graveyard west of town is growing in population, too."

Lorraine Miller gave her husband a cool glance.

Lorraine spoke up. "Gentlemen, it just came to me. South Pass City is where Esther Morris lives, isn't it?"

"She does," replied Nash.

Frank Miller spit in the grass at his feet and said, "I've heard about her. Didn't she have somethin' to do with that nonsense about women and the right to vote?"

"She's the one," Nash said. "And it may be nonsense, but it's now the law, at least here in Wyoming. Not only that, she's justice of the peace for Fremont County. Hard to believe such a thing could happen."

Lorraine smiled and said, "Well, God bless her. It's about time we women were recognized as human beings with rights of our own instead of just being little puppies sniffing at the heels of you men."

"You and my wife would make a good pair, Mrs. Ballard," Snider chuckled.

"Make that a threesome," Nash said. "My Bertha would fit right in, too."

Frank Miller gave his wife a stony look.

"Well, folks," Zeke Halliday said, swinging an empty bucket in his hand, "time to move on. All aboard!"

As the passengers climbed back into the coach, Frank whispered to his wife, "I love you dearly, Lorraine, and you're not a dog sniffing at my heels. But I don't think women have any business meddling in politics."

Lorraine smiled sweetly and whispered back, "Apparently Wyoming's political leaders disagree with you."

The stagecoach arrived in Laramie City just after nine o'clock. The stage that ran between Laramie City and South Pass City was already in and ready to travel when morning came. Passengers and crew told each other good-bye, and the passengers headed for a nearby hotel.

The next morning, the "Ballards" and the two mine owners found that they were the only passengers on this run to Soda Lake, then on to South Pass City. In late afternoon the following day, the stage rolled into South Pass City, and crew and passengers noted the wagon train parked in a circle just outside of town. The mine owners headed for their homes, the crew would spend the night in a back room at the stage office, and the Millers checked in at the Sweetwater Hotel.

5

↑

THE SUN PEEKED OVER the eastern horizon the next morning as Breanna Baylor finished dressing Lawanda Hughes's incision. Carolyne Fulford was placing the baby girl in Lawanda's arms for feeding when Breanna said, "Well, Lawanda, I think you'll be ready to travel tomorrow. It's been five days, and you're healing well. I wish you could wait another five days, but I know the wagon train has to keep moving. You just make sure Larry fixes you a soft bed in that wagon."

"I'm sure he will, Miss Breanna," smiled Lawanda.

"Breanna, you've been awfully busy with Lawanda and so many other patients these five days," Carolyne said. "I didn't want to bother you about the disease prevention principles you said are in the Bible. But since there's no one else to take care of at the moment, would you mind telling me about it?"

"I'd be glad to."

"I'd like to hear it, too," said Lawanda. "It sounds fascinating."

"All right," Breanna smiled, heading to the cupboard where she kept her Bible. She pulled the drawer open and took out her Bible and another large book. She motioned for Carolyne to sit in a chair near the bed and sat down in another chair facing both women.

"This book is called *World History of Medicine,*" Breanna began, "and was written by a Swiss doctor named Erik Heidleman. It's about sixty years old. Dr. Goodwin gave it to me. You see how thick it is...over seven hundred pages. I've been reading it a little at a time for several months. So far, I've only read a few pages since I got here. But first let me read to you from Exodus 15."

Lawanda smiled at Carolyne and stroked her baby's fat little cheek as little Breanna Hughes took nourishment.

"Israel had just crossed the Red Sea and was about to enter its wilderness wanderings. God is speaking to them here in verse 26: *If thou wilt diligently hearken to the voice of the LORD thy God, and wilt do that which is right in his sight, and wilt give ear to his commandments, and keep all his statutes, I will put none of these diseases upon thee, which I have brought upon the Egyptians: for I am the LORD that healeth thee.* The Lord is very clear here. If the Israelites will do what God tells them, none of the diseases that had fallen on the Egyptians would fall on them."

"Miss Breanna," said Carolyne, "while the Israelites were in bondage, did they have the same diseases the Egyptians did?"

"Yes, most likely. And the remedies in the Egyptian medical books had accomplished very little. Often the remedies were worse than the diseases—using lizards' blood, putrid meat and fat, and even donkey dung. Yet here in Exodus 15, the Lord made a wonderful promise. If His people would obey His commandments, He would free them of all the diseases they had known in Egypt.

"God gave Moses a number of commandments, which are part of our Bible today. Though Moses was trained in the royal postgraduate universities of that day and had been taught Egyptian medical remedies, not one time did he ever write anything about lizards' blood or donkey dung! Moses wrote only what Almighty God told him to write. There won't be time to cover all of this, but let me show you two or three things God gave to Moses for the prevention of infectious diseases.

"Take the highly contagious disease of leprosy, for instance. God gave a simple way to stop the spread of that awful disease, and in countries where they have handled it His way, it has been curtailed and even wiped out. In Leviticus 13, God gives Moses and Aaron laws concerning leprosy, and in verse 46, He tells them what to do with the person who has it: *All the days wherein the plague shall be in him he shall be defiled; he is unclean: he shall dwell alone; without the camp shall his habitation be.* What is God's prescription for leprosy?"

"Isolation," said Carolyne.

"Right, that's the key. And leprosy was brought under control in Israel because they obeyed God's command."

"But isn't it true," Carolyne said, "that for many centuries, even after Jesus was here on the earth, millions of people died of leprosy in Asia and Europe?"

"Yes," nodded Breanna. "Heidleman's book addresses that. The physicians on those continents were like so many, even here in our country—they would rather lean on their own intellect than to believe God's Word. The physicians on those continents came up with their own remedies for combating leprosy."

She found the appropriate place in *World History of Medicine* and read, "'Some physicians believed that leprosy was brought on by eating peppers, garlic, and the meat of diseased hogs. Thus they taught that leprosy would be eradicated if people quit eating peppers, garlic, and the meat of diseased hogs.'"

"How ridiculous," said Lawanda.

"Yes, it is. But that's the way it is when men think they're smarter than their Maker. It works the same way with salvation. Men invent all kinds of ways to get themselves to heaven, ignoring or adding to the cross of Calvary. Jesus did all that was necessary to save us when He died and rose again the third day.

"But that's another subject we could talk about for a long time. Getting back to Heidleman's book, he says that although Europe brought its most devastating plagues under control by obeying the biblical command to isolate the diseased victims, other diseases continued to decimate mankind—intestinal diseases such as cholera, dysentery, and typhoid fever."

"That's still a problem, even in the wagon trains," Carolyne said.

"I know," said Breanna. "And so much of it is because people haven't been careful to follow the Bible's teaching about hygiene. The majority of those lives could have been saved if people had only taken seriously God's provision for freeing man of these diseases."

Breanna picked up her Bible again and thumbed to the book of Deuteronomy. "Let me read from another book of Moses. Israel was still wandering in the wilderness, living in camps, and God gave precise instructions about disposing of human waste. Here it is, in Deuteronomy 23:12 and 13: *Thou shalt have a place also without the camp, whither thou shalt go forth abroad: And thou shalt have a paddle upon thy weapon; and it shall be, when thou wilt ease thyself abroad, thou shalt dig therewith, and shalt turn back and cover that which cometh from thee.* You'll notice the place should be outside the camp, and that the waste should be buried. Simple sanitation laws that, when followed, make all the difference in the world. If these rules would be followed by the wagon trains, it would sharply cut down the graves we see along the Oregon Trail."

"I never realized that was in the Bible," Carolyne said with amazement in her voice.

"Me, either," said Lawanda.

"There are a lot of things that people don't realize are in the Bible, but at least some in the medical profession are beginning to take note of what the Bible says about disease prevention. Dr. Goodwin instituted 'running water' washing in his clinic just three years ago and has found the results to be outstanding. It's God's own principle, derived from Numbers 19 and the use of cleansing waters for uncleanness, and it works."

"I hope my father will come to that place in his practice," Carolyne said.

"It's catching on slowly," said Breanna, "but I'm afraid it'll be some time before it's widely accepted."

"It's not only biblical, it's just good sense," Carolyne said.

"You're right. But pride and prejudice will continue to rule until the medical profession humbles itself and wakes up to the importance of handwashing between every patient...and doing it in running water. But I believe the day will come when that practice will be instituted in every hospital."

"I sure hope so," said Carolyne. "In doctors' offices, too."

"I appreciate you washing your hands in running water before you brought little Breanna into the world," Lawanda said.

Breanna smiled warmly and patted the young mother on the shoulder. Lawanda reached over and took hold of Breanna's hand. Tears filmed her eyes. "I love you, Breanna," she said, lips trembling. "I owe my life to you...and so does this precious little baby."

Carolyne put an arm around Breanna and said, "I love you, too. I'm sure going to miss you when we return to the trail tomorrow."

Breanna embraced them and said, "I love both of you...and I'm going to miss you, too."

There was a sudden sound of heavy footsteps in the outer office. Breanna headed for the door, but it came open before she could reach it. Two dusty miners were carrying a third, whose head and face were covered with blood.

"What happened?" Breanna asked.

"I was swingin' a pick," one of them said, "and the head came off and buried itself in the side of this man's skull."

At a quarter after ten the next morning, Breanna Baylor moved slowly out of the clinic. She had spent the entire night laboring to save the life of the injured miner, but he had died a little after seven. The town's undertaker had taken the body away, and Breanna watched the wagon train bearing Carolyne Fulford and the Hughes family pull away only moments later. Carolyne and Lawanda were still waving when they finally passed from sight.

Breanna yawned and went back into the clinic to clean it up, planning to go to her hotel room and get some sleep when she finished. At 8:45 she was about to leave the clinic when a mother brought in her seven-year-old son, who had fallen from a tree. The weary nurse spent the next hour and a half setting a dislocated shoulder and patching up the boy's scrapes and bruises.

Breanna left a note on the office door that in case of an emergency she could be found in room 12 at the Sweetwater Hotel, then walked toward the hotel. The street was busy with vehicles and people on foot. The saloons were already quite busy, and the noise from them filtered onto the street. Breanna was passing the women's ready-to-wear dress shop when Althea Smith, the shop owner, saw her through the window. Althea moved out quickly, calling Breanna's name. Breanna stopped, turned about, and managed a sleepy smile. "Good morning, Althea," she said.

"I've got a sore spot under my arm, Breanna. It's all red. Could you take a look at it for me?"

Breanna yearned for her bed, but smiled and said, "Sure." Althea led her into the shop.

Frank and Lorraine Miller had eaten breakfast at the hotel restaurant and were casually moving down the boardwalk, taking in the sights. Lorraine wore a fancy bustled dress and plumed hat and twirled a parasol on her shoulder.

Frank's interest was in the saloons, where he would soon ply his trade. They were approaching the Buckaroo Saloon when they heard loud, angry voices inside.

Althea Smith buttoned her dress in a small room at the rear of her shop. Breanna had told her the red spot under her arm was just a rash and nothing to worry about.

"I'll go back to the clinic and get you some salve, Althea," Breanna said. "You should apply it three times a day till it clears up."

Suddenly loud male voices were heard on the street, followed by a gunshot. Breanna dashed through the shop to the front door and saw a man down in the dust of the street in front of the Buckaroo Saloon. He had a bullet in his shoulder, and his gun was still in its holster.

Another man stood over him on the boardwalk, holding a smoking gun and swearing at him. Two young women who had been passing the Buckaroo were flattened against the wall, eyes wide with fear. People on the street froze in their tracks.

The angry gunman snapped back his hammer to shoot the wounded man again, but checked himself when the voice of Marshal Bill Stone cut the air, "Hold it right there, mister!"

Stone was moving the gunman's direction from across the street, his own weapon in hand. "Drop the gun!" he commanded.

The gunman, who had the look of a drifter, seized one of the young women and swung her in front of him. He held her in the crook of his left arm and placed the muzzle of his revolver to her head. "Back off, Marshal, or I'll blow her head off!"

Stone halted in the middle of the street. Traffic had come to a complete stop. The marshal glanced at the man who lay bleeding in the dust and said to the gunman, "I don't know what you two were fighting about, mister, but let Katie go. You harm her and you'll hang! Now put the gun down!"

The drifter swore. "This little lady and me are gonna leave town together, Marshal. You or anybody else try to stop us, she dies! Got that?"

"Don't do it, mister!" roared Stone. "You'll only get yourself in more trouble! Let her go!"

The gunman retorted that it would be the marshal's own fault if Katie got killed.

While the two men argued, Breanna looked around for Deputy Frye. Where was he? Two men stood by her, wearing sidearms, but they were frozen like statues. Other men looked on from the other side of the saloon and from across the street, but nobody moved. Breanna turned to the two men at her side and whispered, "Do something! The marshal needs help! If that man takes Katie with him, who knows what he'll do to her?"

Both men gave Breanna a scowl. "Ain't nothin' we can do, lady," said one.

The gunman began to drag Katie Talbot across the boardwalk to his horse. Breanna jerked the revolver from the holster of the man who stood closest to her and moved stealthily up behind the drifter. The swish of her skirt was drowned out by the drifter's voice as he roared, "Don't try to stop me, Marshal, or I swear, I'll kill her!"

Suddenly the gunman felt the cold tip of a gun muzzle press against the back of his neck, followed by the dry, clicking sound of a hammer being cocked. "Take that gun away from her head, mister, or I'll drop you where you stand!" Breanna said.

Katie released a high-pitched whimper.

Color drained from the gunman's face. "Ain't no woman gonna pull a trigger on me."

"You a gambler?" Breanna said. "Don't bet on this one. You'll lose."

Frank Miller stood in shock, eyes wide and glued to the woman who held the gun to the drifter's neck. He had not seen Breanna Baylor since the day he broke off their engagement and walked out on her back in Kansas.

The drifter's pulse pounded in his head. Something in the unseen woman's voice told him she would carry through her threat.

"I'm tired of waiting!" Breanna said. "Drop that gun and let her go!"

The drifter took a deep breath, lowered the gun, and released the girl.

Katie Talbot broke into sobs of relief as her friend took her into her arms. Breanna kept the muzzle pressed to the back of the drifter's neck until Marshal Stone rushed up, took his gun, and handcuffed him.

Stone smiled at Breanna as the drifter turned and scowled at her.

"Good job, Miss Breanna. How'd you like to become my deputy?"

"Don't have time," sighed Breanna, looking down at Harley Cummins, who lay in the dust, bleeding. "I've got to remove a bullet from a miner's shoulder."

Stone ran his gaze over the crowd. "Some of you men carry Harley down to the doctor's office so Nurse Baylor can patch him up."

Four men moved in to pick up the wounded miner, and Breanna turned to follow them to the clinic. She paused in front of the shame-faced man whose Colt .45 she had borrowed and said, "Thanks for the use of your gun." He accepted it silently.

Breanna had taken a couple of steps when Katie called after her, "Thank you, Miss Breanna! God bless you!"

Breanna turned about, smiled, and waved. She was about to turn back when she saw a familiar face in the crowd. Frank Miller! The well-dressed Lorraine clung to his arm.

The sight of the man who had so cruelly jilted her drove an icy needle into Breanna's heart, and the pain showed on her face. Their eyes locked for a brief instant, then embarrassed, Miller looked away.

Breanna wheeled and headed down the street, her mouth suddenly dry, her heart pounding. What was Frank Miller doing in South Pass City? Was that Lorraine on his arm, or some other woman?

Breanna unlocked the door of the clinic and moved inside. She led the men as they carried the wounded miner to the examining table.

Lorraine Miller eyed her husband, who watched Breanna walking away, and said, "So that's the woman you left to marry me. Wonder what she's doing in this town?"

"Apparently she's working for the doctor here."

Lorraine sent a glance after Breanna, then said, "She's a beautiful woman, Frank. I can see why you were attracted to her. She's got guts, too."

Frank did not reply.

It was noon before an exhausted Breanna Baylor climbed the stairs at the Sweetwater Hotel and made her way down the hall near the back of the building to room 12. After removing the bullet from Harley Cummins's shoulder and sewing him up, she left him on the table still under chloroform with his wife by his side. She stopped at the dress shop, gave Althea the salve, and trudged from there to the hotel. Along the street, people congratulated her on the way she had handled the drifter.

Breanna stepped inside the room, closed and locked the door, set her medical bag on a table, and flopped onto the bed. In less than a minute, she was sound asleep.

↓

In a fitful nightmare, Breanna relived the moment the man she had planned to marry sat her down and announced that the wedding was off. She tossed and turned on the bed as she watched Frank walk out the door, knowing he would never return.

She jerked suddenly awake and sat up, her whole body trembling. The sun's rays were beginning to slant through the window. She had been asleep for about two hours.

She rose from the bed and crossed the room, poured water from a pitcher into a tin cup and gulped it down. She went to the window and pulled down the shade, then moved to the dresser, opened a drawer, and picked up a silver disk. She carried it to the bed, sat down, and held it in one hand while running her fingers over the lettering. Breanna didn't need to see it to know what was on the highly polished medallion. It was centered with a raised five-point star, and the letters around its edge spelled out: *THE STRANGER THAT SHALL COME FROM A FAR LAND—Deuteronomy 29:22.*

Breanna lay down, rolled onto her side, and began to weep. "Oh, John, I need you so much! I love you more than anything or anyone else in the world. Please come to me. I need you...I need you."

6

BREANNA BAYLOR AWAKENED at four-thirty in the afternoon, re-pinned her hair, and walked to the clinic. There she found Harley Cummins awake and doing well under his wife's care. Mrs. Cummins had summoned her neighbors, who had come to help her take Harley home, if Nurse Baylor did not object. Breanna consented and said she would come to the house the next day to change his bandages. Mrs. Cummins was to send someone for her if Harley took a turn for the worse.

Breanna cleaned the clinic, left the sign on the door, and at a quarter after five, entered the Bluebird Café to eat her evening meal. There were only a few customers in the place as she made her way to her favorite table in the far corner.

Two men who sat nearby smiled at her and called her by name. Breanna smiled back. One of them said, "I heard what you did this morning, Miss Baylor. I think you ought to let Marshal Stone pin a badge on you!"

Breanna blushed and waved him off.

Waitress Sally Thraemore approached the table, carrying a pot of coffee, a cup, and a menu. "Hello, Breanna."

"Hi, Sally. What's your special tonight?"

"Roast beef, taters, green beans, and apple pie for dessert."

"Sounds good to me. That's what I'll have."

Sally set the cup down and poured it full. She started to turn away, then checked herself. "Say, honey, I heard what you did today for Katie Talbot. That was commendable, but what I want to know is, where were the men?"

"I guess it didn't cross any of their minds to sneak up behind the man, Sally. I'm certainly no heroine. I just did what I felt had to be done."

"Well, you're somethin' special, you are," chuckled Sally. "If the town wasn't already payin' for your meals, you'd get this one free."

Breanna's attention had left Sally Thraemore and was riveted on a couple who had just come in. Frank Miller and the well-dressed woman Breanna had seen with him that morning were sitting down at a table near the front door.

Sally followed Breanna's gaze across the room and asked, "Somebody you know? Must be new in town. I've never seen 'em before."

"Oh. Well…I…ah…I knew the gentleman back in Kansas years ago. The lady, I've never met."

Sally nodded, said, "One roast beef special comin' up," and walked away.

Sally went to the window at the kitchen, turned Breanna's order in to the cook, then carried menus, cups, and a pot of coffee to the Millers. Breanna sipped her coffee and watched as the waitress poured coffee for them, took their orders, then said something and pointed across the room to where she sat.

Both of them looked at Breanna as Sally spoke. When Frank's gaze met Breanna's, it held only a second, and he looked up at

Sally and said something. Lorraine's gaze held firm, even when Breanna looked her straight in the eye. Breanna smiled at the woman, who gave her an arctic glare and looked away.

Breanna saw Marshal Bill Stone and Deputy Wally Frye come through the door, looking for a table. The one next to Breanna was still unoccupied, and the lawmen headed her way. Breanna was glad for their company.

"Evenin', Miss Breanna," the marshal said.

"Good evening, Marshal," she smiled. "Hello, Wally."

"Evenin', Miss Breanna. You look lovely tonight," the young deputy replied, giving her a broad grin.

"Aren't you kind! I don't feel very lovely. Still a bit haggard after a long night without sleep, though I got a little this afternoon."

"I've been hearing a lot about the way you handled Luke Hatch, Miss Breanna," Frye said.

"Oh, is that his name?" she said.

"Yeah. Well-known troublemaker all over the West. Looks like he made trouble in the wrong town this time."

"I'm mighty proud of you, Miss Breanna," Stone said. "Only the Lord in heaven knows what would have happened to that girl if you hadn't intervened. He had me cold. With that gun at her head, there was nothin' I could do but let him take her with him." Stone lowered his voice. "Tell me, Breanna. If he had put a bullet in Katie...would you have shot him?"

"I've never killed anyone in my whole life, Marshal, but I heard a sheriff tell a young deputy one time, 'Don't put a gun on a man unless you're willing to use it.' I think that was good advice."

"That's what I thought you'd say, Miss Breanna," Stone said.

"Well, deputy, let's take a seat over here and see if we can get some supper."

Breanna glanced toward Frank Miller and found him eyeing her coldly. "No need for you gentlemen to sit over there," she said. "Why don't you join me for supper?"

Wally Frye's features lit up. "What do you say, Marshal?"

"Don't mind if we do!" Stone said, and both men sat down.

Sally Thraemore appeared with a tray, bearing Breanna's meal. "Well, I see you picked up some admirers, Breanna."

The nurse's face tinted, but she did not reply.

Sally bent close to Breanna. "The gentlemen over there took a look at you and said you seemed vaguely familiar, but he couldn't remember where it was in Kansas that he met you."

Breanna nodded and glanced toward the man who had jilted her. Frank was bent forward, talking intently to the woman. *On top of everything else, Frank, you're also a liar.*

Breanna stayed at the table while the two lawmen finished their meals. The Millers left without looking her direction again. Later, while Stone and Frye walked her to the hotel, Breanna wondered where Frank and the woman were staying.

At eight-thirty the next morning, Breanna stepped out of her room at the Sweetwater Hotel and was locking the door when she heard a door open in a room farther up the hall toward the staircase. She recognized Frank Miller's voice as he said, "I'll be in a game at the Silver Slipper, Lorraine. After you're done shopping, you can meet me there, and we'll have lunch together."

Breanna froze with her hand on the knob and watched as

Miller closed the door of room number 8 and headed toward the stairs. Since he didn't look back, she finished turning the lock and moved the same direction. She had almost reached the top of the stairs when she heard the desk clerk say, "Beautiful day, Mr. Ballard."

"I'll see about that after a few hands of poker, Benny," Miller laughed.

Breanna slowed up until she heard the lobby door open and close, then descended the stairs. When she reached the lobby floor, she approached the desk and said, "Good morning, Benny."

Benny Freeman, a small, thin man in his late sixties, showed her an almost toothless grin and said, "Same to you, Miss Breanna."

"Benny, that man who just went out. Is his name Ballard?"

"Why, yes, ma'am. Kent Ballard. He and his wife will be guests here sort of indefinitely. He's a professional gambler from somewhere back East. Hopes to win a lot of gold. You know him?"

"He looks a lot like someone I used to know."

Benny grinned. "Well, they say everybody has an identical twin somewhere."

"Mm-hmm," she said, heading toward the door. "Whoever 'they' are."

"Yes, ma'am," the clerk chuckled.

Breanna walked three blocks off Main Street to the Cummins home and changed Harley's bandages. He was getting along satisfactorily, which pleased her. She decided to go by the general store and pick up some supplies she needed for the clinic. *I wonder how much longer it will be until Dr. Everett Wall arrives. With Frank Miller in town, I'd rather be elsewhere.*

She was almost to the door of the general store when it came open and Lorraine emerged, carrying a paper bag. The two women stood face to face, less than ten feet apart.

Lorraine gave Breanna a harsh look and started to turn away.

"Wait a minute, Lorraine," Breanna said, stepping closer to her. "Could we talk? Please?"

"What do we have to talk about?"

"Lorraine, this town is not so big that we won't keep running into each other. Can't we just call a truce or something?"

"What do you mean, a truce?" Lorraine snapped.

"Well, from the menacing looks you've given me it seems that you think of me as your enemy. We've never even met. Why would I be your enemy?"

"Really, Breanna, are you that stupid? I took Frank from you a few days before you were to become his wife. Don't you hate me? Wouldn't you like to scratch my eyes out?"

"No, I don't hate you," Breanna replied softly. "And I don't want to scratch your eyes out. Frank hurt me very much, I'll admit, but I'm over that. And I'm in love with another man...a very wonderful man."

"Well, I'm glad for that. I hope you'll be very, very happy."

"I already am," Breanna replied.

"So then...are you married to this wonderful man?"

"No, not yet. But I hope to be someday, Lord willing."

"Yes, well..."

"Lorraine, I'm puzzled about something. and I wonder if you can explain it to me. I happened to be a few steps behind Frank as he was leaving this morning, and I heard the desk clerk call him Mr. Ballard."

Lorraine's face lost color. "Oh, Breanna. You didn't tell him Ballard isn't our real name, did you?"

"No."

"Oh, thank goodness!" Lorraine gasped.

"If you don't mind telling me, Lorraine, what's this all about?"

Lorraine looked around to make sure nobody was close enough to hear her. "A gang of outlaws is after Frank for something that happened in Cheyenne City. They want to kill him, and we had to leave for Frank's safety. Frank felt it was best that we travel under an assumed name. Please...you won't tell anyone?"

"Of course not," Breanna said. "I don't wish anything bad to happen to Frank."

Lorraine's eyes misted. There was a tiny quiver on her lips as she said softly, "You're not at all what I expected, Breanna."

"And what did you expect?"

"Well, usually when people go over the edge with religion, they get all pious, high-and-mighty, and—"

"Religion?"

"Yes, didn't Frank tell you why he lost interest in you?"

"No, he didn't. He just announced it was over and left. Lorraine, I didn't go over the edge on religion."

"You didn't?"

"No. What I have is salvation, not religion. I came to know the Lord Jesus Christ. He forgave me of all my sins, washed them away in His blood, and made me a child of God."

Lorraine looked at Breanna blankly. "I...I've never heard anything like this."

"I'll be glad to sit down with my Bible and show it to you, Lorraine."

"I've really got to be going now, Breanna. It's been nice talking to you. Thank you for not being bitter and hateful toward me...or toward Frank."

"I might have been before Jesus came into my life, Lorraine, but He has made a big difference in me."

"I'm glad you're happy. But I really must be going." With that, Lorraine wheeled and walked away.

Breanna watched her go, then entered the general store.

Wyoming Overland Stagelines driver Les Jameson drove the six-up team with a steady hand on the lines. Shotgunner Tim Riley sat next to him, the double-barreled weapon cradled in his arms, his head nodding lazily. Les knew Tim wasn't fast asleep, just comfortably dozing.

They were headed west toward South Pass City from Soda Lake, and the hot afternoon sun was lowering, its rays slanting underneath the broad brim of Jameson's hat. He reached up and tilted it farther down on his forehead. Except for a couple of hawks riding the hot air waves, there was no other sign of life around them.

It didn't happen often that the stage ran without at least a couple of passengers, but on this run, all they were carrying was some freight for South Pass's general store. Three passengers were scheduled for the return trip.

They were skirting the Sweetwater River some seventeen or eighteen miles east of South Pass City when Jameson squinted against the glare of the sun, used his hand to help shade his eyes, and noted a wagon train strung out along the bank of the river a couple of miles ahead.

"Tim."

Riley jerked awake, sat up straight, and blinked. "Huh?"

"Got a wagon train up ahead. May be a problem. It's too early in the afternoon for a wagon train to be stoppin' for the night. They haven't formed a circle, either. Somethin's wrong."

"Maybe they're just stoppin' for water," Riley said.

"Could be, but I got a feelin' somethin's awry. Maybe they were attacked by Indians and are lined out along the river to bathe their wounded in the water."

"Well, I guess we'll find out right shortly."

Les Jameson snapped the reins, shouted, "Hee-yah!" and put the team to a gallop. He had spent twenty years in these parts and knew the hazards presented by Indians, wild animals, and the rigors of travel. It was ingrained in him to be alert for trouble.

The bounding coach was within a half-mile of the wagon train when a rider appeared from the river side of the train, galloping toward them. Les kept the team at a gallop until the rider was almost abreast, then hauled rein.

The rider skidded his big bay gelding to a halt, and his face showed that Les Jameson's instincts were still sharp.

"Howdy," smiled the driver. "You got trouble?"

"Yes, sir," said the rider. "I'm Ripley Clayson, the wagon master. We've got a man with a .44 caliber rifle slug in his belly—an accidental shooting. He's still alive, but bleeding bad. Would you have room for him and his wife? I was about to take him into South Pass City on my horse, but it'd be much better if you could take him in the coach."

"We can have him to town in half an hour. I'm sure his wife will want to come along."

"I'm sure she will," Clayson said, relief apparent in his voice. "Come on. I'll lead you to him."

Moments later the stagecoach ground to a halt beside the Wyatt wagon, where Elsie Wyatt knelt at her husband's side. He lay on the grass with a blanket over him. A pale-faced sixteen-year-old boy stood next to them, his face wet with tears. The rest of the crowd stood in a semicircle close by, looking on.

"These men will take you and Jay into town in the stage," Clayson said to Elsie. "They'll have you to the doctor in South Pass City in half-an-hour." He looked around at the crowd. "Let's get Jay into the coach, men. Hurry!"

"Clayson, I should tell you that at present there isn't a doctor in South Pass City," Jameson said.

"There's not? What happened to Dr. Rudd?"

"He took sick and died a few weeks ago. There's a Certified Medical Nurse filling in until a new doctor can get there from back East."

Elsie rose to her feet as four men carried her semiconscious husband toward the coach. "I hope she knows how to do surgery," she said shakily, looking at Jameson. "That bullet is deep in Jay's midsection."

"I know she'll do the best she can, ma'am," Jameson replied.

A skinny little man in his late seventies stepped up. He was wiping sweat from his bald head with a bandanna, holding his hat in the other hand. "I'll go with you, Elsie," he said. "That way I'll be there to help carry Jay into the doctor's office."

"Thank you, Curly," Elsie said, "but you need to drive your wagon. I'm sure we'll have help there."

"It'll be fine, sir," Tim Riley said. "Les and I will carry him in."

"Well, okay, if you're sure you won't need me."

"Appreciate your offer, sir," Jameson said, "but Tim and I will handle it."

Curly nodded and followed as Jay was placed inside the coach. The men laid him across the rear seat, making him as comfortable as possible.

Young Duane Wyatt, looking sick at heart, pressed close to his mother and said, "Ma, I know you told me to stay behind and drive our wagon, but I'd really like to go with you and Pa."

"But, honey," she said, laying a hand on his shoulder, "someone's got to drive the wagon."

"Mrs. Wyatt, I'll drive your wagon for you," said Jerry Adams, one of the men who had carried Jay to the coach. "We all know how bad Duane feels about the accident. He should be with you and Mr. Wyatt."

Elsie managed a weak smile. "Oh, Jerry, that's so kind of you. I really would like to have Duane along, but—"

"You just go on, now," Jerry smiled. "I'll take care of your oxen and the wagon."

Elsie thumbed tears from her eyes and said, "Thank you."

Curly Wesson gave Elsie his hand and helped her into the coach, and Duane climbed in behind her.

As Jameson and Riley climbed into the box, Rip Clayson looked through the window and said, "We'll be praying for Jay. See you both tomorrow. God bless you."

Mother and son nodded, fighting their emotions, and the stage pulled away. Les Jameson cracked the whip over the horses' heads and put them to a full gallop.

7

BREANNA BAYLOR WAS STANDING over a miner sitting in a straight-backed chair near the examining table. His face was battered and bruised, but the pain he felt most was the forefinger he had dislocated in a fight with another miner at one of the mines.

Breanna braced herself, grasped the man's wrist with her left hand, and tightened her grip on the jammed finger with her right. "Now, Ralph, this is going to hurt," she warned.

"It already does," he said, gritting his teeth.

"But not like it's going to when I pull it back in place."

"Are you sure you're strong enough, ma'am?"

Breanna looked him square in the eye. "You want to try it yourself?"

He swallowed hard and shook his head. "No."

"You know, if you miners would grow up and act like mature men, this kind of thing wouldn't happen."

"Gotta get into a fight now and then to show you're tough."

"You're tough, are you?" she asked.

"You bet."

"All right, let's see if you can handle this without passing out."

Breanna gave a quick yank on the finger. It made a cracking sound and popped back in place. Ralph turned white, his mouth sagged, and his eyes rolled back in his head. He swayed and started to fall, but Breanna grabbed his shirt, then eased him off the chair and onto the floor.

Because of the heat, both the door to the outer office and the door to the street were open. Breanna heard thundering hooves and the rattle of a stagecoach. She knew the stage should be stopping a half-block away at the Wyoming Overland office, but she could tell it was drawing up in front of the clinic. She started that direction, then stopped when she heard Ralph Trotter moan. She knelt beside him as he opened his eyes and tried to sit up.

"What happened?" Trotter said, trying to focus on Breanna.

"You passed out."

"I did?" He lifted his hand and looked at the finger. "Is it fixed?"

"Good as new, though it'll be pretty sore for a few days."

The sound of heavy footsteps echoed from the outer office. Breanna turned to see Les Jameson and Tim Riley carrying a bleeding man through the door, followed by a woman and a teenage boy.

Breanna pointed to the examining table. "Put him over there."

Jay Wyatt was completely unconscious, and Breanna could see the wound in his midsection once he was laid on the table. She hurried to the cupboard and pulled out a white apron. "I assume it's a gunshot."

"Yes, ma'am," said Jameson. "The man is Jay Wyatt. This is his wife Elsie and his son Duane. They're part of a wagon train that's headed this way. Tim and I brought 'em in the stage so as to get 'em here as fast as possible."

"Miss Baylor," Elsie said. "They told us your name is Miss Baylor. Am I right?"

"Yes, ma'am. Breanna Baylor. Did these gentlemen tell you that I'm—"

More heavy footsteps were heard in the outer office, then Marshal Bill Stone and Deputy Wally Frye appeared.

"Understand we got a man shot, Miss Breanna," said Stone, pausing just inside the door.

"Yes, Marshal," she replied, "and I've got to go to work on him right away. He's bleeding profusely."

Breanna asked Wally if he would work the pump while she washed her hands. He was eager to help, glad for the chance to be near Breanna. While Breanna washed her hands, Elsie told the marshal how Duane accidentally shot her husband.

Breanna finished washing her hands, laid out the sterilized surgical instruments, then stood beside the table and said, "Mrs. Wyatt, before the marshal and his deputy came in, I was asking if Les and Tim had told you that I'm not a doctor...just a Certified Medical Nurse."

"Yes, they did," Elsie nodded.

"I must tell you that I have assisted qualified surgeons in this kind of surgery many times, but I have done only three on my own. One patient lived, and the other two died. This is a difficult procedure, and he could bleed to death before I'm finished. I need your consent to proceed."

Elsie's lower lip was quivering. Duane had an arm around her shoulder.

"He'll bleed to death if you don't try, won't he?" she asked.

"Yes, ma'am."

"Go ahead then. And please hurry."

"Aren't you going to need help, Miss Breanna?" Wally asked.

"It would be nice, but I'll have to handle it on my own. It would be best if all of you would wait in the outer office. I need the air as clean as possible in here."

Les Jameson led the way, saying, "All right, let's do as the little lady says."

The group collected in the waiting room, and everyone sat down except Duane, who began pacing back and forth. Marshal Stone excused himself, saying he had to get back to the office. Deputy Frye was to return to the office when the surgery was finished and Miss Baylor gave her opinion as to Mr. Wyatt's condition.

Duane wept and paced the floor, repeating over and over that it was all his fault. His mother tried to console him, but Duane wasn't listening. If his father died, he wailed, it would be his own son's hand that killed him. After several minutes, Duane finally grew quiet and sat down.

Three hours after Breanna had begun the surgery, the door came open, and a weary nurse stepped into the outer office. Elsie's heart leaped to her throat. Breanna had discarded the white apron, but there were bloody spots on the sleeves of her dress. Like a courtroom waiting for the verdict from the jury, everyone waited for Breanna to speak.

Breanna sighed, sat down on the corner of the desk, and said, "I think your husband is going to make it, Mrs. Wyatt. It was touch and go for a while, but I was able to stop the internal bleeding in time. I feel sure he'll pull through."

"Oh, thank you!" said Elsie, bursting into tears. Duane could only sob.

Breanna left the desk, put her arms around Elsie and said, "I'll stay the night and watch over him, Mrs. Wyatt. If he's holding steady by morning, then I'll know he's going to make it."

"I'll stay with you," said Elsie, wiping tears. "You're an angel, Miss Baylor. An absolute angel."

Breanna hugged her tight. "Well, I'm not too sure I qualify for that."

"Oh, yes you do!" Duane managed to say. "Pa's going to live because of you. I just know it!"

"I might have a little part in it, Duane," she said, "but your real thanks belongs to the Lord in heaven. He's the One who gives life and sustains it."

"Yes, ma'am," nodded the youth.

The sun was up the next morning with the promise of another hot day. At eight o'clock, Breanna was in the outer office when she saw the stagecoach pull out of town, heading east. She returned to the clinic where Jay Wyatt lay on a corner bed. He had survived the night and was doing well.

"I'll go get us some breakfast, Elsie," Breanna said. "Then I'm going to the hotel and get myself a hot bath."

At ten o'clock, Breanna left her hotel room after bathing and headed down the hall toward the staircase. The door of room 8 came open, and Frank Miller stepped out. Breanna's heart jumped to her throat. Miller's face showed he was just as surprised as she.

Breanna forced a smile and said, "Hello, Frank."

Miller's face took on a stony look. He tried to swallow and

almost choked on the sudden dryness in his throat. "Hello, Breanna."

"Did...did Lorraine tell you we met on the street?"

"Yes."

"She seems like a decent woman, Frank. I hope the two of you are happy."

"Superbly. She tells me you've found a man and are deeply in love."

"Yes."

"Does his name happen to be John Stranger?"

Breanna felt her scalp tingle. "How do you know John?"

"Ran into him in Cheyenne City just before we came here. He was introduced to me as a preacher. I ain't much on religion, and I told him so. In fact, I told him I was once engaged to a woman who got religion, so I dumped her. He asked if her name was Breanna Baylor. When I asked if he knew you, he said he did. 'Quite well,' I believe his words were. Since you told Lorraine you were in love with a wonderful man, I figured you must be in love with this guy."

Breanna's mind was on the race. What kind of coincidence was this? The man who jilted her and the man she had so foolishly sent out of her life had met in Cheyenne City only days ago?

"So you and him gettin' married?" Miller asked.

"If the Lord wills it," she said.

Miller's face screwed up. "Well, hope it works out for you."

"Thank you," she said, and started past him.

"This guy Stranger...He told me preachin' is just part of what he does. What else does he do?"

"Many things. One of them is watching over me."

Breanna wheeled and went to the stairs. She was down them, through the lobby, and out the door before Frank Miller moved.

Late that afternoon, Breanna had just finished caring for an elderly woman and was saying a few final words to her in the outer office when two men appeared at the door, blocking some of the sunlight from the street.

Breanna stopped in the middle of a sentence, looked toward the men, and said, "Good afternoon, gentlemen, I'm Nurse Baylor. May I help you?"

The men moved inside and removed their hats. "My name is Ripley Clayson, ma'am, and this is my friend, Curly Wesson. Yesterday the stage brought a Mr. Wyatt to you with a gunshot wound, and—"

"Oh, of course. You're with the wagon train."

"Yes, ma'am. I'm the wagon master. Is Jay—"

"Mr. Wyatt is doing quite well," she said with a warm smile.

"Oh, praise the Lord!" Clayson said.

"Just one moment, gentlemen," she said, "and I'll take you to him."

Breanna finished giving some advice to the elderly woman concerning her arthritis and told her to come back in a week. The woman thanked her and shuffled out the door.

Breanna was a bit taken with Ripley Clayson. He reminded her a great deal of John Stranger. Though John was taller, Clayson had the same coloring and lean, muscular build. His black hair and mustache were very much like John's.

The smaller man, whom Clayson had introduced as Curly Wesson, made Breanna smile on the inside. He had to be nearing eighty, though he had a boyish grin and a twinkle in his pale blue eyes. He reminded her of an elf or a leprechaun.

Breanna headed for the door that led to the clinic. "In here, gentlemen."

As they followed, Curly laid a hand to his mouth and said, "Cute as she is, I think I'll develop a pain somewhere!" Rip grinned, but did not reply.

Elsie and Duane Wyatt were seated on wooden chairs beside Jay's bed in one corner of the room. When Breanna came through the door, all three looked her direction.

"Rip! Curly!" Duane said, rising to his feet. "Pa's going to be all right! Look at him!"

There was a happy reunion between Clayson, Wesson, and the Wyatts. Elsie and Duane and even Jay couldn't say enough good about Breanna and her surgical skill. Breanna humbly accepted their kind words, but shifted the glory to the God of heaven, who had given her the ability to save Jay's life.

"I wish we had someone like you traveling with us, Miss Baylor," Rip Clayson said. "We've had so many times on this trip that we could have used you."

"Yeah," Curly said. "We had three children and one woman die of cholera when we were about halfway across Nebraska."

"Cholera," Breanna said, as if the word put a bad taste in her mouth. "Deadly stuff."

"Yes, ma'am."

"You have to be so careful about the water as you travel," she said. "Typhoid can come from bad water, too."

"Well, we always take water from the rivers and creeks

upstream from where we camp, ma'am," Clayson said.

"But you must remember that there could be a wagon train camped upstream, or animals dropping feces in the rivers or creeks many miles upstream. Even animals lying dead upstream. If I were riding in your wagon train, all water would be boiled twice before it was used for cooking or drinking."

"I hadn't thought of further upstream," Clayson said. "We'll have to see that it's done like Miss Baylor says, Curly."

"You bet," said the old man. "Sure wish we could kidnap you and take you with us, ma'am." Curly showed Breanna a brown-toothed smile with several teeth missing.

"I'm pretty much needed here, right now, Mr. Wesson." She then turned to Clayson and asked, "How soon are you planning to move on?"

"Well, we've got to pull out tomorrow, ma'am. If we don't keep on schedule, we'll be in trouble when we get to the Sierra Nevada Mountains in California. Snow comes early in the high country."

"Mr. Wyatt, it will be at least two weeks before you're strong enough and healed enough to travel," Breanna said. "Even then, it will be very hard for you. Best thing would be to latch on to another wagon train later."

"But they won't come much later," Jay said. "Whether they're going to Oregon or California, they've got to get over the mountains before the snow flies."

"Well, if you waited even a week, it would be better than going on now. Of course, the best thing would be for you to winter right here and go on to California next spring."

"Can't do that," Jay sighed. "We've got to get to San Francisco this year. I'll be all right. We'll just go with Rip tomorrow."

Breanna shook her head. "Mrs. Wyatt, maybe you should try persuading your husband not to be in that train when it pulls out tomorrow."

"Ma'am," Clayson said, "I have a favor to ask of you."

"Yes?"

"We have a woman in the train who really needs some medical attention."

"Do you know what her problem is?"

"Not exactly, ma'am, but she's pretty sick. I know she's experiencing a lot of pain in her lower back. And she's definitely got a fever."

"How old is she?"

Rip looked at Curly. "What would you say? Fifty-five?"

"Yep, I'd say Hattie's somethin' like that. Three or four years younger than me."

"Yeah, three or four, at least!" Rip said. Then turning to Breanna, he asked, "Could you come out to the train right away, ma'am? Hattie really is in a lot of pain."

"Of course," Breanna nodded, moving to the cupboard where her medical bag sat. "Sounds like possibly a kidney infection if the pain's in her lower back. I'll take along something to help relieve her pain."

Breanna stuffed some small white envelopes into the bag, then spoke once again to her patient. "Mr. Wyatt, I really am serious when I tell you it's best if you don't travel so soon."

"Jay and I will talk about it while you're gone, Miss Baylor," Elsie said.

Breanna nodded, and turned with the bag in her hand. "All right, Mr. Clayson. Let's go take a look at Hattie. What's her last name?"

"Chatsworth, ma'am," answered Clayson. "Her husband's name is Doral. They're moving to California because Hattie has a lung disorder. Her doctors back in Detroit said she should move to the West Coast where the climate was warmer year round."

The occupants of the California-bound wagon train gathered to meet Nurse Breanna Baylor as she walked into the circle of wagons flanked by their wagon master and Curly Wesson.

"I have good news about Jay!" Rip said, halting in the center of the wagon circle. "This is Nurse Breanna Baylor, who's filling in until a doctor arrives at South Pass City. She performed surgery on Jay last night, removed the bullet from his belly, and he's doing fine."

Those gathered applauded and cheered.

"I should explain, however," spoke up Breanna, "that I have advised Mr. Wyatt not to continue on with this train. He must allow himself a couple of weeks to gain strength and give his wounds a chance to heal." Breanna turned to the wagon master and said, "Now, if you'll point me to Mrs. Chatsworth, sir."

Hattie Chatsworth lay in the Chatsworth wagon with her husband and two women sitting beside her. Doral Chatsworth quickly introduced the two women and himself to Breanna. Clara Farnsworth had served as a medical assistant for the Union doctors in the Civil War. Martha Kirkland's husband, Harold, had died of heart failure on the trail ten days previously. Breanna spoke her condolences to Martha, then the women climbed out to give her room to work.

Hattie was pale and quite evidently in pain.

Breanna smiled at her and said, "Hello, Mrs. Chatsworth. My name is Breanna Baylor. I'm a Certified Medical Nurse, and I'm here to see if I can help you. I understand the pain is in your lower back."

"Yes," nodded Hattie.

Breanna laid a hand on Hattie's brow. "You've got some fever, but it's not real high. Any chills?"

"A little, but not much."

"How long have you had the pain?"

"Just about twenty-four hours."

"Can you turn on your side for me? I want you to tell me exactly where it hurts." Hattie bit her lower lip and turned on her right side. "Now, tell me when I touch where it hurts the most."

Within seconds, the spot had been located, and Breanna told Hattie her right kidney was infected.

"Have you had kidney infections before?" asked Breanna.

"No," replied Hattie, lying flat on her back again. "The only real illness I've had is this problem with my lungs."

"Our Detroit doctors said Hattie should live in a warm climate near the ocean," Doral said. "So we're moving to southern California."

"That's good," responded Breanna, opening her medical bag. "I'm going to give her something that will ease the pain and bring down the fever. Since Mrs. Farnsworth has served as a medical assistant, I would like to show her how to administer this medicine so Mrs. Chatsworth can be cared for properly as the train moves on."

"I know she'll be glad to do it," Doral said. He moved to the opening in the canvas and spotted Clara standing a few feet away beside her husband. "Clara, Nurse Baylor would like to speak to you," he called.

"You'll feel better when we get some of this into you," Breanna said, patting Hattie's shoulder.

Clara climbed into the wagon and said, "You wanted to speak to me?"

"Yes. Mrs. Chatsworth has an infection in her right kidney."

"I thought that's what it was," Clara nodded. "How can I help?"

"I have some medicine I want to leave with you for her. It will need to be administered twice daily until the infection is gone. The infection isn't too bad, or she would have a higher fever."

Breanna withdrew several of the envelopes she had placed in the medical bag earlier and handed them to Clara.

"This is pulverized willow bark, Mrs. Farnsworth. Are you acquainted with it?"

"I don't believe so."

"Well, it's an old Indian medicine to relieve pain and bring down fever."

"Indian medicine?" Clara said, concern showing in her eyes.

"White men use it now, too," smiled Breanna, "but it was first known on this continent among the Indian tribes in the East—Delaware, Mohawk, Huron, and Mahican. Goes back to the mid-1600s."

"Really?"

"Mm-hmm. About a hundred years later an Anglican preacher in England was sick with fever and rheumatism. He happened to stick a twig from a white willow tree in his mouth, and after chewing on it for a few minutes, found that his pain was easing and his fever was going down. He was so elated to find relief for his malady that he devised a method of drying and pulverizing the bark, then experimented to discover the best dosage. Little did he realize that the Indians on our continent had already developed this medicine a hundred years previously."

"Isn't that something?" Doral said.

"Within the last fifty years, Swiss and German scientists have combined the willow bark with an extract called *spirsaure*, and just recently named it *salicylic acid*. That's what's in the envelopes."

"I see," Clara nodded. "You say I should give it to her twice a day?"

"Yes. You have a teaspoon, I assume."

"Yes."

"You'll make her a tea with these powders. One spoonful for each cup. A cup at mid-morning and one just before she retires for the night."

"All right."

"Now, let me caution you. I have spoken to Mr. Clayson about this. All water used for drinking and cooking on the trail must be boiled twice before use. Understand? *All* water. Make sure Mrs. Chatsworth's tea is made of twice-boiled water…and she should drink at least eight cups of water a day. That will flush out the kidneys and eventually clear up the infected one."

"I understand," Clara said. "I just wish you were going along to take care of her."

"The whole wagon train would be happy if that were so," Doral said.

Breanna smiled at him, then said to Clara, "I assume you know how to make tea of the powders."

"Yes. I should mix the powders in water, heat it up good—after boiling it twice—then strain the mixture through a thin cloth."

"Exactly! I notice there are milk cows in the train."

"Yes."

"It would be best if you give Mrs. Chatsworth a cup of milk before she takes the tea. The salicylic acid is a bit hard on the stomach. The milk will coat the lining and alleviate any discomfort she might otherwise have."

"All right," Clara said. "It shall be done."

"Good. Now I will leave, and you can begin boiling the water." Breanna turned to Hattie. "I'm leaving you in good hands, Mrs. Chatsworth. You'll be fine."

Hattie drew a rattling breath and coughed. "Thank you so much, Miss Baylor."

Breanna climbed from the wagon, medical bag in hand, and began walking toward Rip Clayson, who stood near. "Kidney infection," she said, "but she'll be all right."

Doral Chatsworth was on Breanna's heels. Before Rip could comment the older man drew up beside Breanna, extended a wad of green bills, and said, "Thank you."

"Oh, there's no need for payment, Mr. Chatsworth. The town is covering my room and board, and buying my medicine."

"But there *is* need, my dear," countered Chatsworth, placing the bills in her free hand and closing her fingers over them. "I need to express my appreciation for what you've done. Thank you so much."

"Thank you, sir," Breanna said, smiling warmly.

"I must commend you, my dear, for how well you are doing in place of a doctor in South Pass City. All of us are grateful to you for saving Jay Wyatt's life. With your talent, you should go back East to medical school and become a doctor."

"You're very kind, sir, but women doctors are almost unheard of in this country. The idea is appealing, but I'm happy being a nurse." She looked at the wagon master and said, "Well, Mr. Clayson, I'd better get back to town."

"I'll walk you back," said Rip.

As they moved through the people, Breanna noticed four young women in various stages of pregnancy. Her heart went out to them, knowing how difficult it had to be to ride in the wagons with all the jolts and bumps. *Brave women,* she thought to herself. *Brave women.*

8

BREANNA BAYLOR AND RIPLEY CLAYSON were just moving outside the circle of wagons when they saw a Conestoga wagon coming toward them out of South Pass City. It was pulled by a foursome team of muscular, well-bred horses.

On the seat were two men with a bonneted woman between them. As the Conestoga drew nearer, it was evident that the younger man was the son of the couple, for his facial features strongly resembled the older man, who sat ramrod straight with the reins in his hands. He was dressed in a snappy gray Confederate uniform with gold braid and a campaign hat to match. The markings on the collar and shoulders of the uniform coat indicated that he was a colonel.

Rip Clayson wondered how the man could stand to wear the coat in the summer's heat.

"You with the wagon train over there?" the man asked as they drew up. His southern accent was heavy.

"Yes, sir. My name's Ripley Clayson. I'm wagon master. And this is Miss Br—"

"Ah, good!" roared the man. "Just the man I want to see! My family and I—Oh! I didn't introduce you. This here's my wife of twenty-four years, Marian...and our son, Jason. My name's

Wade Moore...Colonel Wade Moore. I'm a graduate of West Point, Class of '38. Graduated with my good friend Pierre Gustave Toutant Beauregard and fought beside him in the Mexican War when we were both captains in the U. S. Army. Fought under him as my commandin' general at Fort Sumter, Bull Run, Shiloh, and many other battles too numerous to name."

"What can I do for you, Colonel?" Rip asked.

"Well, sir," said Moore, lifting his campaign hat and dropping it back in place, "we were part of a wagon train that came through here four days ago, headin' for San Francisco. Our wagon's rear axle was comin' apart, and the sawdust-for-brains wagon master wouldn't wait for me to have another one put on. I got a new axle at the wagon works at the west end of town, and now we all are ready to travel. Y'all *are* goin' to California, aren't you? Please don't tell me your headed for Oregon."

"No, sir. We're headed for California, all right. Main bunch of us are going to San Francisco. Some will be dropping off once we're out of the Sierras."

"Well, good! We'll just sign on then if y'all will have us."

"Depends on whether you want to pay my fee," Clayson said. "It's four hundred dollars per wagon from St. Joseph. South Pass City's about halfway, so my fee will be two hundred dollars."

"No problem!" boomed Moore, who was a large, broad-shouldered, thick-chested man.

He swung his leg over the side of the wagon and used the left front wheel for his descent. He pulled out a fat wallet from inside his coat and began counting out the amount, then slapped the money into Clayson's hand.

"Go ahead and count it," Moore said.

"No need," Clayson grinned. "I watched you count it. By the way, we probably won't be pulling out for a day or two, Colonel."

"Why's that?"

"We have a woman in the train who's ailing with a kidney infection and a man who was accidentally shot in the stomach. This lady with me is Nurse Breanna Baylor, who's the acting physician in South Pass City."

Moore touched his campaign hat without smiling. "My pleasure, ma'am. But how can a nurse be a physician? Takes a man to be a physician...and one with a doctor's degree at that."

"You may have missed what Mr. Clayson said, Colonel. He said I am *acting* physician. There's no doctor here because Dr. Rudd took sick and died a few weeks ago. There's another doctor on his way, but until he gets here, this town is stuck with me."

"I see," Moore said, wiping a sleeve across his mouth and mustache. "I meant no offense, ma'am. Just speakin' my mind."

A fool's voice is known by multitude of words, thought Breanna. *Ecclesiastes 5:3.*

"She's mighty good at what she does, Colonel," Rip said. "You were in the War. How many gut-shot men did you ever see make it through surgery?"

"Well, not many."

"Miss Baylor performed the surgery on the man I told you about. He was in bad shape and had little more than a ghost of a chance to pull through. But he's doing quite well."

"But you still have to wait a day to pull out?"

"That's right. I'm not sure the man and his wife will even be going with us. This is Saturday. We'll know more by tomorrow or Monday."

"Well, that's all right, sir," Moore said. "I'm just happy to be in another wagon train." He turned halfway around and looked at his family. "We're happy about this, aren't we Marian? Jason?"

"Yes, dear," Marian nodded.

When Jason didn't respond, Moore's face tightened. "I said we're happy to be in this wagon train, right, Jason?"

"Yes, Colonel," Jason said.

Sunday services were held at the town hall in South Pass City, with most of the people from the wagon train in attendance. Since the town had no organized church or ordained preacher, a few of the laymen—merchants, laborers, and miners—brought Bible messages each Sunday. When the townsmen learned that Rip Clayson always held Sunday services on the trail, they asked him to preach, and he did an excellent job.

On Sunday afternoon, Clayson visited the Wyatts at the clinic and, with Breanna present, tried to convince Jay to winter at South Pass City and join his wagon train when he came through next year. Jay insisted he could travel with Clayson now.

Clayson then tried to talk him into waiting a week or so until the last wagon train of the season came through. Breanna backed Clayson's advice. Stubbornly, Jay held his ground, insisting he could travel with the train when it pulled out.

Breanna and Rip left the clinic and returned to the wagon train, where Breanna checked on Hattie Chatsworth. Clayson saw that Hattie was doing much better and was glad when Breanna said Hattie would be able to travel without too much discomfort if the train waited another day.

On Sunday night, Clayson called the people together within the circle of wagons and announced they would pull out at sunup on Tuesday. The people were glad and voiced it. The loudest approving voice was that of the newcomer, Colonel Wade Moore.

At 6:45 on Monday morning, Marshal Bill Stone approached his office on foot at the same time Deputy Wally Frye angled across the broad street from the Bluebird Café, carrying a breakfast tray.

Stone pulled a key from his pocket and grinned at his deputy. "Why such a sour look, Wally?"

"Aw, I was just wishin' it wasn't gonna be so long till the circuit judge shows up here and passes sentence on Hatch. I'm gettin' tired of haulin' his meals to him. The first week of September can't come too soon for me."

"Well, I've got good news for you, my boy," Stone said. "I happened to run into the Morrises as they were headin' home from the church services last night."

"You mean Morrises as in our esteemed justice of the peace and her husband?"

"You know any other Morrises in this town?"

"No. Just wanted to make sure who we're talkin' about, here."

Stone turned the key, opened the door, and stepped inside. Frye came in behind him.

"So what's the good news?" the deputy asked.

"I was talking to Mrs. Morris about Hatch and telling her I wished the circuit judge was comin' sooner. She said that as justice of the peace, she can handle minor cases. And since Harley

Cummins is doin' fine and the wound ain't serious, Hatch's case is minor. She can hear the case and pronounce sentence."

"Great! Luke'll be on his way to the territorial prison at Rawlins as soon as they can send a U. S. marshal to take him."

"Well, let's go in and tell him he's gonna be facin' the first woman justice of the peace in U. S. history."

At the same time the lawmen were breaking the news to their prisoner, Breanna Baylor left her room at the Sweetwater Hotel and headed for the stairs. She could hear Lorraine Miller humming in room 8 as she passed. Just as she approached room 4, the door came open, and a stout-bodied man in his late thirties stepped out, key in hand.

The man touched the brim of his derby hat, smiled at Breanna, and said, "Good morning, ma'am."

"Good morning," Breanna said, returning the smile. "I don't believe I've seen you before. I'm Breanna Baylor."

"Glad to make your acquaintance, ma'am. My name's Gifford Maston. I'm a drummer. Came in on the last stage."

"Oh? And just what kind of drum do you play?" she asked lightly.

Maston chuckled at her humor. "I sell linens, dress material, and other cloth products, ma'am. Been doing business with the folks at the general store here ever since they opened. If you don't mind my saying so, you are a very lovely lady. If I'd seen you before, I'm sure I'd remember."

"I've only been in town a few weeks, Mr. Maston. I'm a Certified Medical Nurse. South Pass's physician, Dr. Rudd, had a sudden illness that took his life. I'm here to fill in as best as I can until the new doctor arrives. He's coming from Kansas City and should be here within the next few days."

"I see," nodded Maston. "Well, nice to have met you. Oh, I forgot something. Pardon me, but I've got to go back into my room."

"Nice to have met you, too," she said, and headed down the stairs.

Breanna greeted Benny Freeman, who stood behind the desk, and moved out onto the boardwalk. When she closed the door behind her, she found Frank Miller standing alone, hands in pockets, just gazing at the early morning traffic on the street. At the sound of the door closing, Miller made a half-turn and set his eyes on Breanna.

"Hello, Frank," Breanna said and kept walking.

She halted when Miller said, "So how often do you see your boyfriend, Breanna?"

She gave him a tart look and replied, "Not as often as I would like. But he'll probably be showing up here just any time." There was a slight edge in her voice as she added, "He's more than just a boyfriend, Frank."

"Ever think of me anymore?"

"Why should I?" she asked, and started to walk away.

Miller reached out and seized her elbow, spinning her around.

Breanna's face flushed with irritation. "Let go of me, Frank!" she said, tugging against his grip.

Rip Clayson approached the scene, coming from the east end of town along the boardwalk. "Pardon me, but is this man bothering you, Miss Breanna?" he said.

Miller jerked his head around, looked the wagon master up and down, and noted the revolver holstered on his hip. Miller let go of Breanna's arm and eased his hand down where it rested against the bulge of the Derringer in his pocket.

"He *is* bothering me, thank you, Mr. Clayson," Breanna said, "but our conversation is over."

Miller gave her a hard look, then turned and went back into the hotel.

Clayson watched Miller until he disappeared, then turned to Breanna and asked, "Someone you know?"

"Yes. We were engaged to be married once."

"Oh, I see. Are you on your way to the clinic?"

"Yes."

"Well, I'm heading that way, myself. Wanted to see if Elsie Wyatt had been able to convince that husband of hers to at least wait till another wagon train comes along."

"I have a feeling Jay will be in his wagon tomorrow morning with Duane at the reins," Breanna said. "His mind is set on going with you."

It was almost one o'clock in the afternoon when a lone rider trotted his mount into South Pass City from the east and hauled up in front of Marshal Stone's office. The brilliant sun glinted off the badge that he wore on his chest as he dismounted and wrapped the reins around the hitch rail.

Stone's door was open because of the heat. The tall, beefy lawman stepped into the office and found the town marshal bent over his desk, doing paper work.

Stone looked up, noted the Deputy U. S. Marshal's badge on the middle-aged man with the droopy mustache, and rose to his feet. Extending his hand over the desk, he said, "Howdy. I'm Marshal Stone."

"And I'm Deputy U. S. Marshal Claude Olney. I work out of the Greeley, Colorado, office."

"Somethin' I can do for you?" Stone asked.

"Maybe."

Stone gestured toward a chair that sat in front of the desk. "Have a seat."

"Thanks," Olney said and eased onto the chair. He pulled a large bandanna from a hip pocket, removed his hat, and mopped his sweaty brow. "I'm trailing a killer, Stone. I have reason to believe he has either passed through your town or is still here. Name's Frank Miller. Professional gambler."

"Well, we have a lot of those pass through," Stone said evenly, "and we've probably got an easy dozen of 'em in town right now. With all the gold bein' scratched out of the hills around here, it's drawin' 'em like a magnet."

"I can imagine that. This Miller is about five-ten, medium build. Has dark hair...almost black. Wears his mustache real thin. Has extra heavy brows. Eyes are black as midnight. Dresses real sharp. Better than the average professional gambler. I think he's travelin' with a woman. Supposed to be his wife."

"You know what she looks like?"

"From what I was told in Cheyenne City, she's a good-looker. 'Bout five-six or seven. Hair's long and deep-red. You know... auburn. Don't know about her eye color, but they tell me she dresses fancy and wears lots of makeup."

"I know a couple like that," Stone said. "They've been here

just a few days. Stayin' at the Sweetwater, I think. Only their name ain't Miller. It's...ah...oh, what is it? I heard somebody say. Ballard. That's it. Kent and Lorraine Ballard."

"But they resemble this Miller and his wife?"

"Exactly as you described 'em. Early thirties?"

"Yep."

"I'd say you've found your man, Deputy Olney. He wanted for more than one murder?"

"Not as far as I know. There's no record on him. He's originally from Kansas. Took up gamblin' for a livin' five, maybe six years ago. Miller was in Greeley several days ago, doin' some gamblin'. His wife wasn't with him. I understand from folks in Cheyenne City that he often goes off and leaves her to gamble in other towns. They'd made Cheyenne City their home."

"I see."

"Well, as I said, Miller was in my town gamblin' several days ago and got into a poker game with a Jack Lynch. There were plenty of witnesses in the casino to testify as to what happened, and they all told it the same way. Miller accused Lynch of cheating him. When the saloon owner demanded that Miller produce proof, he couldn't do it. He was told to get out and never come back. He lost quite a bundle.

"Later, Lynch and the saloon owner were standin' alone in front of the saloon after closin' time. Shots rang out, and both men went down. Lynch was dead. The saloon owner was wounded but not armed, so he played dead. He testified later that a lone figure emerged from the shadows, cleaned out Lynch's pockets, and ran away into the night. However, the owner made out his face by a nearby street lantern. It was Frank Miller."

"But won't that be the saloon owner's word against Miller's?"

"Would be, but so happens a man and his wife who own a leather shop in Greeley were looking out their window no more than twenty feet from where the two victims went down. Both of them gave a perfect description of Miller's features and the clothing he was wearin' that night. I've been assigned by Chief U. S. Marshal Solomon Duvall in Denver to hunt Miller down and bring him in to stand trial for murder, as well as robbery."

"Well," said Stone, "I guess the first place to look for Miller—alias Kent Ballard—is his hotel room. If he's not there, we'll have to hit all the saloons until we find him."

"'Preciate your offer to help, Marshal," said Olney, "but it's really not your responsibility."

"Hey, I'm a lawman, my friend. We badge toters need to help each other. Besides, that'll put the odds on the side of the law. Two of us against one of him."

"Won't make me mad," Olney grinned. "Let's go."

Frank Miller had played a few hands of poker earlier in the day and found himself losing, so when it was safe to bow out of the game, he did and returned to the hotel.

Lorraine had bathed and washed her hair, and was sitting before the dresser mirror in her robe, brushing her long tresses. Frank was stretched out on the bed, eyes closed, fingers interlaced behind his head on the pillow.

The lobby of the Sweetwater Hotel was unoccupied when the two lawmen entered and approached the desk where Benny

Freeman was preparing a bank deposit. The clerk looked up over his half-moon glasses, grinned, and said, "Good afternoon, Marshal."

"Afternoon, Benny," nodded Stone. "This is Deputy U. S. Marshal Claude Olney. He's on the trail of a man named Frank Miller, who is wanted in Colorado for murder."

"Yes, sir?"

Olney leaned on the counter. "You have a man and woman registered here under the name Ballard, correct?"

"Yes, sir. Mr. and Mrs. Kent Ballard."

"Well, their real name is Miller, Benny," Olney said. "And he's the Frank Miller I'm after. Is he in his room?"

"I believe so," Benny said, fear showing in his eyes. "He came in awhile ago, angry because he's been having a losing streak. He's a professional gambler, you know."

"Yeah, I know," Olney said. "His wife up there, too?"

"As far as I know. I haven't seen her leave."

"What room they in?"

"Number eight."

"All right," Olney said, hitching up his gunbelt. "We're goin' up there right now. If any of your guests come in, send 'em back outside. And if any of 'em come down from upstairs, tell 'em to get outside, too. Understand?"

"Yes, sir," Benny nodded. "And what about me? Should I stay here at the desk?"

"Yes. I need you here to warn people of the danger. Understand?"

"Yes, sir."

"All right, Marshal. Let's go," Olney said.

❧

Lorraine Miller was still brushing her hair and talking to her husband, who lay on the bed, eyes closed.

"Don't take it so hard, honey," Lorraine said. "You've had those days before when you just couldn't seem to pick up a winning hand. It'll be better tomorrow."

"*Tonight*, Lorraine. It'll be better tonight. I'll be in one of those saloons come dark...and my luck'll change."

Lorraine looked at her husband in the mirror. "That's better. Keep a positive attitude. Everything'll be okay. You'll do real good here, and soon we can go back home to Cheyenne City."

Frank did not reply. They could probably never go back to Cheyenne City. He would have to stay ahead of the law. The story he had told Lorraine about Billy Axtell never happened. Billy Axtell didn't even exist.

Lorraine sighed and began brushing her hair again. She jumped with a start when a loud knock came at the door.

Frank sat bolt upright, looked at the door, then at Lorraine, then back at the door. The heavy knock was repeated.

Lorraine saw the fear on her husband's face. "Frank, what's the matter? Why don't you go to the door?"

"Frank Miller!" came an authoritative voice. "Open up! Deputy U. S. Marshal! I want to talk to you!"

Miller sprang from the bed and picked up a Colt .44 revolver from the bedstand.

"Miller!" bawled Olney. "Open the door, or I'll break it down!"

Miller bolted for the room's single window, revolver in hand.

"Frank, it's not Billy Axtell's friends!" Lorraine shouted. "It's a federal marshal. He only wants to talk to you. What are you doing?"

She left her stool in front of the dresser and dashed across the room toward her fleeing husband. Frank had one leg out the window when the door crashed open and the two lawmen rushed into the room, guns drawn.

"Hold it right there, Miller!" Olney roared. "Drop the gun or you die!"

9

LORRAINE MILLER FROZE halfway across the room, still holding her hairbrush, and clasped her robe tight at the neck. She stood facing Stone and Olney, her features rigid and white.

Miller froze with his right leg out the window.

"Okay, mister, drop the gun," Olney said.

Miller swore under his breath and let the revolver clatter to the floor.

"Back out of the window, Miller!" Olney barked. "You're under arrest for the murder of Jack Lynch."

Lorraine stared in open-mouthed astonishment. "Frank, what's he talking about?"

"I have no idea," Frank said.

"No need to lie, Miller!" Olney said. "Three eyewitnesses in Greeley saw you take the money out of Lynch's pocket after you shot him and the saloon owner. They'll nail you in court. There'll be a noose just your size waitin' for you right after the trial."

Lorraine began to whimper. "Frank, what's this all about? You didn't tell me anything like this. What did you do?"

"Murdered a gambler he claimed cheated him, ma'am," said

Olney. "Shot him down in front of the Mustang Saloon. Shot another man too, but he lived."

"Oh, Frank!" Lorraine cried. She turned her back on him and broke down sobbing.

"All right, Miller, get out of the window," Olney said. As he spoke, he pulled a pair of handcuffs from his hip pocket.

Frank's mind was racing. There was no way he would let Olney take him back to Colorado. The Derringer was in his right pants pocket, hidden from view. If he moved fast enough—with the element of surprise on his side—he could take out both men.

"Okay, okay," Miller said, throwing up the hand that was in the room. "I won't give you any trouble."

Miller made as if he was having difficulty getting back inside the room. At the same time he pulled the Derringer from his pocket.

"Come on!" Olney said, waving his gun. Stone stood at his side, his gun ready for action.

Frank Miller slid from the window sill and fired dead-center at Claude Olney's heart.

Olney felt the slug club him in the chest. Reflex squeezed the trigger of his revolver, and it discharged with a roar as his heart exploded, jerking his body. The slug from his gun struck Lorraine in the stomach. She let out a pained cry and collapsed in a heap.

Miller unleashed his remaining bullet on Marshal Stone just as the seasoned lawman spun sideways, and the hot lead buzzed past his ear.

"Okay, Miller!" Stone yelled, lining his gun on the gambler's face. "Drop the Derringer!"

Frank Miller let the Derringer fall from his fingers, then quickly dropped to his knees beside Lorraine.

At that moment a stout-bodied man appeared at the door, took a quick look at the situation, and blinking at the smoke that assaulted his eyes, said, "Marshal, I'm Gifford Maston. Can I help?"

"Yes. Go down the street to the south a block and a half to the doctor's office. There's a nurse there. Her name's Breanna Baylor. Tell her we've had a shooting."

"I know her, Marshal," Maston said. "I'll be right back with her."

"Tell her we've got a woman down, gutshot. And ask somebody on the street to go tell my deputy I want him here fast."

"Gotcha," Maston said, and ran toward the stairs.

Miller shifted his position and placed Lorraine's head in his lap. She was conscious and breathing shallowly.

"You just hold on, honey," Miller said. "They're bringing Breanna."

Lorraine clutched her bleeding stomach with both hands. "Why...did you lie to me, Frank?"

"Ssh. Don't try to talk." Miller looked up at Stone. "Shouldn't we just carry her down to the clinic?"

"I don't want to move her," replied the marshal, still holding his gun on him. "Might do more damage. I want Nurse Baylor to look at her first. She'll tell us what to do."

There were loud footsteps on the stairs, then in the hall, and Deputy Frye plunged into the room. Benny Freeman came in seconds later.

Bill Stone explained what had happened as the two men

stood looking at the dead marshal and the bleeding woman. More footsteps were heard on the stairs. A moment later, Breanna Baylor hurried through the door, carrying her medical bag, with Gifford Maston on her heels.

As she knelt beside Lorraine, Breanna glanced at the lifeless form of Claude Olney. Her eyes met Frank's and held for a second or two, then she turned back to Lorraine and pulled open the robe to examine the damage.

"I didn't want to move her until you said it was all right, Miss Breanna," Marshal Stone said.

"You did right, Marshal," Breanna replied, still probing about the wound. Quickly closing the robe, she said, "However, we need to move her now. I'll need two of you to carry her."

"I'll be one of them," Frank said.

"No!" Stone snapped. "You're goin' to jail!"

"But this is my wife!" Miller shouted, temper flaring.

"And this is a dead lawman here on the floor that you killed!" Stone said. "Whose fault do you think it is that your wife has a bullet in her? *Yours*, mister! Cuff him, Wally, and get him outta here!"

As Frye moved toward him, Miller showed fiery eyes. "Don't you touch me! I'm goin' with my wife!"

Frye whipped out his gun and hissed, "You can go the easy way or the hard way, Miller. Choice is yours."

Frank eased Lorraine's head to the floor and rose to his feet in reluctant surrender. Frye holstered his gun and quickly cuffed Miller's hands behind his back.

Miller shifted his gaze from Lorraine to Breanna and said, "You'll fix her up, won't you, Breanna? She'll be okay. Right?"

Breanna ignored him and spoke to the wounded woman. "Lorraine, the bullet has done a lot of damage to your intestines, and I'm going to have to operate. But first I need your permission. This is major surgery, and I can't guarantee it'll be successful."

"Why do you need her permission?" Frank demanded. "It's got to be done!"

"Because I'm not a qualified surgeon, Frank!" Breanna said. "I'm only a nurse!"

"Well, you did surgery on that man from the wagon train who was gutshot. You saved him, you can save Lorraine!"

"How about it?" Breanna asked, leaning close over Lorraine.

"Yes," she nodded. "Go ahead."

Bill Stone and Gifford Maston picked Lorraine up, following Breanna's instructions, and carried her through the door. Breanna walked alongside them.

"It'll be all right, Lorraine!" Frank called after them. "Breanna will fix you up good as new!"

Wally Frye shoved Miller through the door ahead of him, and Benny Freeman eyed the dead lawman one more time, closed the door, and followed the procession down the stairs.

Moments later, Frye shoved Miller through the marshal's office door, then through the door that led to the cells. Luke Hatch was sitting on his bunk and watched the deputy push Miller into the adjacent cell and slam the steel-barred door.

"Hey, how about these cuffs?" Miller bawled.

"Back up to the bars and I'll take 'em off."

"Careful cuss, aren't you?" Miller said.

"Yeah. Especially with cold-blooded killers."

The cuffs came off and Frye started to leave the cell block.

"You'd better let me know when the surgery is over," Miller said. "I want to know how it went. You hear me?"

"You'll know as soon as we do," Frye said, and walked out.

Moments later Marshal Stone entered the cell block and stood in front of Miller's cell. "The surgery is underway, and we'll let you know as soon as we hear anything. I sent a wire to the chief U. S. marshal in Denver. You'll stand trial right here. Colorado officials will send vital information about the murder in Greeley. Circuit judge will be here sometime the first week of September. Better enjoy these next four weeks, Frank, 'cause you'll hang the day after your trial."

"Lynch cheated me outta four thousand dollars, Marshal!" Frank shouted. "I couldn't let him get away with that! You'd have been mad if it'd happened to you."

"Losin' your temper is no excuse for murderin' Jack Lynch, Miller. Man oughtta have better control of himself. And what about Olney? What were you mad at him about?"

Miller could only stare at the lawman. Emotions warred deep within him, but he had no answer.

Stone turned and left. When the office door snapped shut, Miller swung his fist, swore, and said, "I'll break out of this one-horse jail before September!"

Luke Hatch sat quietly on his bunk, thinking of his upcoming appearance before Justice of the Peace Esther Morris.

Breanna Baylor enlisted the help of Elsie Wyatt as she operated on Lorraine Miller. Lorraine was bleeding profusely and not doing well with the chloroform. Breanna was having a difficult time keeping her under. After over an hour of probing for the bullet, Breanna finally located and removed it. Lorraine began to stir for the fourth or fifth time since Breanna began the surgery.

"More chloroform," Breanna said, looking at Elsie. "Be sure to soak the cloth completely."

Elsie nodded and picked up the bottle of chloroform. She removed the cork and poured the strong-smelling fluid into the folded cloth she had been using. Just before she lowered it to Lorraine's face, Breanna drew in a sharp breath.

"Never mind, Elsie. She's dead."

Elsie's eyes widened above her mask, and her sweaty brow formed deep lines. "Oh, no."

Breanna laid the instrument in her hand on the tray next to the table and sighed with a shudder. "She just bled too much. The slug did too much damage. There was nothing more I could do."

Tears filmed Breanna's eyes as she removed her mask, looking down at the dead woman.

"No one could fault you, honey," Elsie said as she removed her own mask. "Even a qualified surgeon couldn't have saved her. She was torn up too bad."

Breanna's mind went back a few days to the moment she and Lorraine met on the street. She recalled vividly how Lorraine suddenly wanted to leave when the offer was made to sit down with an open Bible. Now, for Lorraine, it was too late."

Breanna took hold of the sheet that lay folded at Lorraine's hips and drew it up over her head.

Footsteps were heard in the outer office, then came a knock at the clinic door.

"Miss Breanna, it's Deputy Frye. May I come in?"

"Yes."

When the door came open, the lawman knew instantly that Lorraine Miller had not survived the surgery. "She didn't make it," he said softly.

"No," replied Breanna, stepping to the water pump and wash basin to clean up. "I thought at the beginning there was a chance, but the bullet was buried too deep. She just bled to death."

"I'm sure you did all you could, ma'am," Frye said.

"Even a doctor couldn't have saved her, deputy," Elsie said. "I saw what that bullet did to Lorraine's insides."

Wally sighed and said, "Well, I'll go tell Miller. I promised him I'd let him know when the surgery was over."

"Wally, I think it would be more appropriate if I break the news to him," Breanna said. "It's always the surgeon who carries the news to the family, whether good or bad. It's only right and proper that I inform Mr. Miller of his wife's death."

"If that's the way you want it, ma'am."

"It would be easier to let you tell him, Wally. But it's my responsibility."

"Yes, ma'am," nodded the deputy. "I'll walk you to the jail, Miss Breanna."

When they reached the jail, Frye opened the door for Breanna and led her across the office to the cell block door. He opened it and said, "Go ahead, ma'am. You can come out whenever you're finished."

Breanna thanked him and headed down the narrow hallway

that led to the cells. Her hands were shaking as she moved into the cell area. There were four cells, but only two were occupied. She hadn't even thought about Luke Hatch being in one of them.

It was Hatch who saw her first, for Frank Miller was lying on his cot, eyes closed, an arm across his face.

Hatch was sitting on his cot. He swore, rose to his feet, and blared, "What're you doin' here, woman?"

Breanna jumped with a start and took a step away from the bars. "I'm here to talk to Mr. Miller," she said with difficulty.

Frank was now up and moving toward the bars. Breanna stepped close to the cell door and started to speak.

"So how's Lorraine?" Miller demanded.

Breanna folded her trembling hands. She breathed through her nose, forcing herself to take deep, even breaths.

"Frank...she—"

"She *what?*" he said, not really wanting to hear it.

"She...died. On the operating table. I did everything I could, but she bled to death before I could get the bleeding stopped."

Frank Miller's eyes widened in disbelief. "She's dead? My Lorraine is *dead?*"

"Frank, I'm sorry. Truly sorry. Believe me, I did all I could to save her. The woman who assisted me would tell you that even a qualified surgeon couldn't have saved her. The bullet had done far too much damage."

"You're lying, Breanna! You let Lorraine die to get back at me for jilting you! That's what you did, didn't you?"

Breanna couldn't speak. She shook her head no.

"Lorraine took me away from you, Breanna, so you let her

die to get back at us! Isn't that right!"

Breanna's lips quivered. She took a short breath and managed to say, "Frank, you know better than that."

"I *don't* know better than that!" Miller was shouting now.

"I did all that was humanly possible to save her, Frank, and God in heaven knows I did!"

Miller swore and shook the bars. "There you go with that religious stuff again! You rotten, murderin' hypocrite! You won't get away with this, Breanna! I'll get out of here, and when I do, I'm comin' for you! I'm gonna shoot you down like a rabid dog. You can bet your bottom dollar on it. There'll be a bullet for you, Breanna! That's a promise!"

Frank's words struck Breanna like sharp stones. Recoiling from their intensity, she took a step back, then turned and ran from the cell block and into the office. Frank was shouting and swearing at her, but she couldn't distinguish his words.

Marshal Stone and Deputy Frye were outside, in conversation with a group of townsmen. Breanna leaned her hands against the top of the desk and burst into tears.

10

↟

BREANNA BAYLOR WEPT for several minutes. She was just getting control of her emotions and drying her tears when Marshal Bill Stone entered the office.

"What's wrong, Miss Breanna?" Stone asked, drawing up short.

"I was just accused of murdering Lorraine Miller, Marshal," Breanna said, sniffing and blowing into the hanky she held in her hands.

Stone's mouth fell open. Eyes wide, he gasped, "You—wha— *murder?* Who—"

"Her husband."

"Miller accused you of murdering his wife?"

"Yes."

"How could he say such a thing?"

"The man has a hair-trigger temper, Marshal. You see, I was once engaged to him."

"You—you were engaged to *marry* him?"

"Yes, sir."

"Maybe you'd better fill me in here," Stone said. He

motioned for her to sit in the chair in front of his desk, then eased into his own chair, removed his hat, tossed it on another nearby chair, and listened while Breanna told him about Miller jilting her to marry Lorraine Williams. She saw no reason to bring up John Stranger, but filled Stone in on her conversation with Lorraine and her confrontation with Miller. Tears surfaced again as she recounted Miller's wicked accusation and his threat to break jail and kill her.

While Breanna dabbed at her eyes, Stone leaned forward and said, "Don't you worry about him, little lady. He won't get out of *this* jail. And once the circuit judge arrives the first week of September, Mr. Frank Miller will hang. He'll have to come back from the dead to bother you then."

"I don't know what's gotten into Frank," Breanna said. "He showed some temper now and then when we were courting, but I've never known him to be like this. It's like he's gone crazy or something. He knows me too well to believe I'd deliberately let Lorraine die."

"Anyone who knows you knows that couldn't be true."

"Maybe…maybe when he cools down he'll change his mind…about hunting me down, I mean."

"Won't make any difference, ma'am," Stone said. "He's not getting out of my jail, and he'll hang before September is ten days old."

Breanna nodded and rose from the chair. Stone stood up too.

"Marshal, will you contact the undertaker and have him pick up Lorraine's body from the clinic? You can talk to Frank about burial arrangements for her."

"I'll take care of it right away, Miss Breanna," he replied.

Breanna headed down the street toward the clinic and was

stopped several times by people asking about the shooting at the hotel and the results of her surgery on the gambler's wife. This only served to keep her emotions at the surface.

She was within a half-block of the clinic when she heard the familiar sounds of the Wyoming Overland stage coming down the street. She turned and saw Les Jameson and Tim Riley in the box.

"Miss Breanna!" Jameson shouted. "The new doctor and his wife are aboard!"

The stage rolled to a stop, and while Jameson and Riley made their way down from the box, a sandy-haired man of about forty stepped out and gave his hand to a woman possibly three or four years younger than he. When she stood in the dust of the street, the man helped two older women from the coach.

Jameson guided Breanna to the man and wife, and said, "Dr. Wall, this is the lady we've told you so much about. She just happened to be passing the stage office as we pulled up."

"I'm so pleased to meet you, Miss Baylor. I'm Dr. Everett Wall and this is my wife, Karen. These gentlemen have told us all about you. If the people of South Pass City feel toward you like Les and Tim do, I may have to hire you as my assistant and put a shingle out with your name on it."

After what Breanna had just been through, it felt good to laugh. She offered her hand to the doctor, then to his wife, welcoming them to the town. Dr. Wall explained that they would be staying at the Sweetwater Hotel until they could find permanent quarters. Breanna offered to go along to the hotel and help them settle in.

Word spread quickly through the town, out to the mines, and to the wagon train that the new doctor had arrived.

That evening, after Breanna had eaten supper with Dr. and Mrs. Wall at the hotel restaurant, she went to her room, lit two lanterns, and sat down on the bed. The quietness of the room closed in on her, and Frank Miller's stinging words assaulted her, reverberating through her mind over and over again.

She took her Bible from the bedstand, wiped tears, and said, "Lord, help me. Frank's got me all upset. I need some peace."

She thought of Jesus' words to his troubled disciples, turned to John 14:27, and read aloud: *"Peace I leave with you, my peace I give unto you: not as the world giveth, give I unto you. Let not your heart be troubled, neither let it be afraid."*

She eyed a notation she had made in the margin next to that verse. *Perfect peace—Isaiah 26:3.* It took only seconds to find the page:

Thou wilt keep him in perfect peace, whose mind is stayed on thee: because he trusteth in thee.

Breanna fell to her knees beside the bed, tears wetting her cheeks. "Lord Jesus, You know my heart. It hurts, Lord, to be accused of letting Lorraine die for spite, when You know I did everything I could to save her. And Lord, I admit it—I'm afraid. I'm afraid of Frank, afraid he could break jail and come after me. O Lord, help me. I need Your perfect peace. I need that right now. I love You, Lord Jesus."

Breanna could almost feel the arms of Jesus close around her, for her heart was flooded with a calm that took away all the hurt and all the fear. A still small voice came, not to her ears but to her heart, saying, "I will take your pain, my child, and I will watch over you. You are safe in My arms." The peace and warmth that flooded her heart was as real as the bed she leaned against.

Breanna breathed a prayer of thanks and rose to her feet. She went to the wash basin, poured water into it from the pitcher, and washed her face. She was drying with a towel when there was a knock at the door. She went to the door and called, "Who is it?"

"Rip Clayson and Doral Chatsworth, Miss Breanna," came the muffled reply. "If it's not convenient for you to talk to us right now, we can come back later this evening or in the morning."

Breanna turned the skeleton key and opened the door. "Now is fine. Come in, gentlemen."

Both men could tell Breanna had been crying. As they entered and she closed the door, Rip asked, "Is something wrong, ma'am?"

"I've...been a bit upset about something, Mr. Clayson, something personal. But I'm doing better now. I just had a good talk with the Lord about it."

"Yes, ma'am. If you'd like us to come back later—"

"Oh, no, please sit down, gentlemen." Breanna gestured toward two overstuffed chairs. "What did you want to see me about? Is there more sickness in the wagon train?"

"No, thank the Lord," Clayson said. "We...ah...we heard that the new doctor arrived this afternoon, and we wanted to know how soon you plan to leave."

"Well, I haven't set any definite date yet, but I'll probably stay another few days to help Dr. Wall get settled in before I head for home."

"To Denver?" Chatsworth asked.

"Yes, sir. I'm based out of Dr. Lyle Goodwin's office there."

Chatsworth glanced at Clayson, cleared his throat, and said,

"Miss Baylor, I would like to make you an offer. I've talked it over with Rip, here, and he's a hundred percent in agreement."

"An offer? What kind of offer, Mr. Chatsworth?"

"You've seen that my wife is not in good health."

"Yes, sir. She should get better, though, when you get her to southern California and the ocean air."

"I'm confident of that," Chatsworth smiled, "but I am concerned about getting her there. She needs the kind of care you could give her if you were traveling with us."

"Oh. Well, I'm sure she could use some special care, Mr. Chatsworth, but—"

"You're aware that Jay Wyatt is determined to go with us in spite of his condition?"

"Yes."

"My deepest concern, of course, is for Hattie. It's imperative that I get her to the warmer climate as soon as possible."

"Of course."

"But I want her to be comfortable and under the best care while I'm getting her there. Am I making sense?"

"Yes. I understand what you're saying. But—"

"If you were to go with us, you could not only take care of Hattie, but you would be there to care for Jay, too. For that matter, there no doubt will be others in the train who'll need your services."

"Yes, Mr. Chatsworth," said Breanna, "but—"

"I'll pay you two thousand dollars to finish the trip with us, Miss Baylor, and I'll pay your railroad fare back to Denver from San Francisco. You can get all the way to Denver by rail from San Francisco now, you know."

"Yes, sir, I know that, but—"

"If my offer is too low, Miss Baylor, I'll make it *three* thousand."

"Oh, Mr. Chatsworth, two thousand is more than generous. Ordinarily it takes me an entire year to come by that much money. The only thing is...Dr. Goodwin might already have work lined up for me."

"I see," Chatsworth said. "Well, let's wire him and find out. I'll pay for the wire."

"Please give it serious consideration, will you Miss Breanna?" Clayson said. "You'd be a real asset to the wagon train, with all the sickness and accidents that happen along the trail...let alone what a blessing you'd be to Hattie and to Jay."

"Words well-spoken, Rip," Chatsworth said. "How about it, ma'am?"

Breanna smiled. "Well, I'd sure like to know that Mrs. Chatsworth gets to California all right...and I wouldn't worry so much about Jay if I was there to look after him. And I sure could use the two thousand dollars."

Chatsworth and Clayson grinned at each other, then Chatsworth said, "Not two thousand, Miss Baylor. I've already opened my mouth and added another thousand. If you go, you'll be paid three thousand."

"That's not necessary, Mr. Chatsworth," she smiled. "Two thousand is—"

"A deal's a deal, ma'am. I will pay you three thousand if you go with us."

"All right, Mr. Chatsworth," Breanna sighed. "I'll wire Dr. Goodwin first thing in the morning. If you want to meet me at the Western Union office when it opens at eight, we'll know before nine, I'm sure, if I'm free to go with you."

"Good!" Chatsworth said, slapping both legs and rising to his feet. "I'll meet you at the telegraph office at eight o'clock sharp."

"*We* will meet you at the telegraph office at eight o'clock sharp," Clayson said.

Breanna walked them to the door and bid them goodnight.

Soon she slipped between the sheets of her bed with the night-cool air coming through the open window and fell asleep thanking the Lord for the perfect peace He had given her.

She awakened early the next morning, having dreamed again about John Stranger riding across the range to take her in his arms on the cabin porch. The dream haunted her while she dressed and fixed her hair. She could almost feel John's presence in the room. Breanna knew if the Lord opened the door for her to make the trip with the wagon train, John would soon know about it. He had his ways of finding out her whereabouts.

As she laid down her hairbrush and pinned the long tresses off her neck, she said, "Lord, if You work it so I can go on this trip, and if John comes near to check on me, would You let me see him face-to-face and tell him how very much I love him? Please, Lord. It doesn't have to be on the porch of a cabin at sunset, but just let us get together...please."

Breanna's prediction came true. Dr. Goodwin's wire was back ten minutes before nine. He *had* lined up more work for her, but in light of the lengthy wire she had sent him, Goodwin said he would assign another visiting nurse to that job so Breanna could go with the wagon train. He wished her well, saying he would see her when she returned to Denver.

"How soon will you be ready to go, Miss Breanna?" Rip Clayson asked.

"I can't just walk away and leave the clinic with Dr. Wall. It's only right that I give him a couple of days of my time to get him settled in. That'll also give Mrs. Chatsworth and Jay Wyatt a little longer to recuperate. Could you wait till Thursday morning to pull out?"

"Well, ma'am, we're already four days behind schedule—but I understand. Okay, we'll pull out Thursday morning at sunrise."

"Good!" Chatsworth exclaimed, clapping his hands together. "Then it's all settled. I'll pay you half the three thousand immediately, Miss Baylor, and the other half when we get to San Francisco."

"There's no need for you to pay me anything now, sir. You can wait until we get to San Francisco...and two thousand is really plenty."

"Don't ever argue with Doral Chatsworth!" he laughed. "You'll lose every time! No, ma'am. You will be paid fifteen hundred Thursday morning, and fifteen hundred the day we roll into San Francisco."

Breanna shook her head in pleasant frustration. "Gentlemen, I brought along a small trunk to carry my belongings. I'll need someone to carry it to the wagon train before we leave on Thursday morning."

"No problem, Miss Breanna," Clayson grinned. "I'll be there at dawn to pick it up."

"Thank you. I'll be ready."

"Why don't you come to the train on Wednesday and eat supper with us?" Doral said. "That'll help you get better acquainted with folks before we actually pull out."

"That sounds like a good idea," smiled Breanna. "I'll be there."

"Tell you what," Clayson said. "It isn't good that a lady should be out by herself at that time of day. I'll come to the hotel and escort you to the train, then take you back to your hotel later."

"You're a gentleman, sir," she said, smiling warmly.

On Wednesday evening, Breanna enjoyed eating with the Chatsworths, Rip Clayson, Curly Wesson, and widow Martha Kirkland, who had cooked the meal for the group. It had been decided that Breanna's trunk would be placed in Martha's wagon, along with a bedroll that would be provided for her. She would sleep in Martha's wagon at night, but she would ride with Curly Wesson during the day. Wesson's vehicle was the supply wagon, including the medical supplies.

Since Colonel Wade Moore never allowed his son to handle the reins of the Moore wagon, Rip talked him into letting Jason drive Martha Kirkland's wagon. Rip wanted men at the reins of all the wagons whenever possible. Breanna learned there were seventy-three people and seventeen wagons in the train.

After supper, around a bonfire, Rip introduced Breanna to the group. He then issued the arrangement of wagons in the train. As usual, Curly Wesson's supply wagon would be out front. The Chatsworth wagon would follow directly behind Wesson's so Breanna would be close to Hattie, and the Wyatt wagon, driven by young Duane Wyatt, would follow next. This way Breanna would be able to slip from Curly's vehicle and check on Jay as needed.

140

Behind the Wyatt vehicle would be the ammunition wagon, which was owned by newlyweds Dean and Darlene Zimmer. Since they had no children, they had space for the heavy wooden boxes of cartridges.

Directly behind the ammunition wagon, Clayson placed the Wade Moore wagon, since they were new to the train. Behind the Moores would be Martha Kirkland's Conestoga, with Jason Moore at the reins. The rest of the wagons—each carrying an average of three children—would follow in order as Clayson assigned them.

With the people gathered, Rip went over what they were to do in case of an Indian attack. They had been fortunate to come this far without trouble, but they must never let their guard down. They must be ready at any time to circle the wagons, and they were always to remain alert.

Rip then described their situation. South Pass City lay almost half way on their twenty-four-hundred-mile journey from Independence to San Francisco. The original schedule had called for them to make the trip in 160 days, from April 27 to October 3, averaging fifteen miles per day. But they were now six days behind. If they could make it over the Sierra Nevada Mountains by September 28, they would be safe from the snowstorms. Should they experience any more delays, they could be in trouble.

When the meeting was over, Breanna moved among the people to get better acquainted. She made sure everyone knew she was there to help all of them, though she would have to give special attention to Hattie Chatsworth and Jay Wyatt. She tried to be especially reassuring to the four expectant mothers who were all due to deliver before the train reached the west side of the Sierras.

✦

Morning came with Breanna once again haunted by her recurring dream about John Stranger. Breakfast was over, and the sun was peeking over the hills to the east as Breanna's trunk was placed in the Kirkland wagon. Inside the trunk was the $1500 Doral Chatsworth had paid her.

Wagon master Rip Clayson then gathered everyone around him, and while heads were bowed, he led them in prayer, asking God's protection as they continued their journey.

They were about to climb into the wagons to roll out, when Curly Wesson hollered, "Hey, Rip! Lookee there!"

All eyes turned to the large crowd coming out of South Pass City. In the lead were Marshal Bill Stone, Deputy Wally Frye, Benny Freeman, and Dr. and Mrs. Everett Wall. They were coming to bid Breanna Baylor good-bye.

The men shook hands with her and the women embraced her, some with tears. Breanna was also teary-eyed. Katie Talbot waited till last, then put her arms around Breanna and wept. "Miss Breanna, I owe my life to you. You're a real angel of mercy. God bless you!"

Katie kissed Breanna's cheek and backed away, wiping tears.

Rip Clayson called for the people of the wagon train to board their wagons. Curly Wesson gave Breanna his hand to help her climb up into the lead vehicle. Rip Clayson, sitting tall in the saddle on his bay gelding, rode to the front of Curly's wagon, and they were under way.

When the lawmen returned to the South Pass City marshal's office, Frank Miller overheard Stone and Frye talking about how much they were going to miss Breanna Baylor and how fortunate the people in the train were to have the young nurse with them.

Don't think you can get away from me that easily, Breanna, Miller thought to himself sitting on his bunk. *I'll catch up to that wagon train and kill you yet!*

11

✦

IT TOOK THE WAGON TRAIN most of the day to move through
South Pass with its rugged terrain, rocky, castle-like walls, and
yawning canyons. It was the last day of July, and the heat from
the sun radiated off the brown sandstone that lined the trail.

Breanna Baylor found Curly Wesson a sheer delight. He had
a keen sense of humor and had her laughing continuously. The
only unpleasant thing about riding with him was his use of
chewing tobacco.

The noonday stop allowed Breanna to check on her two
patients. She found Hattie Chatsworth doing as well as expected,
but she was concerned about Jay Wyatt. The hard bumps were
taking their toll, though Elsie and Breanna had him padded as
much as possible. He was in pain, but trying not to show it.

The wagon train swung out of South Pass about an hour
before sundown and headed south in open, rolling country. To
the east and to the west were ranges of rocky hills that swept for
miles, finally thrusting themselves against towering mountains.

Curly told Breanna they were now in wolf, bear, and cougar
country. Breanna had seen squirrels, groundhogs, beavers, a coyote,
and a porcupine, but no wolves, cougars, or bears. Curly told her
there were both brown and black bears around. She asked about

grizzlies. He informed her that the grizzlies stayed farther north, for which Breanna was thankful.

Rip Clayson went about a mile ahead of the wagon train as the sun was setting and located a familiar spot beside a small stream to make camp. Galloping back, he told Curly of the spot, then rode along the train, announcing to the others where they would be stopping.

Breanna smiled as she watched Clayson in the saddle. Not only did he resemble John Stranger in his appearance, but he also sat astride his horse exactly as Stranger did Ebony.

When the wagons were formed in their usual circle beside the stream and cooking fires were being built, Breanna climbed into the Wyatt wagon to change Jay's bandages. She was concerned because the jolting of the wagon had torn a few stitches loose. Jay endured the sting of the needle while she repaired the damage.

Outside the wagon, Breanna told Elsie her concern that Jay's condition could only get worse. Elsie was deeply concerned also, but she had to go along with her husband's wishes to continue with the wagon train.

Darkness fell while the people ate their evening meal. Stars winked in a moonless sky as the night breeze ruffled the canvas tops and threw dancing shadows from the fires on wagons and people. Under Breanna's directions, the oxen and horses were stationed downstream, and pots and pans were placed over the fires to boil water taken from upstream.

When the meal was finished and all plates and utensils had been washed, Rip Clayson called for a meeting around the large fire in the center of the circle.

Rip stood close to the fire and held a clothbound book in his hand. "Well, we made just about sixteen miles today, which is good…and I am pleased. I talked to those of you who started with me at Independence about this book, but since we have some new people with us, I think it would be good if I go over it again. A refresher would be good for the rest of you, anyhow."

The book, *The Emigrant's Guide to Oregon and California* by explorer Lansford Hastings, was one Clayson carried with him on all his wagon train journeys. It had been published in 1845.

Hastings's book described the Oregon Trail as it began at the banks of the Missouri River and ran across the northeast corner of Kansas, then angled northwesterly across Nebraska into Wyoming at Fort Laramie, then traversed the vast Wyoming Territory through rugged South Pass. From the west end of South Pass, the trail angled southwesterly to Fort Bridger in Wyoming's southwest corner. At the fort, the trail made a sharp turn to the northwest and ran to the north tip of Bear Lake in Idaho Territory's extreme southeast corner.

At the small town of Bennington, the Oregon Trail split in two. The California Trail veered off southwest toward Nevada Territory, and the Oregon Trail went on westward, following the Snake River—which was named by and for the Snake Indians— then turned northwestward in central Idaho toward Oregon.

Clayson reviewed Hastings's vital information about how to survive wilderness travel and talked briefly about the detailed maps of both trails, which included information about river crossings, spring sites, the condition of trails, and the location of important landmarks all the way to where the trails terminated at Oregon City and Sacramento.

"It is 120 miles from South Pass City to Fort Bridger," Clayson continued, "which means we have about a hundred and four miles to go. If we can maintain our schedule, it will take us another seven days to reach the fort. We'll pick up needed supplies there, then push northwestward toward Bennington."

Colonel Wade Moore left his wife's side and stepped close to Clayson. "Pardon me, Mr. Clayson," he drawled, "but speakin' of maintainin' our schedule...I notice there are more people in this train with oxen than with horses to pull their wagons. I know my horses could move faster if they had the chance. Wouldn't it have been smarter for everyone to use horses than all these slow-movin' oxen?"

"Well, Colonel, I don't know how it was with the wagon train you started out in, but they should have told you that though horses can travel faster, oxen have more stamina. You'll see that when we reach the mountains and start climbing those steep passes. But just as important...there are Indians out here, and they wouldn't lift a finger to steal an ox. But if they're in need of horses, they'll shed blood to get their hands on them."

Moore nodded, ran a finger through his bushy mustache, and returned silently to his wife.

Clayson turned his attention back to the group. "Now, I stated this at Independence, but it bears repeating here. There are many dangers on the trail. If anything should happen to me, you are to look to Curly Wesson to guide you. Curly's made the trip with me many times, and he'll keep you on the trail and moving properly. And let me add...if something should happen to Curly, too, you must use Hastings's book to guide you."

Those travelers who had been with Clayson from the beginning had heard all of this before, but having their minds refreshed about what to do if something happened to him and Curly unnerved some of them. One of the men spoke up and said, "Rip, things have gone relatively smooth for us the first half of the trip. You speak of something happening to you or Curly. Is there some particular danger you have in mind?"

"Yes, I do," replied the wagon master. "Actually, there are three dangers that stand out in my mind on a journey like this. The dangers are not just Curly's and mine, they are a threat to everyone in this wagon train. I brought us up because we're your leaders, and our being removed from the picture means leadership has to fall on you men."

Someone tossed fresh logs on the big fire. Sparks flew upward and were carried away by the breeze.

"The first danger is one we've already taken precaution against, and that is the water. Miss Breanna is seeing to it that we double-boil all water to be used for drinking and cooking. To our sorrow, we've already lost four to cholera on this trip, and we don't want to lose any more. A cholera or a typhoid epidemic would be devastating. Miss Breanna, do you have anything to add to what I just said?"

"Only that we must always be very careful to dip our water from upstream when we camp and make sure the animals drink downstream. We must still boil it twice before using it, even if we find a spring that looks clear and clean. Letting down on this just once could start an epidemic and kill us all."

Clayson nodded and said to the group, "I guess that's plain enough. Any questions?"

"Let me add one more thing, Mr. Clayson," said Breanna. "Everyone must also be very careful when you bathe in the streams. Do not let any of the water get in your mouth."

"Good thought," Clayson said. "You mothers with small children will have to watch them closely when they're bathing. All right, let's talk about the second danger. So far our travel has been pretty much on level ground. I know we've had hills and valleys, but soon we'll be in mountain country. There is more opportunity for mishaps in the mountains. We must be very careful. We're even now in bear and cougar country. We must be on the lookout for them and keep our weapons at hand and ready for use."

"What about wolves?" one of the men asked.

"There are wolves here, and we'll have them in the mountains, too," Clayson said, "but wolves will not ordinarily attack humans unless they're at a point of starvation or those humans are seen to be a threat to their young. The only other thing that would cause a wolf to attack a human is if that human is bleeding and the wolf is hungry. To a hungry wolf, the smell of blood is overpowering. Right now they have plenty to eat, so we should have no problem with wolves. When it comes to bears and mountain lions—cougars—we must beware of them at all times. They also are incited by the smell of blood, and we must keep this in mind when we kill small animals for food. We'll need to cover the blood with sufficient dirt to mask the scent."

Rip could tell he had everyone's attention. "All right, let's deal with the third danger—Indians. As has already been said, we've been fortunate so far. The Cheyenne, Kiowa, and Crow could have decided to attack us, as they have other wagon trains across Kansas, Nebraska, and eastern Wyoming. We are now in Sioux, Blackfoot, and Snake country. There are not many Blackfoot this far south, but there are a few. Our greatest danger will come from the Sioux and Snake. The Snake Indians can be vicious if riled and are even more to be feared than the Sioux. But no matter which tribe we may encounter, we must be ready for them. If they attack, the women who can handle guns must do so, as well as the men, and so must the older teenage boys. We'll need all the firepower we can muster. The children and all others not handling guns must lie on the floor of their family wagon. And let me add that I don't expect you women who are with child to handle a gun. You take refuge in your wagons."

Clayson then assigned the men their shifts to be on night watch and dismissed the meeting. He noted that Colonel Moore and his son were in some kind of heated discussion, but paid them no mind.

Later, Breanna was tending to Hattie Chatsworth when she heard Rip Clayson ask, "Is Miss Breanna still in there with Hattie?"

"Yes," Doral Chatsworth replied. "She should be through in a few minutes. I assume you want to talk to her."

"That I do," Clayson said.

"I'm almost through, Mr. Clayson," Breanna called toward the opening at the rear of the wagon. "Give me about two minutes."

"I'll wait, ma'am."

It took Breanna a bit longer than she thought, but soon she and Clayson were walking toward the big fire, which was now dwindling. Other than the men on guard outside the circle of wagons, most of the people had retired for the night.

"You heard what I said about women using guns in case of an Indian attack," Clayson said.

"Yes."

"I need to know if you can handle a gun."

"I can," Breanna replied. "Both rifle and handgun. I've used rifles to hunt small game, and I'm a decent shot. I'm better with a handgun, though all I ever did was shoot at bottles or tin cans. I've never shot at a human being, Mr. Clayson."

"Could you if you had to?"

"I believe I could if it meant protecting others."

"Well, I hope you won't have to, Miss Breanna, but I'm glad you feel you could do it if the need arises."

It was then that Breanna noticed the holstered Colt .45 and gunbelt in Clayson's hand. "I won't load you down with a rifle, Miss Breanna, but I would like you to wear this. It's Curly's spare, and he's pretty small around the waist and hips, so if you buckle it in the last notch, I think you can wear it."

Breanna took the gunbelt in her hands and said, "Tell you what, Mr. Clayson. This much weight on my waist would be cumbersome. If we have an Indian attack, I'll no doubt need to take care of those who get wounded. This gun would slow me down. I'd rather just keep it at my side while I'm riding with Curly and when I'm in Martha's wagon at night."

"All right," he nodded. "But please keep it within reach at all times. I want you to be able to protect yourself if an attack comes. Tell you what—excuse me just a moment."

"Of course," she smiled.

Breanna watched as Clayson headed toward Curly Wesson's wagon and vanished in the darkness. Less than a minute later he reappeared, carrying a small, nickel-plated weapon. Drawing up, he laid the gun in his palm so she could get a good look at it and said, "This is a Derringer, ma'am. It's a .41 caliber. Packs a good wallop. You ever use one of these before?"

"Yes. When Frank and I were courting, he had a .36 caliber single-barrel Derringer. He taught me how to cock and fire it."

"Good. I'd really like for you to have a weapon on your person. Keeping the revolver close at hand is fine, but you're a lot safer if you have a gun on you."

"Is it loaded?" she asked, taking it from his hand.

"Yes."

Breanna slipped the barrel inside the belt of her skirt and asked, "How's that? I think it'll ride there all right."

"Fine," the wagon master replied, reaching into his pocket. He pulled out a handful of cartridges and asked, "Can you carry these on you?"

"I'll put a few in each pocket of this skirt. The others I wear all have pockets, too. I appreciate you looking out for me, Mr. Clayson."

"My pleasure, ma'am. Ah...tell you what..."

"Yes?"

"Could I ask you a personal question?"

"You just did," she said.

"I'm sorry?"

"Well, isn't it a personal question to ask if you can ask a personal question?"

"Yes, ma'am. I guess it is."

Breanna laughed. "I'm sorry. I shouldn't be so ornery."

"No!" he said, shaking his head. "I like a woman with a sense of humor."

"What was it you wanted to know?"

"Oh. Well, I was just wondering if you were attached. I mean, I know you are *Miss* Breanna Baylor...and there's no engagement ring on your finger, so I—"

"I am attached, Rip," she said.

"Oh. May I ask who the fortunate man is?"

"Of course. When I tell you his name, you're probably going to say—as so many others have—that nobody has a name like that. His name is John Stranger."

Rip Clayson's eyes widened. "Did I hear you right? John Stranger?"

"Yes," she nodded. "I told you that you prob—"

"No. That's not what I meant. I *know* John Stranger!"

"You do?"

"Yes'm. About three weeks or so ago we were moving across Nebraska, and he came riding up behind us. He rode alongside me for a little while, and it didn't take long to find out that we were brothers in Christ. I liked him the minute I met him, but I liked him even better when I found out he was a Christian."

"Well, isn't that something?" Breanna said, surprised.

"John sort of became one of us for a couple of days, ma'am. Sure knows his Bible. I assume he must be quite a preacher."

"Oh, yes, he is. Are you saying he traveled with the wagon train for a couple of days?"

"He sure did. Then Curly and Jay Wyatt and I saw him in Cheyenne City a few days later."

"Really?"

"We had to leave the trail and make a circle to Cheyenne City for some supplies. Sure was good to see that long drink of water again."

"He is tall, isn't he?"

"Got me by three or four inches."

"Funny," she said. "The first time I saw you, it struck me that you and John look a lot alike. You even sit in your saddle like him."

"Well, I take that as a compliment, ma'am. He's the finest man I've ever met."

"Yes," sighed Breanna, a faraway look capturing her eyes. "I agree wholeheartedly."

"Do you two get to see each other much?"

"Not as much as I'd like. He does find me quite often, though, and looks in on me."

"Did he swing through South Pass City on his way to Fort Boise?"

Fort Boise. So that's where he's been lately!

"No, he didn't," she said. "He's probably planning to do that when he finishes his business up there. And what about you, Rip? You're a fine man. Isn't there a young woman in your life?"

"Not now," he replied. "There was, though. Her name was Mary. We hadn't become engaged yet, but we were moving that direction. And then...well, Mary came down with pneumonia and died."

"Oh, how terrible, Rip. I'm so sorry. How long ago was this?"

"Four years. And I...I haven't met another woman that I felt I could love as I loved Mary, or who would make the perfect wife for me."

"Rip, you're in the Lord's hands. I have no doubt that He has that right young woman all picked out for you. When His time is right, He'll bring her across your path."

"I know you're right, Miss Breanna," Clayson said. "I've been expecting Him to do that, and I hope you'll take this in the right way. I...I thought maybe it was you. You're certainly a beautiful woman, outside and inside, and I'll admit I was attracted to you, especially when I found out you were a Christian."

"Thank you, you're very kind," Breanna said. "And thank you for being concerned about my welfare and for these weapons."

"You're quite welcome, ma'am. I guess you best get back to the wagon now. It's getting late."

"Yes, I suppose I should. Goodnight, Rip."

"Goodnight, Miss Baylor." Rip stood and watched Breanna make her way through the dark night toward Martha Kirkland's wagon.

The Wyoming sky was heavy and dark when the wagon train pulled away from the stream the next morning. The wind whined over the rolling hills and through the scattered rock formations, bringing with it the smell of rain.

Breanna sat next to Curly Wesson and watched Rip Clayson as he trotted his bay some three hundred yards ahead of the wagon train. The wind tousled her blond hair, and she moved a wisp that had fallen over her right eye.

Curly spat and said, "Fine boy, that Rip."

"Yes, he is," agreed Breanna.

"He's got eyes for you, missy. I guess you know that."

"I had picked up on it a time or two," she admitted, "but it'll be different now."

"Oh? How's that?"

"We had a talk last night when you were already in your jammies, asleep."

"My jammies! I'll have you know, young lady, I don't wear pajamas when I sleep. I believe in undressin' when I go to bed, not dressin'!"

Breanna laughed, and at the same instant, a bolt of lightning slashed the sky ahead of them. The clouds were getting darker. There was a rumble of thunder, but as yet no rain had fallen.

"Anyway," said Curly, "What was you talkin' 'bout?"

"He asked if I was attached, and I told him I am."

"You are? Really?"

"Yes. And I found out that you know the man I love."

"*I* know 'im?"

"His name's John Stranger."

"John Stranger! He's your man?"

"That's right."

"Well, I'll be! That there John Stranger is some kind o' feller, he is. Tell me, does he travel all over the West, preachin'?"

"Well, he preaches a lot of places he goes," Breanna said, "but preaching isn't the main thing he does. He helps people who are in trouble. Of course, when he preaches, he does that, too. Especially people who are in trouble with God."

"In trouble with God?"

"Yes. That's every human being until they know the Lord Jesus Christ."

"Ya mean I'm in trouble with God?"

"You're a sinner, aren't you?"

"Well, I've done my share of wrong, ma'am. No sense in lyin' about it."

"All of us have, Curly," said Breanna.

Curly chuckled. "Not you, ma'am. You're the sweetest li'l thing I ever laid eyes on. You ain't no sinner."

"Oh, but I am, Curly. God's Word says *all* have sinned and come short of the glory of God. That includes me. I woke up to this a few years ago and—"

"I really ain't interested in religion, ma'am," Curly said.

"I'm not either."

"But you just told me what the Bible says. Ain't that religion?"

"No. Religion is built on the traditions of men, Curly. There's a big difference between religion and salvation. God's Word says there is a heaven out there beyond this life, and there is a hell. God is a holy God, and He will not and cannot tolerate sin in His presence. Therefore, if we die in our sins, we have to go to hell. But if we die in Jesus Christ, He will take us to heaven."

Curly shook his head. "I've heard about this before, ma'am, but it's all so confusin'."

"That's because you haven't understood the difference between religion and salvation. It's the Lord Jesus Christ, God's virgin-born Son, who gives salvation. He went to the cross of Calvary, shed His blood, and paid the price for our sins, Curly. It's Jesus who saves the soul and redeems the sinner by His blood."

Curly Wesson was noticeably uncomfortable. "Here comes the rain, Miss Breanna. You'd best put on one o' my slickers and cover that pretty blond head o' yours with that there umbrella right behind ya."

The rain began to come down in sheets. Breanna slid into the slicker and hoisted the umbrella to cover both of them. *I'm not giving up on you just yet, Curly Wesson.*

12

⋏

LIEUTENANT EMERY DODD strained against the rope that wound around his body, holding him in a standing position with his back against the rough bark of the towering pine. The hemp cord encircled his body and the tree several times, and his wrists were lashed to the rope at his sides.

The sound of galloping painted ponies, along with a dozen riderless army horses, was quickly diminishing as the lieutenant stared bleakly at the departing Snake Indians. Red Claw and his three dozen warriors would return later, expecting to find him ripped and clawed to shreds by a bear or cougar.

Dodd's uniform, his face, and his hair were soaked with the blood of the dead antelope the Indians had killed and carried away. They wanted whatever beast smelled the blood and came to investigate to concentrate wholly on the white man. The stench of the blood was making him nauseous. Or was it the growing dread as he listened for the sound of an approaching beast?

The sky overhead was heavy with gray clouds, fringed in threatening black. Dodd wished he was out in the open where the coming downpour would wash the blood off him.

His line of sight trailed to the bodies of his eleven troopers scattered about, all missing their scalps. *Maybe they're the lucky ones,* thought Dodd. *At least they died quickly.*

He shook his head and strained at the ropes again, then reprimanded himself for such a foolish effort. Even a horse could not break one strand of rope, let alone the half-dozen or so that encircled him.

A streak of lightning slashed across the black sky. Seconds later, thunder hammered violently, shaking the tree and the ground. When the sound of the thunder died out, Dodd thought he heard the howl of a big cat deeper in the forest. His heart leaped in his chest and a chill laced through the muscles of his back. The howl seemed to come from behind him. Or was it from the thick forest on the other side of the wagon trail some fifty feet from where he was tied?

Lightning split the dark sky again, followed by a cannonade of thunder. Rain began to fall, but none of it was touching him through the heavy boughs of the big pine. At least if the rain was heavy enough, it might keep the scent of blood from riding the air currents and reaching the nostrils of a bear or cougar.

But if a big cat had already smelled the blood and was on its way, he was a dead man.

He thought he heard a hiss again. If so, the beast was very near. A wave of panic washed over him, followed by a settled, cold dread. He struggled against the ropes, closing his eyes.

There was more lightning and thunder, and suddenly the clouds opened up and sent rain like a waterfall. The roar filled his ears, drowning out all other sounds.

The rain was now dripping from the heavy boughs above him, striking him on the head. Bloody water ran from his hair into his eyes, and he shook his head.

The rain lasted for an hour, then stopped almost as fast as it had started. The clouds soon began to break apart, and little shafts of sunlight lanced the cool air, making bright spots on the wet ground.

Dodd looked around to see if there was movement close to him or in the woods on the other side of the wagon trail.

Nothing.

If there had been a cat close enough for Dodd to hear, surely it would have attacked him by now. Perhaps it had left the area.

One thing bothered him, though. The rain had freshened the antelope's blood. The scent would be stronger than if it had been allowed to dry.

Soon the sun was shining down from a brassy, cloudless sky, and the air began to heat up. A light breeze began to blow, cooling Dodd, whose uniform was soaked all the way through.

His eyes went to the bodies of his troopers again. All but two were married men. Their wives and children—most who lived near Fort Bridger some ninety miles due south—were in for heavy grief. His mind went to his own wife and three children. Would they know the heartbreak of losing husband and father, too?

Time seemed to drag.

Memories of his childhood, courtship, wedding, and sweet moments with his wife and children flooded his mind. He yearned to see his precious family again—to hold each one and tell them he loved them.

His thoughts went back nearly a week to the day he led his unit out of the fort. A patrol of a dozen men was missing. They had gone north four days earlier on a routine mission, and had been expected back in forty-eight hours. When double that amount of time had passed, Colonel Walter Ames had called

Dodd into his office and ordered him to take his patrol and search for the missing men.

On the second day out, Dodd had found the trail of the missing unit and followed it. At midmorning the next day, they found signs of a battle, but no bodies and no horses. Dodd had no choice but to keep moving. He had to have something specific to report to Colonel Ames.

They followed signs deep into Sioux and Snake country, and on the sixth day, as they neared the Sweetwater Mountains, they were ambushed by Red Claw and three dozen of his warriors. Dodd knew it was Red Claw by the description he had been given of him. The Snake leader always wore the stub paw of a black bear on a rawhide thong around his neck. The claws were painted bright red to appear as blood. Chief Red Claw was known for his hatred toward white men, although there had been no Snake uprisings in nearly a year.

Suddenly Dodd's attention was drawn to the deep shadows of the dense pine and aspen across the wagon trail to the west. Something had moved over there. He was sure of it.

He stared, unblinking. There it was again! Something moved, something larger than a beaver or even a wolf.

Suddenly it stood clear at the edge of the trees, just beyond the rutted trail, swishing its long tail and glaring directly at him. A large male cougar!

The cat showed its fangs and hissed.

Rip Clayson trotted his horse back and forth along the line of wagons, noting how quickly the early afternoon sun was drying the ground after the heavy rain.

Breanna Baylor was in the Wyatt wagon, tending to Jay, who was in a great deal of pain. The continuous jostling of the wagon was taking its toll.

The train was skirting the last of the foothills of the Sweetwater Range and was about to make the southerly turn when Curly Wesson called out with urgency in his voice.

Rip spurred his mount and quickly drew up alongside the lead wagon. He found Curly standing up, clutching the reins with one hand and shading his eyes beneath his battered old hat with the other.

"What is it Curly?" Rip asked.

Wesson pointed due south to a spot about three hundred yards down the trail. "See 'em?"

"What?" Clayson asked, lowering his hat to give more shade to his eyes.

"Dead soldiers! Looks like a dozen or so."

Clayson focused on the scattered, uniformed bodies. "That has to be a patrol out of Fort Bridger—at least it's the closest fort around. No doubt they ran into hostile Indians and were out-numbered...probably Sioux or Snake. Don't see any horses around. Indians must've taken them."

Clayson told Curly to draw rein, then looked back along the curved line of wagons and raised a hand, signaling for them to stop. People were clambering out of the wagons, wanting to get a look at the scene at the bottom of the gentle slope.

When Breanna touched ground, Martha Kirkland drew up with Jason Moore flanking her. Jason watched Clayson trot his horse toward the death scene and said to the two women, "We'll go around the bodies somehow, won't we? I don't want to look at them."

"By the looks of the dense forest on both sides of the trail," said Breanna, "I'd say we can't avoid it. I'm sure Rip will want to bury them, anyhow. We can't leave them like that."

"I don't want to look at them!" choked Jason. "I can't stomach anything like that!"

Breanna patted his arm. "Calm down, Jason. Nobody's going to make you look if you don't want to. And I can understand why you wouldn't."

Jason was glad Breanna understood. He wished his father did.

Rip was within a hundred yards of the bloody scene when he spotted two things at once—a soldier tied to a tree on his left and a snarling cougar coming out of the shadows of the forest on his right. Rip skidded the bay to a halt, whipped his rifle from its saddleboot, and brought it to his shoulder. He aimed about four feet ahead of the beast and squeezed the trigger. The rifle barked. The bullet chewed into the rocky ground and buzzed away like an angry hornet. The cat darted back into the woods.

Rip jammed the smoking Winchester into its boot and put the bay gelding to an instant gallop toward the rope-bound soldier.

With his wife at his side, Colonel Wade Moore drew up next to Breanna, Martha, Curly, and Jason, who stood looking at the wagon master as he was dismounting underneath the huge pine tree.

"Looks like Rip saved that bound-up soldier from bein' mauled to death," said the colonel. "Some of the rest of us need to get on down there."

"We'd best wait till Rip gives us the signal to come to him," Curly said.

"Why do that?" objected Moore. "I'm a soldier, and those dead men down there are soldiers." Turning to his son, he said, "Come on, Jason. You and I will go down there and do what we can to help Mister Clayson."

Jason Moore turned white.

Marian said, "Wade, if you want to go in spite of Curly's advice, you go ahead...but don't force Jason to go. You know how the sight of blood affects him."

"Yeah, I know. That's exactly why he's goin' with me."

"Please, Colonel," Jason gasped. "Don't force me to go."

"The only way to get over it is to tackle it head-on, boy. Now c'mon."

Marian knew it would do no good to beg her husband not to do this. Jason had been a grave disappointment to his father because he was mild-natured and not the robust, military type. This kind of thing had been part of Jason's life since he was a small boy.

As Jason obediently followed his father, Breanna stared at the big man's broad back, shaking her head. She wondered how a father could be so cruel to his own son.

Rip Clayson used his knife to free Dodd of his ropes, then helped him sit down on a large rock nearby. The two men introduced themselves, and Dodd explained why he and his unit were in the area and so far from Fort Bridger. He then gave a quick description of the ambush by the Snake Indians.

"So Red Claw himself led the attack?" Clayson asked.

"In person," nodded Dodd. "He didn't take time to introduce himself, but he looked as mean as I've heard he's supposed
to be…and he was wearing that bear's foot he's known so well
by."

"Only one Indian like that," sighed Clayson. "It had to be
Red Claw."

"Snakes haven't been on the prowl for quite a while," Dodd
said. "Of course, I'm wondering if they didn't ambush that patrol
Colonel Ames sent us out to find. Wish I knew what's got them
riled up."

"I don't like the sound of it," Clayson said.

Just then the Moores drew up. Colonel Moore took one look
at the blood-soaked lieutenant and swore, asking how he could
be so bloody and yet apparently unharmed. Dodd made a hasty
explanation.

Moore then stepped to his son and said stiffly, "Jason, quit
actin' like a panty-waist. You need to get a good gander of the
slaughter. Now, I want you to look at those bodies over there and
realize what life and death are all about."

"Please, Colonel, don't make me look!" Jason said. "I can't
stand it!"

Moore seized him by the back of the neck, turned toward the
corpses, and barked, "Look at 'em!"

Jason gave in and opened his eyes. When he saw the crimson
spots where scalps used to be, he clamped a hand over his mouth
and ran for the privacy of a huge pine.

"You sissy!" Colonel Moore shouted. "Why can't you be a
man?"

"Some people have an aversion to such scenes, Colonel,"

Clayson said. "I don't much care to look myself."

Moore gave him a dull look and said, "The only right thing is for us to give these poor soldiers a proper burial, Clayson."

"I'm sure this will meet with your approval, Lieutenant," Clayson said.

"Yes," nodded Dodd. "The quicker, the better."

"I'm going to take the lieutenant to the wagons, Mr. Moore," Clayson said. "I'll send a burial detail down here with an extra shovel that'll fit your hands."

"Good! Send one for Jason, too."

Rip glanced toward the tree where Jason had disappeared. "I don't think he's going to be able to handle a shovel, Colonel." He turned to Dodd and asked, "Think you can walk over to my horse?"

"Sure."

While Colonel Moore looked on, Clayson helped Dodd aboard his bay gelding, and led it away by the reins.

As they moved slowly up the grassy slope, Rip said, "Lieutenant, before the patrol unit that went out a week ago from the fort came up missing, were you aware of any Indian trouble?"

"None other than the normal problems that come up periodically," Dodd said. "There hadn't been any killings or scalpings for almost a year in western Wyoming."

"I understand that Red Claw speaks English."

"Yes."

"He didn't say anything to you that would give you a hint as to what triggered the ambush?"

"No. I asked him about the other patrol, but he ignored me."

Dodd paused a few seconds, then proceeded. "When Red Claw was directing his warriors to tie me to the tree, he was visibly disturbed about something. He used the language of the Shoshoni, which I recognize but don't understand. But I know Mr. Red Claw is one unhappy Indian. Not only that, but he and his braves were wearing warpaint, and they had their ponies painted up. The Snakes are on the warpath."

Clayson shook his head. "I sure hate to bear such news to these people, but they've got to know about it."

The group gathered around Clayson and Dodd as they drew up. Dodd's strength was returning, and he told the people about the ambush. Clayson then sent ten men with shovels to bury the soldiers in a common grave. They also carried rifles in case the Snakes came back. Clayson explained that he would take the wagons down to the burial site, but he didn't want the women and children to see it.

The men and teenage boys who stayed with the wagons kept their weapons in hand and their eyes peeled.

Some of the women offered to wash the blood out of the lieutenant's uniform if one of the men would loan him some clothes. There were several volunteers. Dodd accepted shirt and Levis, and washed up and changed clothes in the back of Martha Kirkland's wagon. While the uniform was being washed, some of the people gathered around Dodd, asking questions about the Indian uprising, wanting to know what had brought it on. The lieutenant gave them the same information he had given to Rip Clayson.

Curly spit a stream in the dirt and said, "Well, if'n there ain't been no Indian trouble in these parts for a whole year, *somethin'* out of the ordinary must've happened to put 'em on the warpath."

✦

By the time the soldiers were buried, the sun was lowering toward the distant mountains to the west. Rip Clayson announced that there was a stream about a mile farther south. They would move there and camp for the night. The wagon train would carry Lieutenant Dodd to Fort Bridger.

After supper, Rip called for a general meeting around the big fire in the center of the wagon circle and briefed the people once again about fighting Indians. "In light of today's incident with Red Claw and his warriors," he said, "there's a good chance we'll come under attack."

"Rip, I don't like to be the one to say this, but maybe we should head back to South Pass City till the Indian problem cools off," Doral Chatsworth said. "Be a whole lot safer there than out here in the wilderness."

"We'd have to winter here if we did that, Doral," Rip said.

"I realize that, and I'd like to get Hattie to California as planned...but better to delay it than not get there at all."

Darrel Day took a step closer to the fire and said, "I want us to get to California safely, too, Doral, but I think our best move is to go on to Fort Bridger. I realize it would be closer to return to South Pass City, but the Snakes can attack us while we're heading back there, too. Why not move closer to army protection?"

"I concur with this man exactly!" Colonel Moore boomed. "Goin' back to South Pass City would be plumb foolishness!"

"I disagree, Colonel," Jason said. "If we go on to the fort, we're vulner—"

"Shut your mouth, Jason! You afraid to fight a few redskins? You can hide in Martha Kirkland's wagon when the Snakes

169

attack. I'm sure there's a girl in the train who can handle your gun!"

Jason went silent and lowered his head.

There was a rumble of voices as men and women discussed their options.

Rip let them talk for a while, then raised his hands for their attention. "I have a rule about things like this, folks. When I lead a wagon train, we always operate as a democracy. The only way to settle this is to take a vote. All those in favor of returning to South Pass City, raise your right hand. All right, all those in favor of continuing on to Fort Bridger, same sign."

The majority elected to go on to Fort Bridger.

As the meeting was breaking up, Wade Moore towered over his son and said loudly, "Why are you always on the sissy side of a matter, Jason? I do declare, you must have a yellow streak down your back a foot wide! Where's your manhood?"

Breanna Baylor felt the heat crawl up her neck and flush her face. Most of the time she kept her mouth shut when angry, but the hurt look on Jason's face was more than she could stand.

She moved directly in front of Colonel Moore and snapped, "Since when are you the model of perfection?"

"What do you mean?"

All eyes turned to watch the confrontation.

"I mean, why do you belittle your son because he's not like you, especially in front of people? Don't you think he has any feelings?"

The colonel cleared his throat nervously. "Well, I—"

"God didn't make everybody with the love for fighting you apparently have! So you're the boisterous, aggressive, soldier type. Bully for you!"

"Well, I—"

"Just because that's the way you're made doesn't mean everybody else is, including your son! Jason is a fine, decent, clean-cut young man. Why don't you look for the good qualities in him instead of trying to find something of yourself in there?"

There was genuine bafflement in Wade Moore's eyes. His mind was spinning, and the rapid-fire licking he was taking from the small woman had him flustered.

"Now, ma'am, I don't rightly cotton to takin' this kind of abuse from a female. I don't appreciate this."

"Oh? Well, I don't appreciate the way you browbeat Jason and make a spectacle of him just because he's different than you, either! Give him some room Colonel! Let Jason be Jason, the person God made him. Don't try to force him into your mold!"

"Are you through, ma'am?"

Breanna thought a moment. "Yes. I've said what I needed to say."

Colonel Wade Moore touched his hat and said, "Then I have other matters to tend to. So if you'll excuse me, I'll do so." With that, he walked away and vanished in the darkness that surrounded the camp.

13

↑

AFTER HIS FATHER DISAPPEARED from sight, Jason Moore and his mother approached Breanna Baylor.

"Miss Breanna, thank you," Jason said. "I've never in my whole life seen my father put in a corner by anybody...until just now."

"Well, you're welcome, Jason. I just felt like I had to say something."

Marian patted Breanna's arm. "My husband has needed a dressing down like that for a long time, Breanna. I love him dearly, but he had that coming, and I'm glad it was you who gave it to him."

Mother and son walked away and were quickly replaced by Rip Clayson and Curly Wesson.

Curly cackled and said, "Well, Miss Breanna, I'll say this for you—you sure got spunk! Boy, did you put that loudmouth in his place!"

"Tell you what," Rip said. "If I had the money, I'd hire you to ride all my wagon trains so you could handle the blowhards for me. Seems like every trip I take, I inherit someone with mouth problems."

"I don't often let off steam like that, Rip," Breanna smiled. "Well, I think I better go see about Jay. He's not doing very well."

"Ride too rough on him?" Curly asked.

"Yes. Just like I told him it would be. But you know how men are—boneheaded and stubborn. If I believed in evolution, I'd say men evolved from mules."

Clayson grinned and said to Breanna, "Do you think it's going to get serious for Jay?"

"Yes, I do. I only hope I can keep him alive till we get to Fort Bridger. He's going to have to stay there until he recovers."

Breanna made her way toward the Wyatt wagon, and several people stopped her along the way to congratulate her on the way she handled the colonel. As she drew near the wagon, she passed a spot where two young people were in heated conversation between two wagons.

"Eddie's in love with Donna, Rhonda!" Jerry Adams said, keeping his voice low. "I don't understand why you bother with him! Besides, if you're my girl as you keep telling me you are, why do you insist on cutting my heart out by flirting with Eddie?"

"I'm not flirting, Jerry," Rhonda Fallon insisted. "I'm just being friendly."

"That's not what it looks like to me or Donna! You know what I think?"

"No, what?"

"I think you flirt with Eddie just to see if you can get his attention on you instead of on Donna!"

"That's not so!"

"Then prove it! Stay away from him!"

Breanna kept moving and couldn't make out what Rhonda said in response. Her heart went out to Jerry Adams. It was apparent that he loved Rhonda and was hurt by the attention she had been giving Eddie Binder. Breanna wanted to sit Rhonda down and give her a good talking to, but figured it was none of her business.

Later, after Breanna had tended to Jay Wyatt, looked in on Hattie Chatsworth, and checked with the four expectant mothers, she was passing Curly Wesson's wagon on her way to bed. Curly was talking with Lieutenant Emery Dodd, who was now back in his uniform.

"Goodnight, gentlemen," Breanna said.

"Goodnight, ma'am," Dodd responded.

"Goodnight, ridin' partner," said Curly. "See ya in the mornin'."

"Riding partner?" the lieutenant asked once Breanna was out of earshot.

"Yep. That li'l cutie-pie rides with me every day, all day long. Sits right next to me on the seat of my wagon, here."

"How come she rides with you?"

"Well, you see, she knows a real he-man when she sees one. Thrills 'er to sit beside me all day…and sometimes it's downright embarrassin'."

"How's that?"

"Well, she's always lookin' at me. Just cain't keep her eyes offa me!"

Dodd chuckled. "Well, on that note, I'm heading for bed. Goodnight, Romeo."

Curly laughed and climbed into the back of his wagon.

✦

Steel-rimmed wheels grated on rocks and pebbles the next morning as the wagon train rolled southwestward. Lieutenant Dodd rode in the seat of the Jay Wyatt wagon beside young Duane. Elsie was inside with her ailing husband.

Rip Clayson rode back and forth along the wagons, chatting with people and answering questions. It was midmorning when he drew up beside the lead wagon on Breanna's side and smiled at her. Curly was saying something to her, but let it trail off when he saw Rip pull close.

"Curly talking your leg off?" Rip asked.

"Not really," Breanna smiled. "He worries me, though."

"What do you mean?" Rip asked.

"I'm afraid one of these times he's going to forget which way to spit, and I'm going to get a face full of tobacco juice."

Rip laughed.

"Well, how would you like to live in such danger twelve hours a day?" Breanna said in mock agitation.

Curly laughed, slapped his leg, and said, "Don't you worry your purty li'l head, honey! I know my left from my right!"

"I'd think anyone smart enough to know left from right would be smart enough not to put that awful stuff in his mouth," Breanna said.

Curly looked past Breanna to the wagon master. "Ain't she a cutie, Rip? She talks like that 'cause she's really crazy about me."

Breanna dug an elbow into his ribs. "Don't flatter yourself, you old coot!"

"Y'hear that, Rip? She says I'm cute!"

"Your hearing's bad, too," Breanna said.

The three of them had a good laugh together, then Rip asked Breanna, "You see the colonel this morning?"

"Mm-hmm."

"He speak to you?"

"No, but he gave me an icy look."

"If he gives you any trouble, I want to know it."

"I don't think he will."

"He'd better not," Curly said, "or he'll have me on his case!"

"Yeah," laughed Rip, "he'd be in real trouble facing an old Indian fighter like you!"

"You better believe it!" Curly said, turning to spit.

"Have you been in battles with Indians, Rip?" Breanna asked.

"A few. The worst was—"

"I've been in more," Curly said.

"I won't argue with that," Rip said. "You've been around so long, you fought the great-great-grandfathers of the Indians who roam these hills today."

"Humph! I ain't so old."

"Just how old are you, Curly?" Breanna asked.

"He's older than dirt, ma'am," Clayson snickered.

"You've done it now, you young whippersnapper!" Curly said.

Breanna laughed till the tears came.

Curly mumbled something indistinguishable, then said, "Let's get serious, now. This Indian fightin's no laughin' matter."

"Tell me about the Snake Indians," Breanna said. "I've never seen one as far as I know. Are they really as mean as people say?"

"Any of the Indians in these parts can be mean," Rip said, "the Sioux, the Cheyenne, Ute, Kiowa, Crow, Blackfoot, Comanche, regular Shoshoni, and Apache. They all can be vicious when they're on the warpath. But from everything I know, the Snakes are the worst. The Apaches probably come the closest to them for brutality, like what Red Claw did to Lieutenant Dodd."

"Yeah," put in Curly. "Them 'Paches like to stake white men out on anthills in the blazin' sun and stuff like that. But one thing I'll say for the 'Paches...they won't do to white women what the Snakes do."

"What do you mean?" asked Breanna.

"Well, ma'am, this is a li'l delicate. Are ya sure ya want to hear it?"

"Yes, I do."

"Well, in the 'Pache religion, they have a powerful hatred for adultery. A man is s'posed to keep hisself to just his wife, and likewise a woman to her husband. If a 'Pache man and woman are guilty of adultery, they're put to death."

"Like the people of Israel in Bible days," mused Breanna.

"I don't know about that," Curly said, "but they really frown on it amongst the 'Paches. They'll use rawhide to tie the adulterer and the adulteress together face-to-face, put 'em out in the hot sun, and let the rawhide dry up. When it does, it squeezes down so hard on 'em, they die."

"Oh, how awful!" exclaimed Breanna. "Of course, in Bible days they stoned them to death. That's a pretty horrible way to die, too."

"Don't doubt it," Curly said. "Anyway, as I was sayin', with the 'Paches a man is s'posed to keep hisself to just his wife, so they don't molest white women."

"I see," said Breanna. "But the Snakes are different?"

"That's right. Them Snakes have no conscience at all when it comes to white women. When they capture a white woman, they'll...well, I think you can imagine the terrible things they might do to her."

Breanna's features paled and she looked toward Rip.

"I've warned the other women in the train about it," Rip said. "If the Snakes attack us, you be sure to stay close to a man for protection. If they should capture you and take you with them, it would be a fate worse than death."

"Oh, Rip, we need to do everything we can to make sure every woman and girl is fully protected," Breanna said. "We can't leave any of them vulnerable to such a thing."

"I agree. Everyone in the train has been fully instructed about this."

As the day progressed, dark clouds began to collect in the sky, and by evening it looked like more rain was on the way.

After supper, Jerry Adams sat with Rhonda Fallon on a huge rock, holding hands. Others were milling around within the circle of wagons and talking by the fire.

"I'm going to the wagon for a drink of water," Rhonda said. "I'll be right back."

"Don't be gone long. I'll waste away to nothing if you're gone more than ten minutes."

Rhonda giggled and walked away toward the Fallon wagon. There she dipped a tin cup in the barrel that hung on its side.

The water had been boiled twice, as ordered by Nurse Baylor, and Rhonda was glad it was safe to drink. The cholera-caused deaths in Nebraska still haunted her.

As she made her way back to Jerry, Rhonda found Eddie Binder in her path, talking to Duane Wyatt. From the corner of her eye, Rhonda could tell Jerry was watching her.

She glided up beside young Binder, gave him a warm smile, and said, "Hello, Eddie. You sure do look fine when you're driving your daddy's wagon. It's like...like you were king of the world up there on that wagon seat."

Eddie cleared his throat nervously. "Oh, I don't know about *that.*"

Rhonda moved a little closer. "Oh, but you do," she said, reaching out and touching his cheek.

Jerry Adams slid off the rock, eyes glued on Rhonda. Someone else had been watching, too. Donna Day had fiery red hair and the temper to go with it. She surprised Rhonda by stomping up behind her just as she was taking her hand away from Eddie's cheek and snapping, "Keep your hands off Eddie, you hussy!"

Rhonda whirled and said, "Who are you to tell me what to do? I don't see your name written on Eddie! I can touch him if I want!"

"Listen, sister!" Donna snarled, hands-on-hips. "We've been over this before! Eddie likes me, not you! Now stay away from him!"

Rhonda looked at Eddie. "Tell me you want me to stay away from you, Eddie. We're good friends, aren't we?" As she spoke, she extended her hand and stroked his cheek.

Donna reached out and grabbed Rhonda's wrist, yanking her

hand away from Eddie's face. "I told you to keep your hands off him!"

Eddie blinked. "Rhonda, I—"

His words were interrupted when Rhonda gave Donna a stinging slap across the face. Donna struck back, her fist hitting Rhonda square on the jaw, knocking her down.

Both sets of parents dashed to the scene, having been told their daughters were fighting. Jerry Adams stood close by, not knowing what to do.

Donna had Rhonda on the ground, and Rhonda was doing her best to get her fingernails in Donna's eyes. Donna pulled her head out of reach and punched Rhonda again, then sank her fingers in Rhonda's hair and yanked her head back and forth.

Rhonda managed to scratch Donna's face. Donna felt the burn of the fingernails and clawed at Rhonda, raking her left cheek and drawing blood. She grabbed hair again and twisted hard.

Chuck Fallon and Darrel Day moved in quickly. Darrel gripped his daughter's shoulders and shouted, "Donna, that's enough! Get off her!"

Donna let go of Rhonda's hair, breathing hard, and stood up.

Chuck took his daughter by the hand and helped her to her feet. "Now, what's this all about?" he demanded, looking at both girls. They were bleeding from the scratches on their faces, their dresses were dirty, and Rhonda's hair was a mess.

By this time a crowd had gathered. Breanna had been in Hattie Chatsworth's wagon and drew up as Eddie Binder was telling of Rhonda's flirting and the trouble it was causing between Donna and him.

Eddie looked at Rhonda and said, "This is partially my fault.

I wanted to be a friend to you, Rhonda, and I didn't want to hurt your feelings by telling you to back off when you came around acting sweet. But I'm telling you now…I'm in love with Donna. I don't want any other girl's attention or affection, including yours."

"You get that, sister?" lashed Donna.

"All I was doing was being friendly," Rhonda said.

"Well, you were *too* friendly," Donna said.

Rhonda knew Jerry was standing on the other side of her parents, who looked on, dumbfounded. Looking past them she said, "Jerry, you know all I was doing was trying to be a friend to Eddie, don't you?"

"I don't know, Rhonda," Jerry said quietly. "I think an awful lot of you, but you have a way of making me wonder just where we stand."

Rhonda's lower lip was quivering. "Can we…can we talk about it?"

"Before there's anymore talk, I think both you girls need attention from Nurse Baylor," Molly Day said.

Breanna led Rhonda and Donna to Curly's wagon so she could take care of their scratches, and the parents talked among themselves with Rip Clayson in their midst. They all agreed they would do their best to keep anything like this from happening again.

The mothers then went to the lead wagon to check on their daughters. They found Breanna dabbing iodine on the scratches and talking to the girls in a low, steady voice.

"Rhonda, I've noticed you with Eddie on several occasions. The way you were acting toward him was certainly not in line if you're supposed to be Jerry's girl. I know flirtation when I see it, and you were flirting."

Louise Fallon kept silent. She knew her daughter had the tendency to flirt, and had talked to her about it before. She hoped that Breanna's words would sink in. She saw a pout was forming on Rhonda's face.

"Look me straight in the eye and tell me you were just being friendly to Eddie, Rhonda," Breanna said.

The girl's pout grew more pronounced, but she did not reply.

"Rhonda, Jerry Adams is a very nice young man. He has a genuine interest in you, and he deserves honesty. If you're going to be his girl, then be his girl. If you don't care that much for him, fine...but be honest and tell him so, straight out. Don't play with his feelings and dangle him on your string."

"Miss Baylor is making good sense, honey," Louise said. "Haven't I told you the same thing?"

Rhonda met her mother's gaze, then gave a small nod.

When the nurse's work was done, Molly Day said, "You've been given some excellent advice from Nurse Baylor, Rhonda. I'm sorry you and Donna had to have this confrontation, and I hope there'll never be another one."

Again, Rhonda only nodded.

Donna moved close to Rhonda and said, "It's a long way yet to California. I'd like to be your friend, if you'll let me."

Rhonda met Donna's gaze, then turned to her mother. "Can we go now? I want to get to bed." As she spoke, she walked away.

Louise embraced Donna and said, "Thank you for your attitude, honey." Then she thanked Breanna and hurried after her daughter.

Before everyone in the camp was asleep, the heavy night sky came alive with lightning. Thunder boomed and rain began to fall. It rained hard all night, but the sky was clear at dawn, and the world smelled fresh and clean. The air was cool, and every-one wished it could stay that way.

During breakfast, Jason Moore found Rip Clayson eating at the tailgate of Curly Wesson's wagon alone. He was unaware that his father was standing near, on the outside rim of the wagon circle, having drawn guard duty from 3:00 A. M. to sunrise.

"Good morning, Jason," Rip said as the young man approached.

"Good morning, sir."

There was a hint of hesitation in the young man's voice, and Clayson picked up on it. "Problem?" he asked.

"Well, sort of."

"I've got big ears."

Jason cleared his throat nervously. "Well, sir, it's just that...well, I've got this fear about what'll happen if the Indians attack us."

"So do I," Rip said, then finished the last of his coffee.

"*You* have fear about fighting Indians?"

"Sure do."

"I thought—"

"That experienced Indian fighters went into battle unafraid?"

"Well...yes, sir. I guess."

"Wrong, Jason. I don't talk about it much, but I fought in the Civil War. Union side. Under General McClellan, then various others that President Lincoln moved in and out of leadership. I know what it's like to go into battle against Rebels...and as you already have heard, I guess, I've been in some battles with hostile Indians."

"Yes, sir. I didn't know about the Civil War."

"Hasn't your father explained how a man feels before a battle? I mean that every man is scared?"

"Well, sir, he never talked to me about it much, but I do recall him saying if a man is afraid to go into battle, he's a coward."

Rip nodded and set the coffee cup on the lowered tailgate, next to his empty plate. "I can picture him telling you that. Now, Jason, you're not a child anymore, or I wouldn't go any further with this. But since you're a man, I'll tell you that if your father ever went into battle without fear, he's the only man I ever heard of that did."

Jason squinted and cocked his head. "You're serious?"

"Dead serious. Just because you have fear about an Indian attack doesn't mean you're a coward. Not at all. It's normal to feel some fear. Completely normal. You see, a person shows what they're made of when they do what they have to do in spite of their fear. Heroes are made in time of battle when a frightened man goes above and beyond the call of duty and does his job."

A smile worked its way across the young man's face. "I never heard it that way before. I—"

"That's enough of that tommyrot!" boomed Wade Moore, coming around the wagon. The colonel's veins stood out on his forehead and neck as he spat at Clayson, "What's this hero stuff you're tellin' my boy, mister? What kind of soldier were you, bein' afraid to go into battle?"

"A normal one, Colonel. And I'm the same way about fighting Indians."

Moore shook his head in disgust and turned to Jason. "I heard what you told him, boy! Scared of fightin' Indians, are you? You're nothin' but a snivelin' coward, Jason, and I'm ashamed to call you my son!"

Jason wheeled and walked away. Rip thought he had seen tears in Jason's eyes just before he spun around.

The colonel mumbled something under his breath as he watched Jason go, then turned to face Clayson. "You quit puttin' sissy ideas in his head, y'hear?"

"Any man who says he has no fear of going into a battle, whether it's Indians or enemy soldiers, Colonel, is a fool or a liar! Which are you?"

Moore held the wagon master's unblinking stare for a long moment. Then he grunted and stormed away.

Twenty minutes later the wagons pulled out and began the day's journey.

As usual, Rip Clayson trotted his mount back and forth along the line of wagons, talking to their occupants. Each time he drew near the Moore wagon, Marian gave him a smile, but the colonel ignored him.

In the seat of the lead wagon, Breanna said to Curly, "I've thought a lot about what you and Rip told me about the way Snake Indians treat white women. Do you have any idea how many warriors this Chief Red Claw might have around here?"

"Not a clue," the old man replied, turning to spit. This time the whole wad went. Curly reached into his shirt pocket and pulled out a plug of tobacco. He grinned at Breanna and extended it toward her. "Wanna chaw?"

"Oh, ugh!" she said, turning her head away.

The old man cackled, bit off a chunk, and put the plug back in his pocket. "Don't you worry none 'bout them Snakes, honey. If'n they attack, you just stay close to ol' Curly. I'll pr'tect ya."

"I wasn't just thinking of myself," she said softly. "There are a lot of women and girls in this train. I'm concerned that if the Snakes come in large enough numbers, they could overwhelm us and take every female they want."

"I don't think they've got that many, honey," replied Curly. "From what that there lieutenant said, the bunch that was with Red Claw was about three dozen. It wouldn't be no pushover to take on that many, but with the men and women we got who can use a gun, I don't think they'll overwhelm us."

"I hope you're right," Breanna said, adjusting herself on the seat after the wagon had hit a hard bump. "Even more, I hope they don't come after us at all."

"I'll buy that," Curly said, turning and spitting.

Breanna looked at him with smiling eyes but a turned-down mouth. "Must you do that?"

"Oh, yes, ma'am," he grinned, wiping the juice on his sleeve. "Why?"

"'Cause it'd make me sick if I swallered it!"

14

THE MORNING SUN worked its way higher in its wide arc across the Wyoming sky as the wagon train climbed a steep incline out of a grassy draw. When the lead wagon topped the rise, a wide, sweeping valley spread out before them. It was lush with long, dark-green grass, and the mild, vagrant winds made the grass look like great waves of the sea.

The valley stretched eastward with round, undulating hills as far as the eye could see, and westward to a range of blue-cast mountains that worked their way in a half-horseshoe shape to the south. A few miles north, the valley began a gentle rise toward the southern swing of the mountains. At its lowest point, a wide river snaked its way eastward through the valley. The grassy land was dotted with patches of blue spruce, Ponderosa pine, and aspen. Wild berry bushes surrounded some of the patches, and a variety of wild flowers decorated the open areas.

"Oh, how beautiful!" Breanna Baylor exclaimed. "If I were looking for a place to settle down and make my home, this would be it!"

"It shore is a gorgeous place, all right," Curly said, "but have you ever seen Jackson Hole?"

"No, but I've heard it's a beautiful valley, too. Is it prettier than this?"

"Shore is. The Snake River winds its way through that gorgeous valley for over fifty miles. Has flowers and grass and trees just like you're lookin' at, but what really takes your breath are them Teton Mountains. Whooee! I'll tell you! The Almighty outdid Hisself when He put that place together!"

"The Almighty, Curly?" Breanna said. "You believe in the Almighty God who created this earth and the whole universe?"

Curly turned his head and met her searching gaze. "Well, shore. I ain't no atheist. Man'd have to be plumb loco to believe that there Charlie Darwin stuff." He reached into the pocket of his worn-out denim vest, pulled out a pocket watch, and said, "Be just as sensible as me tryin' to tell you that the parts of this here watch come together all by theirselves."

"Now, that's good thinking," smiled Breanna.

"Just stacks up, the way I see it," Curly said. "Anybody with a brain in his skull would say that behind this here watch was a watchmaker. I gotta say the same thing 'bout this earth and the universe around it. The Almighty did it, all right. He's the Designer and the Worldmaker."

"I'm glad you see that, Curly," Breanna said. "Do you understand that the Designer and Worldmaker became a human being and came into the world to provide a way of salvation for sinners?"

Curly's scraggly eyebrows arched. "The Creator became a human bein'?"

"That's right. His name is Jesus Christ. He not only is the great God of the universe, but He's the only one who can cleanse and forgive our sins so we can go to heaven when we die."

Breanna turned in the seat and opened her medical bag,

which contained a small Bible. "Here, let me read you something."

Curly had always been afraid of anyone using the Bible on him. He swallowed hard. There would be no escaping it this time. He wouldn't hurt Breanna's feelings for anything.

"You see, Curly, the same God who created this universe also authored this Book."

"Yeah? I thought men wrote it."

"Men penned the words down, yes," she nodded, "but the Lord gave them the words so they would be perfect and inspired...and we could bank our eternal destinies on it."

"Guess if He could make the universe, He wouldn't have any problem doin' that."

"No, He wouldn't. Listen to this, Curly. It's speaking here of the Lord Jesus Christ. *For by him were all things created, that are in heaven, and that are in earth, visible and invisible, whether they be thrones, or dominions, or principalities, or powers: all things were created by him, and for him.*"

"Hmm—and that's talkin' 'bout Jesus Christ?"

"Yes, it is."

Breanna turned pages again and read Curly the story of Jesus' virgin birth, pointing out His purpose for coming into the world. She then told him in brief of Jesus' ministry on earth, of His death on the cross of Calvary, and of His resurrection. She read him two verses about the need to believe in Jesus, then closed the Bible.

"So what do you think, Curly?" she asked softly.

Curly gripped the reins so hard his knuckles were white. After a long moment, he said, "Well, Rip has talked to me 'bout this on several occasions, but I'll have to confess...I ain't never let him go near as far with it as you just done."

"Any questions you'd like to ask?"

Curly stared at the broad valley ahead. "Not...uh...not right now."

"Would you say that the story of Jesus and His love for us is just a fairy tale?"

"Well...no. I wouldn't say that."

"Then you believe it's true?"

There was a mysterious burning sensation somewhere deep within Curly Wesson. He had never been so uncomfortable in all his life, yet he knew the strange feeling was more than simply Breanna's persuasive powers. Was it the Almighty who was causing him to be so disturbed? He needed time to think it through.

"What's the verdict, Curly?" asked Breanna. "Is it true, or is it a fairy tale?"

"Miss Baylor!" came an excited male voice from Breanna's side of the wagon.

She turned to see Lorne Clymer running up to her, his eyes wide. Lorne was the husband of Amanda Clymer, who was expecting her second child but was not due for another two weeks.

"What is it, Lorne?" Breanna said, leaning from the seat.

"I think Amanda's having labor pains, ma'am. Would you come and look at her?"

"Of course. Curly, would you stop the wagon? I have to see about Amanda."

The train was halted while Breanna went to the Clymer wagon and examined the expectant mother.

Curly was trembling inside. He pondered what Breanna had

read to him from the Bible, and the things she had told him about Jesus Christ. If it was true, for certain an old cuss like Curly Wesson was in trouble with God.

After some twenty minutes, Rip Clayson rode up to the lead wagon and said, "We'll be able to pull out shortly, Curly. Miss Breanna is on her way now."

"Amanda okay?"

"Seems to be."

"She ain't gonna deliver?"

"Not yet."

Breanna drew up on the other side of the wagon and climbed aboard.

"No baby yet, Rip tells me," Curly said.

"Not yet, but soon."

"No problems, though?"

"I don't think so. The baby might just come a little early."

"Good," Curly nodded. "Well, let's move on."

Rip Clayson decided to ride ahead for awhile. As they descended into the valley, Breanna cast a long look at the broad river. "What river is that, Curly?"

"That's the Big Sandy, honey. The Little Sandy flows into it from up north beyond them hills off to your right. We're too far from it to tell for sure yet, but it looks like it's runnin' purty full."

"The heavy rains, I guess."

"That'll do it. That rain water's gotta go somewheres when it comes down like it's been doin'."

"Will it be a problem for us, Curly? Getting the wagons to the other side, I mean."

"Could be. We'll just hafta tackle that big ol' bear when we get down there."

Three hours later, the wagon train reached the bank of the Big Sandy River and found it near flood stage. Rip Clayson knew that even if there was no additional rain, it would take the river three or four days to return to its normal level. They could not afford the delay. The river would have to be crossed.

It took nearly four hours to get all the wagons across the Big Sandy. Eight families had milk cows tied on behind their wagons. The cow belonging to a family named Maxwell—with six children—became disoriented in the crossing. Her halter broke, and she was swept away, bawling, in the swift current.

The Anthony Singfield wagon collided with another wagon near the far shore, breaking a wheel. The Singfields had four children and another on the way. Bea Singfield was nearing the end of her eighth month and was shaken hard when the two wagons collided. While the wheel was being repaired in the falling darkness, Breanna tended to Bea, expressing hope that the jolt would not cause her to deliver early.

The wagon train made its usual circle on the south bank of the Big Sandy and fires were built for cooking. While the food was being cooked, Breanna visited Amanda Clymer and her other two expectant mothers to make sure they were all right after the river crossing. Kitty Harbison was in her seventh month with her first child, and Effie McFadden was nearing term with her third child. All were doing fine.

Breanna had time to check on Hattie Chatsworth before supper and found that her lungs were a bit congested. A good rubdown eased her breathing.

After supper, the weary nurse climbed into the Wyatt wagon to check on Jay. Elsie and Duane looked on from the front part of the wagon while Breanna examined him by lantern light. Jay's color was not good, and he was experiencing a lot of pain. Breanna put a fresh bandage on the incision and sighed. Jay could see the concern in her face.

"What's the matter?" he asked.

"Jay, I think you're bleeding internally. The jostling of the wagon is just too much for you. I wish you had listened to me and stayed in South Pass City."

"What can you do, Breanna?" asked Elsie. "Is there any way you can tell for sure that he's bleeding?"

"Only when his midsection starts to swell from the blood filling it up."

"Won't he bleed to death if that's the case?" Elsie asked.

"It's...it's my fault," Duane said. "If only I—"

"It's *not* your fault, son!" Elsie said, patting his hand. "It was an accident. Nothing more...nothing less."

"That's right, Duane," Jay said. "Please don't blame yourself."

Duane bit his upper lip and closed his eyes.

"Is there nothing you can do if Jay *is* bleeding internally?" Elsie said to Breanna.

Breanna glanced at her patient, then looked Elsie in the eye. "Honey, I'll have to open him up again and see if I can stop the bleeding. I'm not a surgeon. I don't know how well I'll do the second time. All I can do now is keep a close watch on him."

The majority of the people were gathered around the main fire talking to Lieutenant Emery Dodd about Indians. The lieutenant felt he would be doing the people a disservice if he held back on telling them how vicious Chief Red Claw was known to be. He described some of the Snake leader's atrocities against white people in the past five or six years, especially white women. Kitty Harbison turned pale and asked her husband to take her to the wagon.

Moments later, Clara Farnsworth appeared at the Wyatt wagon and said, "Excuse me, folks."

"What is it, Clara?" asked Elsie.

"It's Kitty Harbison. She needs Breanna."

"What's wrong, Clara?" Breanna asked.

"Abdominal pains."

"The baby?"

"Could be."

"All right. I'm through here for now. Let's go."

Breanna told the Wyatts she would be back to check on Jay before bedtime, and that if he seemed to get worse, Duane should come and get her. In less than a minute, Breanna was at the rear of the Harbison wagon and found Bud sitting beside his wife, reading to her from the Bible.

"Hello," Breanna said. "May I come in?"

"Please do," Bud smiled.

Breanna mounted the wooden steps at the rear of the wagon. Bud moved the lantern a little closer to Kitty and laid the Bible on top of a small box. He gestured toward a short stool that sat by the cot where Kitty lay and said, "You can sit here, Miss Breanna."

"You're having abdominal pains, I understand," Breanna said.

"Yes," Kitty replied. "Not real bad, but enough that Bud

thought we should have your opinion."

"I realize this is your first baby, Kitty," said Breanna, "and you're due in another month or so...but would you say what you're experiencing is the beginning of labor pains?"

"I'm not sure. It could be just an upset stomach."

"Well, let's see how things look."

Bud decided to leave the wagon while Breanna made her examination. Ten minutes later he returned just as the nurse was covering Kitty with a light blanket.

"So what do you think, Miss Breanna?" he asked.

"It's definitely not the beginning of labor, Bud. I think it's just nerves."

"Nerves?"

"Yes. She's worried over the threat of what Red Claw and his warriors might do if they attack the train."

"I never realized that fear could cause pain like that," Kitty said.

"Emotional stress can cause all kinds of physical problems," Breanna said.

"What can we do, ma'am?" asked Bud. "The threat is on us."

Breanna ran her gaze to the Bible Bud had laid on the box. "More of what you were already doing."

Bud grinned and picked up the Bible. "God's Word really can help, can't it."

"More than most people realize," Breanna smiled.

"Miss Breanna, we really haven't had a chance to talk to you about ourselves. Whenever you've been here to the wagon, it's always been a quick check on Kitty, and you had to be somewhere else. Rip Clayson told us that you're a Christian."

"That's right," said Breanna. "The born-again, blood-bought kind."

"Us, too."

"I thought you might be when I saw you reading to her from the Bible. Could I share something with you from the Word of God that has been a real strength to me?"

"Sure," said Bud, handing the Book to her.

Breanna turned to Isaiah 26:3 and told them how the verse had helped her lay hold of God's perfect peace. They talked about it for a while and prayed together. Breanna was about to leave when Duane Wyatt appeared at the rear of the covered wagon. When Breanna saw his face in the lantern light, she knew Jay had taken a turn for the worse.

"Ma sent me, Miss Breanna. Pa's pain is worse, and he's swelling up in his middle."

"All right, Duane," Breanna said, picking up her black bag. She bid the Harbisons goodnight and quickly descended the wooden steps. A numb feeling settled in her chest. The thing she had feared was upon her.

"Miss Breanna, how am I going to face this if Pa dies?" Duane said as they walked across the circle toward the Wyatt wagon.

Breanna switched the bag from one hand to the other, put an arm around Duane's shoulder, and said, "You can't blame yourself, Duane. I realize the gun was in your hand when it went off, but you didn't cause the wagon to hit the rut. It was just one of those freakish things that happens. You mustn't punish yourself. It wasn't your fault."

"Yes, but—"

"Miss Breanna!" Rip Clayson's voice cut across Duane's words as he drew up behind them. "It's Amanda Clymer. Lorne asked me to find you. Amanda's about to deliver!"

"Oh, dear," Breanna said, putting the fingers of one hand to her forehead. She thought a moment, then spoke to Duane. "Find Clara Farnsworth and tell her I've got to do surgery on your father. I'll need her help. Tell her she'll find the necessary items in the box of your wagon. Tell her to get herself scrubbed up. She knows how to do that. Get a couple of the men to help lay your father on the tailgate of the wagon. I'll need three lanterns for light. I must see about Amanda first, then I'll be there."

"Yes, ma'am," said Duane, and started away.

"Duane, you get your dad on the tailgate and the lanterns in place," Rip said. "I'll deliver the message to Clara and carry the box from Curly's wagon to yours."

The youth nodded, fear stamped plainly on his face, and darted toward his wagon.

"Thank you, Rip," Breanna said and headed for the Clymer vehicle.

Ten minutes later, Jay Wyatt was ready for surgery. Clara Farnsworth was scrubbed, and the surgical instruments lay on a sterilized cloth next to Jay on the tailgate, along with needles, thread, cloth squares, towels, and a bottle of chloroform.

Elsie and Duane stood beside Jay, worry evident on their faces. Elsie held her husband's hand and spoke soft words of comfort. Several other people stood close by, including Rip Clayson, Curly Wesson, and Lieutenant Dodd.

All eyes turned to Breanna as she rushed in and said to Clara, "Everything ready?"

"Yes."

Breanna moved up to the tailgate of the wagon, and Elsie and

Duane stepped aside to allow her to stand over Jay. She saw that his swollen midsection was much worse than it had been when she looked at him no more than an hour before. He was bleeding profusely.

"What about Amanda?" Elsie asked while the nurse probed her husband's middle.

"She's having contractions every three minutes. The membrane has already ruptured. She could deliver within an hour or so. I've got two experienced midwives with her who can handle the birth unless complications arise."

Elsie nodded. "What do you think, here?"

"I've got to open him up in a hurry and see if I can locate the bleeder. Clara is going to put him under while I get scrubbed."

Jay spoke weakly, "Miss Breanna...do I...do I have a chance?"

"Of course, but time is of the essence. You try to relax."

"Miss Breanna...if something should happen and I don't make it, don't take any blame on yourself. If I'd only listened to you, this wouldn't have happened."

"Perhaps not, Jay. But right now I need to ask you to stop talking so Clara can administer the chloroform."

Clara Farnsworth had Rip and Curly ready to pour twice-boiled water over Breanna's hands while she scrubbed them with lye soap. While she scrubbed, Rip said, "Miss Breanna, I wouldn't have your job for all the tea in China."

"Me, neither," Curly said.

"We all do what the Lord equipped us to do and what we enjoy doing the most," Breanna said. "I won't say that medicine is always pleasant, but when you can help the sick and save lives, it's very rewarding."

"A little taxing on the nerves sometimes, though, huh?" said Curly.

Breanna looked up and smiled at him. "You might say that."

The curious crowd kept their distance from the Wyatt wagon but watched as Breanna began her work. Elsie and Duane stood closest, holding on to each other. Clara Farnsworth was next to Breanna, following Breanna's instructions and making sure Jay stayed under.

Breanna accepted the metal hemostats one at a time from Clara, clamping the vessels and arteries as she reopened the incision. When that was done, she directed Clara to sponge away blood with clean strips of cloth while she gingerly probed with her fingers for the bleeder.

The night was cool, but perspiration beaded on Breanna's brow and her heart thudded against her ribs. There was so much blood. *Where was that bleeder?*

Breanna was alert to the rhythm of Jay's breathing. It was acceptable for the first few minutes, but as she continued to probe without success, it suddenly became sporadic.

Clara's gaze swerved to Breanna, and she saw a shadow of apprehension behind the nurse's eyes.

Jay's breathing stopped.

Breanna's face paled and a tiny gasp escaped her lips.

Clara's eyes widened. She knew Jay Wyatt had just died.

Elsie and Duane clung to each other and stared in disbelief as Breanna straightened her back and shook her head. She reached for a towel and began wiping blood from her hands.

She slowly turned around. "I'm...sorry. I couldn't find the bleeder in time."

15

✦

BREANNA BAYLOR WAS CALLED to the Clymer wagon, where she delivered a beautiful baby girl while Lorne stood nearby, holding their eighteen-month-old son.

There were mixed emotions in the camp. Jay Wyatt had left the world and the Clymer baby entered it, all in a matter of minutes.

They buried Jay Wyatt the next morning. Rip Clayson conducted a brief service, reading from the Bible, and had Bud Harbison close in prayer. Elsie clung to Breanna with one arm while she held her son with the other. Duane took his father's death very hard, still shouldering the blame.

When the train pulled out, Lieutenant Emery Dodd was at the reins of the Wyatt wagon. He had volunteered to drive, allowing mother and son to mourn in the back of the wagon. Breanna rode with them. Mother and son had not slept during the night. When they seemed settled enough, Breanna gave them sedatives, and by midmorning they were both asleep.

Breanna dropped from the Wyatt wagon and made her way to the Clymer vehicle to check on Amanda and the newborn baby. Donna Day had volunteered to take care of the Clymer's little son in the Day wagon, freeing Lorne to drive.

Breanna found mother and baby doing well, and after spending a few minutes with them, she returned to her normal spot in the lead wagon beside Curly Wesson.

Two days later, the wagon train wound its way through the rugged mountains that made up the half-horseshoe to the south and came out in relatively flat, more arid country. There was less grass and fewer shrubs and trees. Giant rock formations rose up like towering sentinels on the southern and western horizons. It was almost four o'clock in the afternoon.

Rip Clayson rode alongside Curly's wagon, chatting with the old man and the nurse. Suddenly, movement caught his eye on the sun-washed land straight ahead.

"What is it, Rip?" Breanna asked.

"Something out of the ordinary is moving out there. I can't make it out yet."

Both Breanna and Curly concentrated on the spot where Rip was looking.

"Oh, I see it," said Breanna. "It's just a speck, but it seems to be moving."

"That's about all I can tell at the moment, too," Rip said.

"Well, I can tell ya what it is," Curly said.

"Oh?" Rip and Breanna said together.

"Shore, it's a fly a-crawlin' on a rock five miles away."

Breanna drove an elbow into Curly's side. "Who do you think you're kidding? You couldn't see a fly on a rock five *yards* away, let alone five miles."

"Oh, yeah? I got eyes like a eagle!"

"You also have a tongue like a salamander!"

"Hear that, Rip?" Curly said. "She's got it real bad for me, I'm a-tellin' ya!" He leaned over and spit.

"I've got it bad for you, all right," Breanna sighed. "And it gets worse every time you do that."

Curly and Rip laughed, then the three of them concentrated on the movement ahead of them. The speck had divided into two men who were moving toward them on foot.

Twenty minutes brought the lead wagon and the two men within thirty yards of each other. One of them was limping.

Clayson motioned for the wagons down the line to halt. "Haul up, Curly. I want to talk to them."

The two men were no more than fifteen yards from Curly and Breanna when Rip met them. One looked slightly older than the other, though both were in their early twenties. They were dirty, unkempt, and slender.

"What say, Curly?" asked Breanna in a hushed tone, studying them.

"I don't like the looks of 'em."

Breanna did not respond, though she felt the same way.

The older one had greasy, matted hair protruding from under his sweat-stained hat. It was evident he had not visited a barber in months. The other had a ruddy complexion, deep-set eyes, and buck teeth. Orange-red hair, as long and filthy as his partner's, dangled from under his hat brim. The stubble on his face was as red as his cohort's was black.

"Howdy," the dark one said. "Name's Max Rule. Pal here is D. J. Danco. We're fur trappers. Been workin' the ponds along the Green River to the south and were doin' quite well until a bunch of Snake Indians came along. Stole our furs, guns, and horses."

Breanna didn't like the way both men were looking at her. She turned and acted as though she was searching for something in the wagon.

"You the wagon master?" Rule asked, bringing his gaze back to Clayson.

"Yep. Snakes, eh? We've heard they're on the warpath."

"Well, you can believe it," Rule said.

"Any idea what sparked it? They've been pretty peaceful for almost a year."

"No idea at all. Just up and started unleashin' their wrath on whites all over this part of Wyomin'." After a brief pause, he said, "Say, I didn't get your name."

"Clayson. Ripley Clayson."

"Headed for Oregon or California?"

"California."

"Well, uh…Mr. Clayson…I wonder if you could spare D. J. and me some food? We haven't eaten in three days."

Rip had an uneasy feeling about Rule and Danco, but he couldn't let hungry men starve when there was food available. He held up the train long enough to persuade some of the travelers to share some hardtack and beef jerky with the two men.

Rule accepted the food with a broad smile. "Haven't got any spare whiskey, have ya?"

"Nope," Clayson said. "We don't have whiskey on this train…spare or any other kind. When I lead a wagon train, one of my rules is no liquor."

"Too bad," Rule grunted.

"No. Very wise," Rip said, heading for his horse. "Now, we've got to get moving again."

Max Rule and D. J. Danco exchanged glances.

"Say, Mr. Clayson, I was wonderin'..." Rule said, moving up close as Clayson settled in his saddle. "Would you...uh...allow us to travel in this here wagon train with you? Them Snakes might just decide to come after us."

"Exactly where are you fellas heading?"

"We were headed for Granger."

"Granger?" Rip knew the small town of Granger lay on the wagon trail between where he sat and Fort Bridger.

"Yeah. We plan to buy us some more horses, guns, and trappin' equipment there."

Clayson gave the dirty man a wary look. "You're not making sense here, Max. Granger is south of here. When we spotted you, you were heading north."

"Oh. Well...uh...you see, we were headin' south toward Granger, then we happened to look behind us and seen your wagon train. So we turned around, hopin' you'd let us have something to eat."

"And we're much obliged for the food," Danco said.

"Yeah, but we'd be even more obliged if you'd let us ride along as far as Granger," Rule said.

Most of the people in the wagon train were standing in a half circle watching the two men. Rip looked around and said, "What do you folks think? They'll have to ride with some of you."

"I object, Clayson," Colonel Wade Moore said. "Why should

we share our food and the wagons we paid hard-earned money for with the likes of these riffraff?"

Moore looked around for moral support, but no one spoke their agreement.

"We can't leave them out here for the Snakes to track down, Rip," Earl Maxwell said.

"Earl's right, Rip," Darrel Day said. "We know the Snakes are on the warpath. These men are human beings... *white* human beings. Only right thing is for us to give them protection."

In spite of Colonel Moore's loud objections, the people voted to take Rule and Danco as far as Granger. Moore stomped away, muttering. Clayson assigned Rule to ride in the seat of the Wyatt wagon beside Lieutenant Emery Dodd, and Danco to ride in the seat of the Kirkland wagon beside Jason Moore. Martha volunteered to travel inside her wagon.

As the train moved out, Curly said, "Miss Breanna, I don't like the way those two looked at you."

"I don't either," she replied.

"You just be wary of 'em, won't ya?"

"I will," she replied, touching the handle of the Derringer that secretly rode at the waistband of her skirt.

The sun had dropped below the western horizon and twilight was on the land before Rip Clayson called for the wagons to halt and make a circle for the night. He was trying to make up as much lost time as possible.

Elsie Wyatt volunteered to feed Lieutenant Emery Dodd, since he was driving her wagon, and offered supper also to Max

Rule, which he gladly accepted.

D. J. Danco was invited for supper by Martha Kirkland, who also would feed her driver, Jason Moore, and Nurse Breanna Baylor. While Jason built a cook fire for Martha, Danco planted himself beside the wagon. Breanna was busy looking after Hattie Chatsworth and the three expectant mothers, and would be there by the time supper was ready.

Danco talked with Jason and Martha as they prepared the meal, and his speech was liberally sprinkled with profanity.

"D. J., there's a lady present," Jason said. "You shouldn't use that kind of language at all, but most certainly not in front of a lady."

"Thank you, Jason," Martha said.

Danco bristled and swore again, saying he always talked that way, even in front of his mother.

Colonel Wade Moore was passing nearby and heard the foul words, then heard his son say, "Look, D. J., I'm sorry you had no more respect than that for your mother, but I'm asking you not to talk that way in front of Mrs. Kirkland."

"Jason!" boomed the colonel, moving in and standing over Danco, who was still sitting on the ground.

"Yes, Colonel?" Jason said.

"That's not how you handle a situation like this."

"Sir?"

Moore looked down at Danco and said, "Stand up."

"Huh?"

"I said stand up!"

"Now look, mister, I don't know who you are or why you're in that Confederate uniform, but I don't have to obey anything you say."

The colonel seized Danco by the front of his shirt with one hand and raised him to his feet. Danco's eyes bulged at the man's strength.

"Now, Jason," Moore drawled, "whenever you hear a man use profanity in front of a lady, you don't *ask* him not to talk that way. A real man will do this."

The colonel rammed his left elbow into Danco's stomach. The blow drove the air from Danco's lungs and sent him sprawling. Moore stepped quickly to where Danco lay, jerked him to his feet, and punched him in the face. Danco went down flat on his back and stayed there. He was out cold.

Rip Clayson arrived on the scene, scowling. "What's going on here?" he demanded.

Max Rule came charging up, having seen the incident from the other side of the circle. He pointed a stiff finger at the colonel, called him a vile name, and blared, "What did you hit my partner for?"

"Y'all see these ladies around here?" Moore replied.

"Yeah. So?"

"So your partner used profanity in front of Mrs. Kirkland like you just did so loudly in front of her and these other ladies. I was just givin' my son a lesson on what to do when a man fills a lady's ears with that kind of language."

The last three words were just coming out of the colonel's mouth when his fist shot out and struck Max Rule, who went down in a heap. Both Danco and Rule lay unconscious,

Clayson looked at Moore and said, "Colonel, I appreciate your concern for the ladies' ears, as any gentleman would...but maybe you should have warned them once and demanded an apology to the ladies before resorting to fisticuffs."

Moore grinned. "Why, Mister Clayson, that's exactly what I did. What you saw *was* my warnin'. If the ladies don't get an apology when these men come to, you'll see what the warnin' was about."

"Mr. Clayson, I'm in total agreement with the colonel on this," Lieutenant Dodd said. "These two must be made to apologize to the ladies."

"Oh, they will," Clayson said. "I don't object to the colonel's defense of the ladies' ears. I just think he might have been a little slower to resort to force."

Breanna joined the crowd, and one of the women explained to her what had happened. She went over to the two men who lay sprawled on the ground and looked down at them. D. J. Danco was coming to. A moan escaped his lips as he rolled his head back and forth. Max Rule was also beginning to stir.

"Looks like they'll be all right," Breanna said, looking at Rip.

"Good, but if they refuse to make an apology, they'll be on their way real quick."

When Rule and Danco were fully conscious and on their feet, Rip demanded that they apologize to the women. Both of them bristled at first, but when they were told they would be off the train if there were no apologies, they both gave in and did so.

Later that night, when the people had gone to bed, six men were at their posts on the outer edge of the circle, keeping watch on the first shift. The main fire in the center of the circle was dying out, and the only light was from a myriad stars overhead.

Curly Wesson's post was at his own wagon. The horses, oxen, and milk cows were in a rope corral a few yards away. The old man could hear snores coming from various places within the camp.

Suddenly there was a series of yaps somewhere in the night, followed by a long, mournful howl. It seemed to come from the forested hills to the east. Seconds later, there was an identical reply, which Curly was sure had come from a huge jumble of rocks off to the west.

Curly gripped the rifle in his hand and listened to the stillness of the night. Less than a minute had passed when the same yapping and howling came from somewhere to the south.

Curly knew Rip Clayson was on watch at the Kirkland wagon a few yards away. Hastening that direction, he could make out Clayson's form in the gloom. Rip was on his feet, watching Curly come toward him.

"You hear those coyotes?" whispered Curly.

"Yeah," Rip whispered back. "You thinking the same thing I am?"

"Must be. You don't seem very relaxed."

Two more forms drew up. It was Matt McFadden and Colonel Wade Moore.

McFadden whispered, "Rip, what do you think? Those really coyotes?"

"Didn't sound like the real thing to me nor to Curly."

"That's what I thought too. If those are Indians—"

McFadden's words were cut off by another coyote sound that came from the forested hills to the east. The four men stood in absolute silence and waited. There was an answering call again from the huge rock formations to the west.

Soft footsteps were heard, and a dark form came from between two wagons. It was Lieutenant Emery Dodd, who was not on watch.

"The howls woke me up," Dodd whispered. "I don't think those are furry-bodied critters."

"I don't either," Rip whispered back.

"You think they'll attack, Lieutenant?" McFadden asked.

"No way to know for sure. They could be trying to unnerve us, or they could be signaling for attack."

"You mean an attack in the mornin'," Moore said.

"Not necessarily," Dodd said.

"Lieutenant, aren't you aware that Indians won't attack at night?" Moore said. "It's their religion. I've read about it. They believe that to be killed in battle at night will lock their souls in a halfway spot between earth and the happy hunting ground forever. They fear this, so they will not attack at night."

"That's true of many tribes, Colonel," Dodd whispered, "but it doesn't hold true for all of them. All Indians don't adhere to their ancestors' religion or superstitions. I don't know about Red Claw and his warriors, but if they're not tied to the Shoshoni religion, they just might attack at night. We've had Crow and Blackfoot who have attacked forts at night in Wyoming."

Others from the train joined them, including some women. In the group were Breanna Baylor and Martha Kirkland. Everyone who had heard the sound of the coyotes or been awakened by fearful whispers gathered to hear what Rip Clayson had to say.

Clayson left the sentries at their posts and met with the people in the middle of the circle. They were told that the sounds might be genuine coyote howls, but there was no way to be sure. Everyone in the camp would have to be awakened and told to be on guard with guns ready.

This was done, and at 2:30 A.M., fear settled like a cold blanket on the wagon train. They had tried to keep from waking the children, but they had been unsuccessful. All over the camp, frightened children cried while fearful parents tried to comfort them.

Extra ammunition was pulled from the Zimmer wagon, and Rip Clayson doubled the guard.

At 3:45, Bud Harbison found Breanna and asked her to come to the wagon. Kitty was terrified and having abdominal pains. Breanna climbed into the wagon and found that Kitty was going into labor, though she estimated that the baby would not come for several hours. Breanna stayed with her the rest of the night.

When the sun rose the next morning, the weary, frightened people were relieved that no attack had come. Clayson and Dodd warned them to stay alert while they ate breakfast.

Jason Moore delivered Breanna's breakfast to her at the Harbison wagon. Kitty begged the nurse not to leave her. The pains were growing closer together, and because this was her first child, she was especially anxious.

While the women cleaned up after breakfast, the men hitched up the teams to make ready to pull out.

Max Rule had noticed Rhonda Fallon and found her quite friendly. While she was at the side of her wagon, placing cooking utensils in a wooden box, Rule stepped up and said, "Mornin', good-lookin'."

"Good morning to you," Rhonda said, giving Rule a warm smile. "Rough night, wasn't it?"

"Aw, didn't bother me much. I've been up against Indians plenty of times. They ain't so tough."

"My, my, a real man of experience. I'd sure like to hear about some of the battles you've been in."

"Well, maybe we can arrange for a little private session," Rule grinned.

"Hey!" Jerry Adams said as he moved up close. "What's going on here? Rhonda, you shouldn't be talking to this guy."

"Oh?" Rule said. "And just why not? You own her, do you?"

"She's my girl!" Jerry said. "Ask her!"

"That true? You his girl?" Max said, turning to Rhonda.

Suddenly the voice of Rip Clayson roared through the camp. "Indians! They're attacking! Everybody in your place!"

Terror was mixed with resolve as the people hurried to their assigned places. On the rolling plains to the south, a band of war-painted Indians thundered toward the circled wagons, whooping and waving rifles over their heads.

16

✦

THE EARTH TREMBLED under the thundering hooves of three dozen whooping, yelping Snake Indians as they bore down on the wagon train.

Rip Clayson saw Curly Wesson take Breanna Baylor under his wagon; everyone else took refuge in the family vehicles, the women and children lying low in their wagons while the husbands made ready to fight from beneath.

Rip Clayson quickly found Jason Moore and told him the two of them would fight side-by-side from under Martha Kirkland's wagon. Martha was already down there with a rifle in her hands.

A small child could be heard crying from a nearby wagon as Curly lay beside Breanna and saw her holding his spare Colt .45 revolver in two trembling hands. Her black medical bag was at her side.

"Don't you worry none, honey," Curly said. "Ol' Curly's here with ya. I ain't gonna let no Injun get ya!"

Breanna nodded, but could not work up a smile.

"You'll be okay, honey. Just wait till you get a clear shot at one o' them savages and aim somewhere above his waist. Whether he's facin' ya or got his back to ya, let 'im have it!"

The Snakes were now less than a hundred yards away. Suddenly Bud Harbison rushed up behind them, knelt down, and gasped, "Miss Breanna!"

Breanna twisted around to see who it was. "Oh, no," she said. "Don't tell me the baby's coming!"

"Yes, ma'am! And I mean it's coming now!"

Rifles were already starting to bark, and men were shouting back and forth to each other as the Indian ponies closed in.

"All right," Breanna said, backing out on her hands and knees. "Curly, I've got to take care of this."

"Sure, honey. You bring that new life into the world, and I'll see if I can send a few redskins to their happy huntin' grounds!"

The whooping and yelping of the Indians was punctuated with the sharp sound of gunfire as Breanna ran across the open area in the wagon circle with Bud Harbison. She had the medical bag in one hand and the .45 in the other.

When they reached the wagon, Indian bullets were already striking canvas, wood, and dirt all around the circle. Bud picked Breanna up and set her in the wagon. "I'll be underneath, ma'am, if you need me!"

When the Snakes were within forty yards, they suddenly divided and began to circle the wagons. Guns from both sides were unleashed full force.

Curly drew a bead with his .50 caliber buffalo rifle and dropped the hammer. The Indian arched his back as the slug plowed through his chest and exited his back. His rifle slipped from his fingers, and he reeled off his painted pony. He was dead before he hit the ground.

The battle raged, guns roared, and children cried out with fear. The smoke-filled air was alive with the bloodcurdling war cry of the Snakes.

Jason Moore lay next to Rip Clayson, frozen with terror. The rifle in his hands might as well have been a tree limb. He was so frightened, he couldn't fire it. Rip blasted away, swiftly working the lever of his Winchester .44.

Lieutenant Emery Dodd was bellied down under the Wyatt vehicle with Elsie on one side and Duane on the other. Mother and son both fired rifles at the galloping Indians.

Dodd looked past the painted ponies and their riders to a rocky knoll some six hundred yards to the south. There Red Claw, the young Snake chieftain, watched the battle from a safe distance. He was recognizable from that distance by his albino horse and by the long feathered headdress that he wore. Dodd pointed the chieftain out to Elsie and Duane.

"Why doesn't he come and fight?" asked Duane.

"He's not about to risk his own skin!" Dodd shouted. "Figures he's too important!"

"Wish I had a cannon!" Duane said.

Inside the Harbison wagon, Breanna prayed earnestly as she brought Kitty's healthy baby girl into the world. Twice, bullets ripped through the canvas above them, but neither one came close to the women or the baby.

The firing stopped abruptly, with only a few parting shots from the wagon train as the Indians galloped southward and disappeared behind a series of bluffs.

Six Snakes lay dead. Others had been wounded, but were picked up and carried away when the Indians left.

Mothers soon had their children quieted, and in the relative silence, Kitty Harbison's baby girl's voice was heard in the tight, quavering wail common to newborns. Several women gathered at the wagon to see if Kitty and the baby were both all right.

Howard and Bertha Lewis had been killed in the fighting, leaving behind three small children. Other families quickly volunteered to care for the orphans.

Another man, Will Powers, had also been killed, leaving behind his wife, Celia, and two young daughters. Several people gathered with them to try to give comfort.

One man had been wounded in an arm, and two women had been splintered with wood from bullets that had barely missed them. While Breanna cared for them, Lieutenant Dodd talked with Rip Clayson in the center of the circle. Jason Moore stood next to Rip with his unfired rifle in his hand.

"It was Red Claw, all right," Dodd told Clayson. "No mistake about it. He always rides that albino horse, and I've never seen him without that full headdress."

"What do you think? Will they come back?" Clayson asked.

"Without a doubt, but there's no way to know when. I think we surprised them with our fire power. Most wagon trains don't use the women to bear arms."

"I don't know why," Clayson said. "Most of them can handle a gun just fine."

Just then the colonel drew up and glared hard at his son. "Well, Jason, how many Indians did you shoot?"

Jason tried to speak, but no words came.

The colonel snatched the rifle from Jason's hands, lifted the chamber to his nose, and sniffed. "You didn't even fire this gun, you yellow coward!"

"Easy now, Colonel," Rip said. "This was Jason's first time to face an enemy. I've seen men freeze like that before. He'll do better next time."

Wade Moore spit, threw the rifle down, and stormed away. "I'm ashamed to have a coward for a son!" he yelled over his shoulder.

When the colonel was out of earshot, Jason fought tears and said with a tremulous voice, "I wish I'd been one of those killed today."

Rip laid a hand on his shoulder. "Don't talk like that, Jason. You'll have another chance to fight the Snakes. And next time you'll do better."

Clayson made the rounds, telling everyone they would wait an hour or so before pulling out. If Red Claw and his warriors did not return by then, they would move on.

The wagon master looked in on Breanna to see how she was doing with the wounded and to commend her for the job she did in delivering Kitty Harbison's baby.

Breanna smiled back at him. "Nothing spectacular on my part, Rip. The baby decided now was the time to be born. All I did was be there to greet her."

"Well, I suspect you did more than that. But whether what you did was spectacular or not, I thank you just the same."

Many of the men waited between the wagons and watched for another attack. Rhonda Fallon passed by where Max Rule was watching and said, "Hello, Max. I'm glad you made it through the fight."

"I'm glad you did, too," Rule grinned. "Hey, maybe when we get to Granger you and I should—"

"Rhonda, get away from that man!" Jerry Adams yelled, dashing up. "He's bad medicine!"

"Bad medicine, eh?" Rule said. "Well, Rhonda doesn't seem to think so, do you, honey?"

"She's not *honey* to you, Rule! You stay away from her, or I'll bust your head!"

"If you think you're man enough, hop to it, sonny!"

"Hey!" Rip Clayson shouted. "What's going on here?"

"This man's botherin' Rhonda and pushin' himself on her," Jerry said.

"I ain't botherin' her!" Rule said. "She's real friendly. If I was botherin' her, she wouldn't be so nice to me. I never made a move toward her till she gave me the eye."

Rhonda's face crimsoned.

Chuck and Louise Fallon were now on the scene. Chuck faced his daughter and asked, "Did you give him the eye?"

Rhonda nervously ran her tongue over her lips. Her voice was subdued, like a small girl's. "No, Daddy. I smiled at him, but I didn't mean anything by it."

Rule turned and scowled at her, calling her a liar with his eyes.

Rip Clayson spoke sternly. "Rule, you're off the train. Get out!

"Aw, now, Mr. Clayson, this ain't fair!"

"I said get out!"

"Please, Mr. Clayson, don't do this. If those savages out there find me and D. J. alone, they'll kill us! You'll be guilty of murder if you put us out!"

Rip thought on it, then said, "All right, I'm going to give you one more chance, Rule. Now you listen to me. If you get within thirty feet of Rhonda just once, you're gone. I don't want you even looking at her. Stay completely away from her. Do you understand me?"

"Yeah," Rule said quietly.

"I can't hear you!" Clayson said.

Rule met his stern gaze. "Yeah!"

"Yeah, what?"

"Yeah, I'll stay away from Rhonda!"

"All right. Now go about your business."

Rule ignored Rhonda, but gave Jerry Adams a hard look as he walked toward his partner.

"Hold it!" Clayson said. "No more trouble, Max. I mean with *anybody*...or you're afoot and on your own. Do I make myself clear?"

"You do," Rule nodded grimly.

"All right."

Rule wheeled and walked away and was joined by a limping D. J. Danco.

"I want to talk to you at the wagon," Chuck Fallon said to his daughter.

"Come on, Rhonda," Louise said, taking Rhonda by the arm.

When both parents were alone with their daughter, Chuck said, "Rhonda, I am sick and tired of you flirting with every man that comes along."

She started shaking her head and opened her mouth to speak.

"Don't deny it, girl," Chuck cut her off. "You've done it too many times to convince me that you're innocent."

Rhonda avoided her father's eyes.

"And another thing," Chuck said, "I detest the way you treat Jerry. He's a fine young man, and it's evident he cares very much for you. Why do you insist on cutting his heart out?"

Rhonda stared at the ground and did not reply.

"Well, let me tell you something, young lady. You either start treating Jerry right, or you tell him you're through with him."

Rhonda raised her eyes to meet her father's, then looked away quickly.

"I mean what I say, girl," Chuck said. "You better think about it." With that, he walked away.

Louise put an arm around her daughter's shoulder and said, "Come on, honey, let's talk about it. Your father is absolutely right, and I want to help you understand."

There was a pout on Rhonda's mouth as the two of them entered the wagon.

Rip Clayson decided to give it a little longer before pulling out. He would have a burial service for those who had been killed in the attack. A burial detail—which included Rule and Danco—worked at digging graves, while others kept a sharp lookout for another attack.

When the graves were finished, the bodies were lowered into the ground amid wails and tears. The graves were filled, and Clayson stood over the mounds and opened his Bible. He was just starting to read when one of the men on guard shouted, "Here come the Snakes again!" The Indians could be heard whooping and screeching as they thundered toward the wagon circle from the south.

The people scattered, took up their guns, and dashed to their posts. Just as Jason Moore was about to slide under the Kirkland wagon, he happened to glance toward his father's wagon and found the colonel's disapproving eyes on him. Jason pulled his gaze away and slid underneath. He made up his mind he would not freeze this time.

Breanna was under the Wesson wagon with Curly. The old man had his buffalo gun cocked and ready for action. Breanna held the Colt .45 in both hands, cocked it, and lined it where the Indians would be within a few seconds. She hated the idea of killing another human, but she knew she had to help defend herself and the others from attack. Suddenly a charging warrior was in line with her gun. She squeezed the trigger, and the bullet hit him in the right armpit, causing him to drop his repeater rifle and almost fall from his horse.

Rip Clayson blasted away from beneath the Kirkland wagon. He was pleased that Jason Moore was firing, too, and commended him for it. Martha told Jason that his father would be proud to hear he was bravely fighting the Indians. She would make it a point to tell the colonel.

The air was filled with smoke, and the acrid smell of burnt gunpowder stung their nostrils. A bullet chewed dirt and kicked dust in Jason's eyes.

"You okay?" Rip asked.

"Yes, sir. Just a little dirt in my eyes. I'm fine."

At the Wesson wagon, a Snake bullet struck the metal rim of one of the wheels and caromed away angrily. Breanna fired at another Indian who was bent low on his horse, and missed. For a brief moment, the smoke cleared and Curly caught a glimpse of the Snake chief astride his albino horse on the knoll where he appeared before.

"Looky there, Breanna!" Curly exclaimed, pointing to the mound. "That's Red Claw!"

Breanna looked at Red Claw and felt a chill on the back of her neck as she thought of what Dodd had said about the Snake chief's atrocities against white women.

Two galloping horsemen suddenly blocked Breanna's view of Red Claw. Curly's gun discharged, spewing a cloud of smoke. When the smoke had drifted away, a Snake lay flat on his back with a .50 caliber slug in his heart...and Red Claw was gone.

Rip Clayson estimated that Red Claw had come against the wagon train with no less than fifty warriors, but the Snakes were paying a heavy price for this attack. Suddenly they wheeled and rode south to get out of rifle range. Curly's big .50 boomed above the other guns, and a Snake took a bullet in the back. He jerked and bounced to the ground. His pony galloped away, following the others.

Soon the Indians were out of rifle range and gathered at the base of the knoll where Red Claw had appeared earlier. The chief was there to confer with them.

People began to crawl out from under their wagons. When Rip Clayson saw it, he rolled free of the Kirkland wagon, leaped to his feet, and shouted, "Get back in your places! They'll come back as soon as they regroup!"

Colonel Moore was on his feet, helping Marian to back out from under their wagon. "They didn't come back quickly the last time," Moore said, frowning at Clayson. "It's uncomfortable under there for my wife!"

"It's also a lot safer!" Clayson said. "Get her back under there! The rest of you, too!"

"How do you know there comin' again?" Moore demanded.

"Are you blind? Last time they rode out of sight. Take a look out there! They're regrouping. They'll be back any minute!"

No sooner had Rip's words left his mouth than the Snakes came galloping toward the train once more. People scrambled back under their wagons.

"I don't know how much more of this I can take, Rip!" Martha said.

"Hang in there. We're going to make it!"

A series of whooping yells pierced the air as the ponies divided and once again began to close in on the wagons. Guns roared, blue-white smoke filled the air, and bullets whined. On the outer rim of the Snakes, Rip caught a glimpse of the albino horse and its colorful rider. Red Claw was waving a feathered rifle and shouting encouragement to his warriors.

Suddenly Rip saw a lone Snake running into the circle of wagons on foot. Before he could bring his Winchester around to fire, Rip saw Eddie Binder halfway out from under a wagon, taking aim. Eddie fired, and the Indian went down in a heap.

Two more Indians deserted their horses and came into the circle, guns blazing. Darrel Day shot one of them, but the other one fired and hit Eddie, dropping him on the spot. Donna Day saw it happen from under the Day wagon and screamed. She wanted to go to Eddie, but her mother restrained her.

More savages were coming into the circle. Men left their wives under the wagons and met the Snakes in hand-to-hand fighting. Rip joined the hand-to-hand battle, while Martha and Jason continued to fire at circling Snakes on horseback.

Jason emptied his Winchester and twisted around for a box of cartridges to reload. He saw his father battling a husky Snake while another Indian was sneaking up behind him, knife-in-hand. Jason rolled out from under the wagon, jumped to his feet, and dashed toward his father.

Marian Moore watched from underneath her wagon, eyes wide, heart pounding, as Jason tackled the bronze-skinned man and began to wrestle for the knife.

The colonel, teeth clenched, sweat drenching his face, used his brute strength to twist the Indian's revolver toward his stomach and drop the hammer. The gun roared and the husky Snake buckled.

Wade Moore's head whipped around just in time to see another Indian drive a knife into Jason's back. The colonel swore, brought the revolver up, and fired twice in rapid succession. Both Indians went down. Jason Moore lay face-down with the Indian's knife buried in the center of his back. Marian was screaming in horror.

Colonel Moore was about to see to his son when another Snake came at him, knife blade flashing in the sun. They met head-on in a death struggle.

At the Wesson wagon, Breanna and Curly were busy firing at the mounted Snakes outside the circle. The hammer on Breanna's Colt .45 snapped down on a spent cartridge. The buffalo gun boomed beside her as she shouted, "Curly, I need more bullets!"

Just then a hand seized Breanna's ankle with a steel grip, and she found herself being dragged from under the wagon. She whipped her head around and saw the painted face of a warrior. He had an evil look in his eye, and she knew he meant to capture her. She felt panic and terror whirl through her mind. She wanted to scream, but her throat was locked tight.

She tried to fight the Indian off. As the strong hands of her abductor forced her toward an opening between two wagons, she suddenly remembered the Derringer tucked under the waistband of her skirt.

The Indian now had her arms pinned to her sides and was lifting her feet off the ground. A prayer for God's help flashed through Breanna's mind. She writhed and kicked for all she was worth as the Snake carried her between the wagons. The jerking of her body had him a bit off balance, and he stumbled over the tongue of a wagon. When the Indian went down, Breanna whipped out the Derringer and fired point-blank into his chest. She didn't wait around to see if he was dead.

While the battle raged around her, Breanna had the presence of mind to pull another cartridge from her skirt pocket and reload the small handgun. Just as the bullet slipped into place, she noticed that Curly was out from under his wagon, battling a young, muscular Indian who was trying to drive a knife into his heart. The old man was no match for the Snake. Breanna ran toward them, raising the Derringer, but she was afraid to fire, fearing she might hit Curly.

Suddenly the old man spit a brown stream in the Indian's eyes. Still gripping his knife, the Indian backed away, wiping his eyes. Curly was winded and a bit lightheaded and unable to press his momentary advantage.

It took the Snake only seconds to regain his vision. There was murder in his eyes as he ejected a wild cry and set his feet to charge Curly.

He never got the chance. Breanna's Derringer fired, dropping the unsuspecting warrior.

Gasping for breath, Curly looked at Breanna in amazement.

Suddenly, as if they had heard some secret signal, the Snakes inside the circle broke off fighting and dashed between the wagons. One of them was shot down as he ran. Outside the circle, the whooping and firing stopped. Painted ponies galloped away to the south into a shallow draw, up over a hill, and disappeared.

17

↑

THERE WAS CHAOS IN THE CAMP. Frightened children were wailing as adults tried to calm them. Six Indians lay dead inside the circle, and the sight of them added to the children's fear.

Unbelievably, the only fatality in the wagon train was Jason Moore. There were a few minor wounds that the people were taking care of themselves. Eddie Binder was the most seriously wounded with a bullet in his left shoulder. He lay on the ground, bleeding and in pain. Young Binder was traveling to California with a family named Donaldson, and both husband and wife were kneeling beside him as Breanna Baylor examined him.

"Eddie, I've got to go after that slug immediately," she said, pressing a cloth to the wound. "Lead poisoning will set in if I don't get it out soon."

Clara Farnsworth was summoned, and a couple of men carried Eddie to the Wesson wagon and laid him on the tail gate. While Clara was getting the needed materials ready for surgery, Breanna enlisted Jerry Adams to pour water for her while she scrubbed her hands.

Breanna could see Rip Clayson standing over Marian Moore, who sat on the ground holding the lifeless body of her son, weeping and wailing. The colonel was next to Clayson, his shoulders drooped. Martha Kirkland was there also, as were several other people.

The cries of terrified children were still in the air.

Lieutenant Emery Dodd and five other men carried the dead Indians outside the circle. Rip Clayson had asked Dodd to oversee the job and to count the total number of Snake dead. As before, the Indians had taken their wounded with them.

Breanna had finished scrubbing when Curly Wesson stepped close and said, "Little gal, I owe you my life. That Snake would have killed me if you hadn't shot 'im. How can I ever thank you?"

"No need, Curly," Breanna smiled, moving toward the tailgate of his wagon. "You'd have done the same for me."

"Well, of course."

"You helped yourself a little," she said over her shoulder as he followed.

"Oh, you mean spittin' in his eyes?"

"Yes," she said with a laugh.

"So, you see? That there 'nasty habit' helped save my skin!"

"Maybe this time—but it's still a nasty habit," she said.

Curly hauled up short of the tailgate, knowing it was off limits when Breanna was using it as an operating or examining table. Breanna let Clara administer the chloroform, and when Eddie was under, she began probing for the slug in his shoulder.

Marian Moore rocked Jason in her arms and stared into space. Her wailing had been reduced to a low, heart-rending sob. More travelers had gathered and stood looking on sadly.

"I don't know what to do for her," the colonel said, turning to Clayson. "I don't think she even knows I'm here." His face was a mask of sorrow and guilt.

Rip glanced toward the Wesson wagon, then back at Moore. "I want Miss Breanna to look at her. I think it's best that we not disturb her now."

Clayson left the colonel standing there and went to a group of men, asking them to dig a grave for Jason. While other men kept a watch for Indians, the gravediggers went to work.

Clayson then moved about the camp, checking on those with minor wounds. When he was satisfied that they were not seriously hurt, he breathed a prayer of thanks to the Lord that there were so few casualties when the fighting had been so fierce.

Breanna stitched up Eddie Binder's wound, then asked Richard Donaldson and Darrel Day to carry Eddie to the Donaldson wagon. As Breanna began washing her hands, Rip moved up and asked, "He going to be okay?"

"Yes," Breanna said. "Eddie's young and strong. He'll be fine."

"I checked the others. Looks like we're in pretty good shape, especially after an attack like that."

"Yes, I've been thanking the Lord for that."

"Me, too." Rip paused, then said, "Marian Moore seems to be in some kind of shock, Miss Breanna. Could you look at her now?"

"All right," she said, picking up a towel to dry her hands. "What about the colonel? How is he?"

"Very quiet right now. He hasn't said much."

Breanna brushed a wisp of hair from her forehead. "From what I can pick up, Jason saved the colonel's life."

"Yes. And gave his own."

"Brave young man."

"I knew he had it in him."

Breanna turned to Clara, who was cleaning up, and said, "Thank you for your help. I need to see to Marian Moore. Can you finish up here?"

"Of course," Clara smiled. "You go on."

All eyes were on Breanna as she knelt in front of Marian, who was still rocking her dead son.

"Marian, can you hear me?" Breanna said.

There was no change. It was as if no one was there at all.

Breanna tried again, even waving her hands to get Marian's attention, but to no avail. She rose to her feet and shook her head. Rip was standing next to Wade Moore, whose features were like granite.

"Marian is in emotional shock," Breanna said, running her gaze between the two men.

"Will she be all right?" the colonel asked.

"I'm sure she will. Right now her mind is numb, trying to cope with the pain."

"What can be done to bring her out of it?"

"Nothing medicinal. Just love and care. She could come out of it any minute, or she could stay like this for several days. If she's treated kindly, she'll come around and be like always. She—"

Wade Moore moved past Breanna, leaned over to place himself in Marian's line of sight, and said, "Marian, it's Wade. I'm right here with you. Do you know me?"

Marian stopped rocking Jason. She cocked her head one way,

then the other, and slowly focused on her husband's face. Her eyes widened, then narrowed. "You! You called my son a coward!" The colonel started to speak, but she cut him off, hissing, "Jason was no coward! You hear me? He was no coward!"

"Marian, I—"

"If he hadn't risked his own life to save yours, you would be dead, Wade…instead of him!"

"Marian, listen to me. I—"

"Get out of my sight! Get away from me! Go away!"

Marian broke into sobs. Wade Moore stood there dumbfounded.

Breanna stepped up beside him and said, "Colonel, I'll stay with her. It's best you leave until she settles down. She'll be better, now that she's come to tears. She'll get it cried out, then you can talk to her."

Moore nodded and walked away without a word.

The group that was gathered around moved away. Rip Clayson looked toward the men who were digging the grave and could see they were making good progress. At the same time, he saw Lieutenant Dodd coming toward him from between two wagons and went to meet him.

As they drew up, Dodd said, "Mr. Clayson, there are a total of eleven dead Snakes. And we found one alive out there. Apparently Red Claw and the others thought he was dead."

"How bad is he?"

"Bullet in the chest," Dodd said. "We've got him just the other side of the Adams wagon over there."

"Is he conscious?"

"Yes."

"Bring him inside the circle and lay him down. I'll have Miss Breanna take a look at him. I need him alive so he can answer some questions."

"Will do," said the lieutenant, heading back toward the Adams wagon.

Clayson wheeled and hurried to Breanna, who was sitting on the ground beside Marian. Clara Farnsworth was seated next to Breanna.

"What is it, Rip?" Breanna asked.

"They've found one of the Snakes alive. He's got a bullet in his chest, but he's conscious. I need you to take a look at him. You've got to keep him alive until I can talk to him and find out what started the Snakes on the warpath."

Breanna nodded, turned to Clara, and asked her to stay with Marian. Then she followed Rip as he headed toward Dodd and two men who were laying the wounded Indian on the ground near the Adams wagon.

Breanna knelt beside him and made a close inspection. The Indian was barely conscious. His eyes were glassy.

"The bullet is close to his heart, but apparently didn't hit it," Breanna said, looking up at Rip. "I'll have to do surgery immediately."

"Let me try to talk to him," said Rip, kneeling beside her.

"I don't think he can answer you. If I'm going to save his life, I must operate now."

The eager wagon master leaned close and spoke to the Indian. "Can you hear me, fella?"

The man tried to focus on Rip's face, but there was a glaze over his eyes. He worked his lips, made a grunt, then stared emptily at him.

"Okay," sighed Clayson. "You're right. He's not able to talk. Do your surgery and see if you can save him."

Dodd and another man carried the Indian to the tailgate of Curly Wesson's wagon, and Breanna began preparing once again for surgery. She asked Rip to have another woman stay with Marian and to send Clara to help her.

People began to gather at the Wesson wagon, Max Rule and D. J. Danco among them. Clara prepared the instruments and the chloroform and Breanna scrubbed her hands. Colonel Moore approached her with a scowl on his face.

Breanna marveled at how quickly he had recovered from his wife's scathing remarks. "I'm busy, Colonel," she said.

"I can see that. It's what you're busy *about* that has me concerned."

"Saving a human life? That concerns you?"

"Savin' a stinkin' *Indian's* life. *That* concerns me, ma'am. And there are some other men here who are concerned, too. We think you ought to let the dirty scum die."

"Let him die?" Breanna gasped.

"Yes, ma'am. He's the enemy and must not be allowed to live."

Curly Wesson was pouring the water over Breanna's hands as she scrubbed. "Who's these other men who are in agreement with you?" he said.

"Mister Rule and Mister Danco over there."

Curly scoffed. "Same fellas you didn't want in the train to begin with! Sorta fickle ain'tcha, Colonel?"

"You must let the savage die, ma'am," Moore said.

Breanna looked around for Rip Clayson, but he was nowhere

to be seen. "You're bothering me, Colonel. Go away. I'm busy."

"Now, look, ma'am, this Indian attacked us with intent to kill. One of his pals killed my son. He deserves to die!"

Breanna finished scrubbing. Curly set the bucket down and said to Moore, "The lady told you she's busy, Colonel. Why don't you go comfort your wife?"

"You mind your own business, old man! I was talkin' to the nurse!"

Breanna looked at Clara, who stood at the tailgate with a cloth over the Indian's face. "He under?"

"Yes," said Clara.

"Miss Baylor, if that savage lives, he'll kill more white people!" Moore said.

Breanna picked up the instrument she used to probe for bullets. Without looking at Moore, she said, "This man is a human being, Colonel. My life is dedicated to saving human lives...and I'm going to save this one if God will allow it."

"Well, aren't you the high and mighty one? I saw you shoot and kill a human bein' a little while ago, and I was told you shot and killed another one, too. What's so different about this one?"

"It galled me to have to take those lives, Colonel," Breanna replied, keeping her back to him. "But with one it was to save Curly's life, and the other one was self-defense. We're not in battle now, and this wounded man is no threat to any of us. As a nurse, I must do my best to save him."

"But he's a savage killer!" Moore said. "You ought to let him die!"

Breanna turned and looked the colonel square in the eye. "If I just stand here and let this man die when there's a chance his life can be saved, it would be the same thing as murder. Now, I'll thank you to let me get on with my work."

At that moment, Rip Clayson appeared, having caught Breanna's last words. "I take it you are objecting to this Indian's life being saved," he said to Moore.

"That is correct! He came at this wagon train intendin' to kill us, didn't he? And one of his fellow savages killed Jason, didn't he?"

"Yes, but the Indian is our prisoner now, Colonel. You understand about prisoners, don't you? In a time of war, prisoners are to be given medical attention and treated humanely. Isn't that so?"

Moore set his jaw, glared at Clayson for a moment, shot an angry glance at Breanna's back, and stomped away.

Rule and Danco eased back from the scene, finding a place of privacy where they could still keep the Wesson wagon in view.

"If she keeps that savage from dyin', we'll have to kill 'im before he can talk to Clayson!" Rule whispered.

"Yeah, he might not be able to identify us by face," Danco said, "but he sure can tell Clayson what started the Snakes on the warpath. It would throw suspicion on us, that's for sure!"

"Tell you what," said Rule, "he may live through the surgery, but he'll be one dead redskin before mornin'."

The sun went down while Breanna labored to save the Indian's life. She finished her work by lantern light and left her patient with Clara while she headed for Rip Clayson, who was at the central fire. Most of the people were gathered there, except for the men on watch and those who were unable to be out and about.

"I was able to get the bullet out all right, Rip," Breanna said. "He's resting well. Unless he has complications, you should be able to talk to him in the morning."

"Good," said the wagon master.

"I'm going to stay up with him just in case a problem develops," she added.

Rule and Danco overheard Breanna and glanced at each other. "We'll have to figure a way to lure her away some time in the night," Danco whispered.

As the people made their way to their wagons, Rip stepped close to Breanna and said, "Tell you what, ma'am. I'll sit up with the Indian, and you get some sleep. If there's any problem, I'll awaken you."

"No offense, Rip," Breanna said, "but I could recognize problem symptoms much quicker than you. That young man came very close to dying. I want to make sure he lives."

"No offense taken," Rip grinned. "I won't argue with you on that. I'll just sit up with you, then. You'll need some company."

"All right," she smiled. "If you wish."

Deep into the night, Rule and Danco crept through the camp, intending to divert Breanna and suffocate the Indian. They were surprised to see that Rip Clayson was with Breanna. They waited and watched almost until dawn, and realized Clayson was there for the duration of the night. They could only hope the Indian died before he gave any information to Clayson.

Soon the eastern horizon turned a dull gray. A few low-lying vapors took on the same hue, gradually changed into orange-red puffs, then slowly evolved into cotton-white clouds.

As people arose from their cots and bedrolls, Rip Clayson moved about the camp, saying he wanted to get the train in motion by no later than nine o'clock. As soon as they had the burial service for Jason Moore, they would move out.

Clayson then returned to the Wesson wagon where he found the Indian awake and Breanna talking to him. Curly had removed his cot from the wagon and allowed the Indian to spend the night on it. Breanna and Rip had sat in chairs next to the cot.

"Here he is now, Little Wolf," Rip heard Breanna say as he moved up beside the cot.

Rip dropped onto the chair where he had sat all night and looked at the Indian, then at Breanna. "So his name's Little Wolf?"

"Yes. He's a bit groggy yet, but we've been talking some."

"He knows English?"

"Yes. Speaks it quite well."

"Good. That'll help."

"Do you know his language?"

"Enough that I could've understood him if he didn't know English."

"Mr. Clayson wants to ask you something," Breanna said to Little Wolf.

The Indian was young, probably in his late teens or early twenties. He nodded, set his eyes on the wagon master, then looked back at Breanna and said, "I must ask a question of you."

"All right."

"You are white woman. You have medicine hands. Little Wolf be dead now if you not save my life. You save my life only because Mr. Clayson want ask me question?"

"No, Little Wolf," Breanna replied. "I would have done everything I could to save your life because human life is sacred to the great God of heaven who gave it. I am a Christian first, and a nurse second. It was my duty to do all I could to keep you alive."

"Christian," the Indian said softly. "Little Wolf believe in Sky Father, but our medicine man say white man's God speak with forked tongue."

"That is not true," Breanna said. "I'll admit that many white men speak with forked tongue, but those who lie to the Indians and steal their land from them are not Christians. The Christians' God is the true and living God. He speaks only the truth." Breanna paused, then said, "Mr. Clayson is also a Christian, Little Wolf. He needs to ask you something."

"I live because of your medicine hands," Little Wolf said. "I give you that name from my heart. Medicine Hands."

Breanna smiled. "Thank you, Little Wolf. I am honored."

The Indian then looked at Clayson. "You have question for me?"

"Yes, Little Wolf," Rip said. "The Snake warriors have not been on the warpath for better than a year. Now they attack and kill us. Why is Red Claw on the warpath?"

Little Wolf licked his lips. "I have water, please?"

Breanna had a canteen beside her chair. After Little Wolf had taken a drink from it, he said, "Many suns ago—maybe twenty—we camp with squaws and children where Big Sandy River meet with Green River many miles south of here. Snake girl, not yet twenty grasses old, bathe alone by bushes at river. Her name Sparrow Wing. Two white men"—Little Wolf's dark eyes flashed with fire—"two white men take Sparrow Wing into brush. Both violate her. Beat her without mercy when she scream. Some of my people hear screams, run to help. By time they arrive, white men on horses, crossing river to get away.

242

Warriors fire at them. Hit horses, possibly men. They fall into river, never come up. Warriors believe they drown. Sparrow Wing die next day from beating. Red Claw furious. Go on warpath. Say kill all whites!"

A strange feeling come over Rip Clayson. Turning to Breanna, he said, "I'm going to talk to Rule and Danco."

Max Rule and D. J. Danco were frightened when Rip Clayson took them aside and told them the story he had just heard from Little Wolf. They covered their fear by acting insulted that Clayson would think they were the two rapists. Rule even got a bit huffy, saying that the Indian himself said the white men went into the river and never came up. Though he was still suspicious of them, Clayson accepted their word since he could not prove otherwise.

Breanna had just finished changing Little Wolf's bandage when Rip returned. Dan and Sally Adams, Jerry's parents, were standing nearby. They had offered to let Little Wolf ride in the back of their wagon, where Sally and Jerry would look after him.

"Is he able to travel?" Rip asked.

"It won't be good for him," Breanna said, "but I know we must move on. He insists we should just leave him here. He says Red Claw and the other warriors will find him when they come to pick up their dead."

"What do you think?"

"I think he'll die if he doesn't have proper care. We had best take him with us. Who knows when Red Claw might show up here?"

Colonel Moore was standing close, listening. Moving in, he spoke in his blaring way, "Tell you what, Clayson! Since Miss Baylor has gone to the trouble of saving the Indian's life, we ought to take him along as a hostage. Maybe we could hold Red Claw at bay if he knew we had this warrior of his and would kill him if the Snakes attacked the train again."

"Colonel Moore, I am not a savage," Clayson said. "I will not hold Little Wolf as hostage and kill him if his chief attacks."

Moore's features stiffened. "Now look, Clayson! I'm a soldier, an officer! I say we use ever'thing at our disposal to get us through this Indian country alive. If it means holdin' a stinkin' redskin hostage to save lives, we ought to do it!"

"Okay, Colonel. Let's say we do that...and when Red Claw comes at us, we hold up a big sign that says if they come an inch closer, we'll kill Little Wolf. Do you really think that'd stop him?"

"Yessir!"

Rip turned to the Indian and said, "Little Wolf, you heard what the colonel said. If we did such a thing, would Red Claw turn and ride away?"

Little Wolf rolled his head on his pillow. "No. Any man who thinks he would, he not understand Indian thinking. White man very sentimental. Not so, Indian. Red Claw would attack anyway. If save Little Wolf, good. If not, no matter. Main thing in Red Claw's mind is kill whites. It is best you leave me here."

"He's lyin'!" Moore blurted. "Just tryin' to save his own skin! If Red Claw saw we had him and would kill him if he attacked, he'd back off!"

Rip turned to Emery Dodd and said, "Lieutenant, you've had plenty of experience with Indians. Is Little Wolf lying?"

"No. He's telling the truth. Our holding him hostage

wouldn't even slow Red Claw down."

Moore walked away muttering.

Little Wolf spoke. "Mr. Rip Clayson, it is best you leave me here. It not be long until Red Claw come." He turned his eyes on Breanna and said, "When Little Wolf tell Red Claw how Medicine Hands save life of Snake warrior, maybe he not be in mind to attack wagon train again."

"We won't bank on that," Clayson said, "but since you prefer, we'll leave you here."

Breanna, Clara Farnsworth, and Sally Adams made Little Wolf as comfortable as possible while preparations were made for Jason Moore's burial service.

Rip Clayson stood over the blanket-wrapped body at the grave and read from the Bible. Breanna was beside Marian with an arm around her while the colonel stood on her other side, hands folded and shoulders slumped. Rip gave Jason a hero's burial, recounting his unselfish deed in saving the life of his father.

It was nearly ten o'clock when the wagon train pulled out, leaving the grave behind.

18

↑

LATE IN THE AFTERNOON, Rip Clayson was riding ahead of the wagon train as it wended its way south. He was thinking of Little Wolf, who lay under a tree amongst his dead comrades. His mind also went to the Moores. Marian had not yet spoken to her husband since the tirade she had unleashed on him that morning.

Clayson was about half a mile ahead of the train when he topped a gradual rise and saw a cluster of dark objects about two miles away. Being familiar with the trail, he knew it was something that was not ordinarily there.

He wheeled the bay and trotted back to the train. He reined in at the lead wagon and said, "Curly, there's something strange on the trail a couple miles ahead."

"Whattya mean?"

"Dark objects. That's all I can tell. They weren't there when we came through here last time. Keep moving, but watch me. If it's what I think it is, I may want you to haul up before these wagons get there."

With that, Rip galloped south at full speed.

Breanna looked at Curly. "What does he think it is?"

"Well, purty miss, I think he thinks it's a wagon train that's been burnt out by the Snakes."

"Oh, I hope not! How awful!"

"More awful than you can imagine, honey. Let's wait and see."

Rip Clayson's heart sank as he neared the scene. His worst fears had been realized. There were ten wagons, some on their sides, some upside down. All but two were charred heaps. No animals were in sight. It was apparent that the train had been attacked when camped next to a small creek lined with heavy brush.

The smell of death hung like a bitter pall in the air. Bodies of men, women, and children were scattered over the area. Most of those who were not burned had been scalped. As Rip dismounted, his eyes fell on a hideous sight near the heavy brush that lined the creek.

A rage washed over him and a moan escaped his lips. Quickly, he made his way to one of the covered wagons that had not been burned and found two blankets. He hurried to the sight that so upset him and used the blankets to cover two bodies. This was Red Claw's ultimate brutality.

Rip looked back toward the north and saw that the wagon train was now about a quarter of a mile away. His horse suddenly nickered, bobbed its head, and looked toward the bushes that edged the creek. Then Rip heard it. The cry of a tiny baby.

Rip's heart quickened pace as he ran toward the bushes. The baby let out another wail as he reached the bushes and found a path that led down to the creek. Suddenly he stopped. There in the thick brush near the water's edge was a young woman, her face filled with fear. The baby was wrapped in a small blanket and held close to her bosom.

When she saw Clayson, tears welled up in her eyes and she gasped, "Oh, thank God! I heard a horse nicker, and I was afraid the Indians had come back!"

"Ma'am, I'm wagon master of a train coming through right now. I'm going to go signal my lead driver to stop the train before it gets here. I don't want the people to see this. I'll be right back. Don't you worry, now. We'll take care of you and your baby."

The young woman wiped tears and nodded, relief evident in her hazel eyes.

Rip scrambled up the path between the bushes and ran toward the oncoming wagon train, waving his arms and shouting for Curly to stop. They were some 250 yards from where he stood. Curly got the message and immediately drew rein. The other wagons followed suit.

Rip cupped his hands around his mouth and shouted, "Curly, I don't want any of the women and children to see this! Send six men and tell the others to stay on guard! Red Claw could show up at any time! And send Miss Breanna! I need Miss Breanna!"

Curly was having a hard time getting it all, but Rip could tell that Breanna had. She took a few seconds to repeat it to him, then grabbed her black bag and slid down from the wagon seat. Curly dashed back toward the long line of wagons.

Rip stood and waited for Breanna. When she was within forty yards, he saw six men heading toward him, walking shoulder to shoulder.

As Breanna drew up, Rip said, "I hate to make you look at this, Miss Breanna, but there's a young mother and her small baby still alive. I think they're all right, but I wanted you to take a look at them. They're over this way," said Rip, leading the way, "down by the creek."

Breanna followed, her eyes roaming the hideous scene. "You think this is Red Claw's doing?" she asked.

"Definitely," Rip replied over his shoulder.

Lord, how can they be so cruel? Breanna wondered. Suddenly her eyes fell on one of the wagons that had not been burned. It looked vaguely familiar. Where had she seen that wagon before? It stood out because of the metal rings that encircled it at top, middle, and bottom. She had never seen one like it, except—

"Rip! I know this wagon train!" she gasped, stopping in her tracks.

"You do?"

"Yes! It was at South Pass City just ahead of you! I…I did a Cesarean section on a young mother and—"

Breanna's head swung back and forth as she studied the scattered bodies. She was trying to see if she could identify those of Larry and Lawanda Hughes, little Breanna Hughes, or Carolyne Fulford. None of those whose features she could make out were any of the four. The charred bodies were so blackened, most of them were unidentifiable.

Breanna's eyes fell on two forms covered with blankets. Rip noticed her looking at them and said, "I covered them."

"What—?"

"You don't want to know."

"What do you mean?"

"Remember what I told you Red Claw and his warriors do to white women?"

"Yes."

"Teenage girls. They were left to bleed to death after those savages—"

"Oh." Breanna's stomach wrenched.

"The mother and the baby are down here," Rip said, moving into the path between the bushes.

Breanna was right behind him. Before she saw the young woman with the baby, the young woman saw her.

"Breanna!" came a cry of surprise and gladness.

"Carolyne!" Breanna gasped.

Carolyne Fulford was on her feet with the baby in her arms, tears brimming in her eyes. Breanna dashed to her, laid the medical bag down, and wrapped her arms around Carolyne and baby Breanna Hughes. Carolyne broke into sobs.

"I see you two are acquainted," Rip said, allowing a thin smile to curve his lips.

Breanna wiped away her own tears and said, "Yes. This is Carolyne Fulford, Rip. And this is the baby I told you I delivered by Cesarean section in South Pass City. But Carolyne is not the mother—"

Breanna looked into Carolyne's tear-dimmed eyes.

"They're both dead," Carolyne said with quavering voice. "Everybody in the train is dead except baby Breanna and me."

"Baby Breanna?" Rip asked.

"The parents named her after me," Breanna said.

Rip looked at the tiny child in the blanket. "Bless her little heart. That'll give her a lot to live up to."

Breanna gave him a warm look, then asked Carolyne, "How did you manage to escape?"

"I happened to be at the Hughes wagon holding little Breanna when the attack came. Flaming arrows rained out of the sky, then guns began to roar. I saw the Indians swarming in. Larry and Lawanda were at another wagon, talking to an older couple. They started running for their own wagon, but they didn't make it. I saw them both go down. There was a lot of dust and smoke, and I ran from the wagon with this baby in my arms. I don't even know how it happened, but we ended up down here by the creek. The Indians never saw us and didn't know to look for us. I went up after the Indians left and saw that there were no survivors."

"It was Red Claw, wasn't it?" asked Rip.

"Yes. I heard the wagon master shout out that name a few seconds after the attack had started. He told us earlier that Red Claw and his warriors were in the area."

"I felt sure this was his work," Clayson said.

"Oh, Breanna," sighed Carolyne, "I'm so glad you were able to lead Larry to the Lord. At least we know that he and Lawanda are in heaven together."

"Yes. Thank the Lord."

"Rip, we're here!" a male voice called from above them.

Clayson looked up at Dean Zimmer and said, "Dig a common grave, fellas. We have a lady and a baby alive down here, but everyone else in the train is dead. I'm going to take these two to our train. Come on back when you're done. I don't want the women and children to see the carnage."

Rip and Breanna entered the wagon train with Carolyne and the baby, and the people gathered around. Breanna introduced Carolyne and explained how they came to know each other. She told them who the baby was, then Rip gave the people a brief description of the massacre. He did not tell about the two teenage girls.

When the burial detail returned to the train, Rip led the wagons out. Breanna and Carolyne rode in a wagon that had been owned by a couple killed in the first Indian attack. Jerry Adams had been driving it since. A cow had been milked, and Carolyne spoon-fed the milk to the baby.

When the sun had been down for a half hour, Rip led the wagons into a circle by a bubbling spring. Water was put on to boil. During the evening meal, the harried travelers shared their fears about another Indian attack.

Rip Clayson ate with Carolyne Fulford, Breanna Baylor, Martha Kirkland, and Curly Wesson. While they ate and talked, Breanna could tell that Rip was taken with Carolyne. Curly noticed it, too. Twice he and Breanna shared furtive glances, winking at each other.

The watchmen took their places after supper, and soon the people were bedding down for the night. Breanna made a bed in the spare wagon, telling Carolyne she would sleep with her the first night. Baby Breanna was fed and soon asleep.

The two women lay in the dark and talked. In their brief time together at South Pass City, they had not discussed their personal lives. As they talked, Carolyne learned about the mysterious man in Breanna's life, and in turn, Breanna learned that Carolyne was on her way to San Francisco to look up a man named Randall Perkins.

Both Carolyne and Randall had lived in St. Louis. They had met at a church social, had fallen in love, and soon were engaged. Randall was a mathematics instructor at Bedford College in nearby Florissant. Shortly after they became engaged, he was offered a professorship at a new college in San Francisco, which he accepted. He told Carolyne he would go there, get established, then send for her. They would be married upon her arrival.

Months passed, and Carolyne never heard from Randall. Worried that something had happened to him, she wrote the college, asking about him. The college gave her letter to Randall, and finally Carolyne received a reply. In his letter, Randall explained that he needed more time to get settled before she came and told her to wait till she heard from him. Six months went by, and no more word came from Randall. In spite of pleadings by her parents, Carolyne had joined the wagon train, riding with some casual friends who were going to northern California. She would surprise Randall by showing up on his doorstep.

Breanna was silent for a moment, then said, "Carolyne, do you want my opinion about this delay in your hearing from Randall?"

"Why, yes."

"Okay. I smell a rat."

"Pardon me?"

"Honey, this isn't normal. Tell me, why did your parents object to this trip? The hazards, or Randall's mysterious silence?"

"Both."

"So they smelled a rat, too?"

"I guess you could put it that way. They tried to convince me that he's already married or at least engaged, and doesn't have the courage to own up to it."

"That's what it sounds like to me. I'm afraid you're in for a broken heart. If the man really loved you, he would want you with him."

Carolyne was silent for a moment, then said in a broken

voice, "Oh, Breanna, I've had the same thoughts, too...but I've got to know for sure what's going on."

"I understand, but I think you'd better brace yourself for a jolt. If the man wanted to marry you, you wouldn't have to chase him down."

Carolyne was about to comment when the howl of a coyote cut through the night. A chill crawled over her skin. "That coyote sounds so lonely," she said. Hardly had she spoken, when the sound of another coyote came from the opposite direction. "Must be his mate. Guess they'll get together now."

Breanna wondered if the howls were really coming from coyotes.

Rip Clayson moved amongst his watchmen, making sure they were on the alert. He had just spoken to Anthony Singfield and had turned to move on when the howls filled the night. He froze on the spot, listening.

"What do you think?" asked Singfield. "Coyotes or Snakes?"

"I wish I could tell you it was coyotes for sure, but I've got a gut feeling it's Red Claw and his bunch. Stay alert."

"Will do," Singfield said.

Rip moved on to Dan Adams. "How you doin', Dan?"

"All right. I got a feelin', though, that those aren't coyotes."

Suddenly there were whoops and screams from the darkness, the thunder of hooves, and the bark of Indian rifles. The men on watch returned fire. Everyone else in the camp came awake in a hurry, grabbing their guns and hurrying to their posts.

Five riders came from somewhere in the darkness with blazing arrows notched in their bows. The arrows were shot into the air, arched against the black sky, and began falling toward the canvas-covered wagons.

"Fire arrows!" somebody shouted.

In the spare wagon, Breanna shouted for Carolyne to hold the baby and lie flat.

"What are you going to do?" Carolyne said.

"I'm going to send some bullets—"

Suddenly Breanna realized she had left the Colt .45 in Curly's wagon. She pulled the Derringer from the waistline of her skirt and crawled to the rear of the vehicle, where she saw the gun flashes of the mounted Snakes as they circled the wagons. Breanna soon used up the bullets she carried in the pocket of her skirt.

The attack lasted only a few minutes, but when the Snakes rode away, three wagons were on fire. Two of the fire arrows had dropped harmlessly inside the circle. Rip Clayson organized a bucket brigade to draw water from the spring, and soon the fires were extinguished. The damage was minor and could be repaired in a short time with extra canvas from Curly's supply wagon. A quick check revealed that no one in the train had been hit.

"That oughtta settle your thinking about Indians attackin' at night, Colonel," one of the men said to Wade Moore. Moore did not reply.

Once the children were assured that the Indians were gone, most of them went back to sleep. The only adults able to sleep were Hattie Chatsworth and Eddie Binder, who had been given sedatives before settling down for the night.

Breanna went to Rip Clayson and told him she was out of bullets for the Derringer. Rip went to his saddlebags, grabbed a handful of cartridges, and gave them to her. He also reminded her to keep the revolver with her at all times.

Rip gathered the people in the center of the circle and told them they should be ready for another attack. The fire arrow assault was probably a forerunner to another full-scale attack.

Weary, discouraged men and women gathered at the Zimmer wagon to load up on ammunition. Dean Zimmer sought out Rip Clayson, who was in conversation with Lieutenant Emery Dodd.

"Excuse me, Rip," Dean said, "but I thought I should tell you the ammunition is getting low."

"I'm not surprised. Let's hope Red Claw eases off pretty soon."

"If he doesn't, we're going to be in trouble," Zimmer said. "I'd say about three more attacks like we've had, and the supply will be depleted."

Rip scrubbed a hand over his tired face, then rubbed the back of his neck.

Dodd looked at the exhausted wagon master and said, "I'm going to head for Fort Bridger and bring help, Rip."

Rip shook his head. "I appreciate the offer, Lieutenant, but the fort is nearly sixty miles from here. A lone man would be open prey for the Snakes."

"I'm willing to take that risk. Granger's only about twenty-five miles. Once I get there, I can borrow a horse. I can make it to the fort in a day from there on horseback."

"Lieutenant, I won't let you leave here on foot. If you go, you'll take my horse."

"But you need the horse," Dodd said. "You dare not be without it."

"I won't dispute that, but it's critical that we get help. If you're game to take the risk, I'd sure be fool not to let you go."

"Then I'll do it," said the lieutenant.

There was a slight hint of gray along the eastern horizon as Rip Clayson gathered the people together and explained that Lieutenant Dodd was going to ride for Fort Bridger and bring back the cavalry. This news brought encouragement, and they all bid the lieutenant Godspeed as he mounted and rode away.

Clayson then told the people the train would pull out after breakfast. He had a feeling the Snakes would attack again soon, but there was no way to know how soon.

Fires were built, and the women prepared breakfast. After everyone had eaten, the women cleaned up while the men stood on the outside of the wagons, peering across the rugged land for any sign of Indians.

The sun was throwing a fan-shaped shaft of yellow light skyward through broken clouds when Doral Chatsworth shouted, "Here they come!"

Once again the people dashed to their battle stations. Frightened children were rushed into the wagons and flattened on the floors.

Carolyne Fulford lay on the floor of the spare wagon, holding the Hughes baby and praying. Jerry Adams was underneath the wagon, speaking words of encouragement to her, knowing she was especially frightened because of the ordeal she had gone through with the other wagon train.

Breanna was at her station beside Curly Wesson under his wagon. He had a large wad of tobacco in his mouth and was chewing vigorously as the Snakes thundered in. Guns roared, terrified children screamed, and kill-hungry Snakes whooped and screeched.

Rip Clayson's forces—though never far from the edge of

panic—fought like seasoned soldiers. Indians toppled from pintos, and gunsmoke was everywhere. Clayson had joined Jerry Adams under the spare wagon. Above the rattling of rifles and revolvers, he could hear the periodic big boom of Curly's buffalo gun.

While Curly blasted away, Breanna saw a warrior directly in front of her whose pinto had been shot in the hindquarters. The terrified animal was shrieking and spinning in a circle. Its rider leaped from its back and fell flat on the ground.

The Snake rolled and settled on his belly, looking around. When he saw curly and Breanna under the wagon nearest him, he swung his rifle around, bringing it to bear.

Curly was busy firing at the mounted Snakes. Breanna gritted her teeth and lined the Colt .45 on the Indian. She dropped the hammer, the gun bucked against her palm, and the slug ripped through the Indian's upper left arm. He howled and jerked from the impact. Eyes wild and full of murder, he fired at Breanna. His wound, however, threw off his aim, and the slug chewed wood just above Breanna's head, spraying her with splinters.

The Indian struggled to jack another cartridge into his rifle. Breanna took aim and dropped the hammer again. The empty, hollow click that came from the Colt sounded louder to her than if it had fired. She had lost count of her shots.

Breanna dropped the revolver as if it had suddenly turned red-hot, reached to her waist, and pulled out the Derringer. There was no time to take careful aim. She fired a split second before the Indian did. Her slug centered his forehead, causing him to flinch, and his shot went wild.

The sight of it chilled Breanna's blood. A tiny sob broke in her throat.

259

"That's good shootin', honey!" Curly shouted.

As the Snakes rode around the circle, they fired not only at the men and women underneath the wagons, but under directions from Red Claw, also fired directly into them.

Hattie Chatsworth took a bullet as she lay on the floor of her wagon. Her husband, who was firing underneath, heard her cry out, but the Indians were coming too fast and furious for him to leave his post and check on her.

At the spare wagon, Carolyne Fulford lay flat, hugging little Breanna Hughes to her breast. The roar of battle had the baby crying at the top of her lungs. Carolyne took some comfort in the knowledge that Rip Clayson was fighting directly below her. Somehow she felt safer with him close by.

Suddenly Carolyne looked up to see a wild-eyed warrior peering at her through the rear opening of the canvas. He was about to climb in after her. A shrill scream came from her throat.

Underneath the wagon, Rip Clayson saw the bare legs and moccasined feet of the Indian leave the ground just as Carolyne screamed. He swung his gun around and fired, but missed.

In a flash, Rip was out from under the wagon. He was like a maddened beast. This Indian had somehow known Carolyne was inside the wagon and had dared go after her. Rip grabbed the warrior by an ankle and yanked him hard to the ground. The Indian rolled and jumped to his feet.

Rip sent a quick fist to his jaw, knocking him down. The Indian screeched and started to get up. Rip moved in quickly, sank his fingers into the man's long black hair, and punched him again. The Indian went down hard and his head struck a rock. He did not move.

As sudden as before, the Snakes galloped away, heading

south. Red Claw appeared on his albino horse, wearing the full headdress. He met his warriors at a spot safely out of rifle range, and they rode out of sight.

19

THE INDIANS PAID ANOTHER HIGH PRICE for attacking Rip Clayson's wagon train. Five of them lay dead after Red Claw and the others were gone.

One of the three orphaned children had been killed by a bullet that had chewed through the side of the wagon he was hiding in. Hattie Chatsworth had died shortly after the bullet had struck her in the back. Breanna Baylor embraced the weeping Doral Chatsworth, doing what she could to comfort him. Bud Harbison had been creased by a bullet on his left side. Kitty was seeing to him until Breanna had done what she could to comfort Doral.

Soon Breanna was at the Harbison wagon to examine Bud and clean and bandage his wound. Though the wound was only superficial, Breanna told the young man it would take him a couple of weeks to get back to normal.

Burial services were held for Hattie Chatsworth and the little boy. There was much sadness, and many tears were shed. In his closing prayer, Rip Clayson asked the Lord to get Lieutenant Dodd to the fort safely and bring the cavalry.

When he finished praying, Rip told the people that he knew they were weary. He wished he could let them stay where they were and rest for a day, but they were already more than a week behind schedule. They would have to keep moving. They should reach the fork of the Green and Big Sandy Rivers by midday tomorrow. They would cross the Green River and head for Granger. The closer they could get to Fort Bridger, the quicker they would have cavalry protection.

By the time the wheels began to roll and the wagon train moved out, the wind was picking up and dark clouds were coming in from the northwest. Since he was without his horse, Rip Clayson decided to ride in the spare wagon. He placed it second in line, behind the Curly Wesson wagon, and sat in the seat beside Jerry Adams. Carolyne Fulford rode in the back, holding little Breanna Hughes.

Whenever Rip turned to check on Carolyne or say something to her, he found her eyes on him. Whenever their eyes met, he felt a strange warmth flow across his chest and settle in his heart. He had met many fine young women, but none ever stirred him like Carolyne. He loved her winsome smile, the way she styled her long, dark-brown hair, and the way she carried herself with such grace and elegance. She truly had a sweet spirit about her, and best of all, she knew the Lord and made her love for Him quite obvious. Rip wondered if she was promised to a man.

The clouds grew heavier as the morning wore on. At about ten o'clock, a jagged bolt of lightning lashed across the sky. A sharp clap of thunder followed. Those who walked alongside their wagons or rode in the seats began to put on their slickers, as did everyone in the three wagons whose canvas tops had burned. There had not been time yet to repair them.

Moments later lightning flashed again and the rain began to fall in torrents. Horses neighed and oxen lowed in complaint at the sudden downpour. Men on foot climbed into their wagons.

Though the heavy storm made traveling a bit slower, Rip Clayson was thankful for it. Red Claw and his warriors would not launch an attack in this kind of weather.

The wagon train moved steadily until darkness began to fall. Rain still pounded the earth. Everyone knew there would be no hot meal at the end of this day. They would have to be satisfied with beef jerky and hardtack.

When darkness fell, everyone stayed in their wagons. Those whose tops had been burned sought shelter with others in the circle of wagons.

Breanna braved the storm to look in on Eddie Binder and Bud Harbison. Rip Clayson also made the rounds to make sure all was well, then returned to the spare wagon. He found Carolyne alone with little Breanna Hughes. Someone had brought milk, and Carolyne was feeding the baby by lantern light.

"Where's Jerry?" Rip asked, climbing inside.

Carolyne smiled her winsome smile. "Attending to a necessary situation."

"Oh, what?"

"Rhonda Fallon."

"I should've known. That young man really has been smitten by her. I just wish Rhonda would treat him better."

"You mean there's a question about how she feels toward him?"

"Let's just say Rhonda seems to have eyes for others."

"Poor Jerry. I think I may know a little how he might feel."

"Oh?"

Carolyne gave Rip a sideways glance, then looked back at

baby Breanna. "It's a long story. Are you sure you want to hear it?"

"Yes, I'm sure."

Carolyne told Rip the story she had told Breanna the night before. When she finished, Rip sat quietly for a moment, then asked, "Miss Carolyne, what will you do if you get to San Francisco and find that Mr. Perkins indeed has someone else, or at least has changed his mind about you?"

Carolyne was burping the baby, patting her on the back. She stared at the floor of the wagon and did not respond.

"Miss Carolyne?"

Slowly, she brought her gaze up to his.

"You're a wonderful young lady, Miss Carolyne. You don't have to take that kind of treatment from a man. I'm sorry if this offends you, but Randall Perkins doesn't deserve you."

Tears misted Carolyne's eyes, but she did not pull her gaze from his.

"The Lord has a man picked out for you, Carolyne—one who will treat you right, love you with all his heart, and want you to be with him no matter where he is or what the circumstances might be."

Carolyne's lips were quivering as she laid the baby in a small box that served as a crib. Little Breanna was satisfied and almost asleep.

Carolyne turned back to face Rip, looking at him through a wall of tears. She wished she had met this fine man a long time ago. When she raised a hand to her cheek to brush away the tears, Rip left the stool and folded her into his arms. That was all it took for the broken-hearted young woman to break into sobs.

"It's all right, Miss Carolyne," Rip said, holding her tight. "Go on. Cry it out."

Carolyne's sobbing gradually subsided and became soft snif-fles. Rip still held her tight and was about to speak again when he heard Curly Wesson's voice at the rear of the wagon.

"Hey, Rip! Miss Breanna asked me to come and tell—oh, 'scuse me! I didn't realize I was buttin' in. I'll come back when you're through."

Both Rip and Carolyne turned and looked at the old man. Rain was pouring off his dirty crumpled hat.

"It's all right, Curly," Clayson said. "I was just comforting Miss Carolyne. She's had her heart broken and—"

"Hey, young feller! You don't have to explain that kinda stuff to me. Fiddlesticks! If I was nearer Miss Carolyne's age, I'd find a reason to hug 'er meself!"

Rip eased his hold on Carolyne and said, "So what is it you want, Curly?"

"What?"

"You came to the wagon, looking for me."

"Oh! Well...actually I didn't. I came to give Miss Carolyne a message from Miss Breanna."

"Yes, Curly?" said Carolyne, enjoying the strong arms that still held her.

"Miss Breanna axed me to come n' tell ya that she'd spend the night here with ya if'n ya wanted her to."

"Why, of course," smiled Carolyne, freeing a hand to wipe tears from her cheeks.

"All right, I'll let 'er know. She said if'n ya did, to tell ya that she's havin' to do some minor repair on Eddie Binder's wound, but she'll be here in about a half hour or so."

"That'll be fine, Curly. Tell her I'll just keep her with me every night till we get to California, if she'll let me."

"Well, she usually sleeps in the wagon with the widder Kirkland, ma'am, but you gals can wrangle that out."

"Thank you for bringing the message, Curly," Carolyne said.

"Oh, you're welcome, ma'am," Curly chuckled. "Now you two can get back to huggin'."

Carolyne's face tinted.

"Didn't mean to embarrass nobody, but I will say you two look real good together." With that, Curly turned and left.

Rip eased back to the stool where he had been sitting and said, "I'm sorry if you were embarrassed."

"Oh, I wasn't really. He seems like such a dear man. Certainly he didn't get the wrong idea."

"Of course not," Rip said, smiling at her. "Well, I guess I'd better get ready to put the camp to bed."

"Don't drown out there."

"I'll try not to."

He was about to swing his leg over the tailgate when Carolyne said, "Rip..."

"Yes?"

"Thank you."

"For what?"

"For caring what happens to me...and for a shoulder to cry on."

Rip Clayson released a smile that reached all the way to his chocolate-brown eyes. "You don't have to thank me for caring, Miss Carolyne. I find that quite easy. And as for the shoulder—if you need it again, it's here."

She gave him a sweet smile. He touched his hatbrim and went over the tailgate into the storm.

The rain was still pouring down when Carolyne and Breanna lay on their cots in the dark. Baby Breanna was fast asleep. Carolyne told Breanna that she had told her story to Rip Clayson, and that he had responded with kindness and compassion.

"He's a fine man, honey," Breanna said. "When the Lord brings the right Christian woman into his life, he's going to make her a wonderful husband."

Carolyne was silent for a long moment. Then she said, "Breanna…the Lord knows the truth about Randall."

"Yes, He does."

"And like Rip, He has a plan for my life."

"Yes."

There was a brief pause. "Breanna…"

"Mm-hmm?"

"I…well, I wouldn't tell this to anyone else, but from the first moment I saw Rip coming down that path toward the creek where I was hiding with the baby…"

"Yes?"

"I…felt something strange in my heart. Like Rip was a knight in shining armor."

"That's a good way to put it," Breanna said, enjoying a secret smile in the darkness. "Carolyne, you deserve a good man like Rip Clayson—someone who'll treat you better than Randall Perkins has."

After a few seconds of silence between them, Carolyne said, "Well, I guess it's time to meet the sandman, Breanna. See you in the morning."

"Goodnight," Breanna said.

Carolyne lay there, her mind filled with Rip Clayson. She thought again of his strong arms around her and of how he had smiled at her when she thanked him for caring about her. Just before drifting off to sleep, she thought, *Carolyne, what did you ever see in Randall Perkins anyhow?*

Breanna Baylor found herself inside the jail at South Pass City, looking through the bars into the angry eyes of Frank Miller.

"You rotten, murderin' hypocrite!" he roared, shaking the bars. "You won't get away with this, Breanna! I know you're leavin' this town when that doctor gets here, but there's nowhere you can go that I won't find you! You got that? This one-horse jail can't hold me. I'll get out, and when I do, I'm comin' for you. I'm gonna shoot you down like a rabid dog! You can bet your bottom dollar on it. There'll be a bullet for you, Breanna. That's a promise!"

Breanna sat bolt upright on the cot, coming fully awake in an instant. The inside of the wagon was pitch-black. It was still rain-ing outside, though not as hard. She had no idea what time it was, but lay back down. She could hear the shallow breathing of the tiny baby and the deep, even breathing of Carolyne Fulford.

"Lord," she whispered, "I need Your peace again." She thought of John Stranger for a moment, then put her mind on the Lord Jesus, and was soon peacefully asleep.

The sky was still cloudy when daylight came, but the rain had stopped.

Breanna looked in on her two patients, then crossed the circle to eat breakfast with Carolyne and Martha Kirkland. Doral Chatsworth saw her and angled toward her from his wagon. "Miss Baylor, may I see you for a moment?"

"Of course."

"I had a talk with Mr. Clayson, and I'll be leaving the train when it gets to Fort Bridger. With—with Hattie gone, I have no reason to go on to California. I have family back home, so I'll return there as soon as possible. Mr. Clayson says there are army units moving back and forth continually between the East and Fort Bridger, so as soon as I can, I'll hop on with an eastbound unit and go home."

"I'm so sorry about Hattie, Mr. Chatsworth," Breanna said. "And I can understand why you would want to go back home. We'll miss you on the rest of the trip."

"Thank you," he said with a slight smile, then reached in his pants pocket and pulled out a wad of currency. "I want to pay you the other fifteen hundred I owe you."

"I'm not going to let you pay me when I didn't finish the job," Breanna said shaking her head.

"It's not your fault," he countered, taking her hand and stuffing the money in it. "There's seventeen hundred here. That'll pay you what we agreed and more than buy your railroad ticket back to Denver."

"But Mr. Chatsworth, I can't—"

"Hush, child," he said softly. "A deal is a deal. Discussion closed."

"Thank you, sir. But—"

"Ah, ah, aahh!" Doral said, waving a finger at her. "I said the discussion is over." With that, he wheeled and walked away.

Breanna went to the Wesson wagon and placed the money in her trunk along with the amount Chatsworth had paid her before they left South Pass City.

The rain had been heavy and the ground was soaked. Mud caked on the hooves of oxen and horses and on the wheels of the wagons as the train pulled out. Breanna was back beside Curly, and Rip Clayson was in the next wagon, sitting beside Jerry Adams. Jerry noticed that Rip spent more time talking to Carolyne than he did facing forward. His own mind was on Rhonda Fallon. Though he had repeatedly confessed his love for her, she would not commit herself to him. But Jerry loved the girl with all of his heart. He would remain patient and win her over.

The morning dragged by slowly under the cloudy sky, but there was no more precipitation.

Curly and Breanna rode in silence. Breanna was thinking about the nightmare and praying that the Lord would protect her if Frank somehow was able to escape. Around noon, the wagon topped a hill and two swollen, turbid rivers came into view, forking due south of them.

"On, no," Curly said.

His words caught Breanna's attention. "The Green and the Big Sandy?" she asked.

"Uh-huh. And look at 'em. These rains have really got 'em full. Rip's gonna have to make a big decision here. Fast as that water's movin', and deep as it is, it could wash these wagons downstream in a hurry."

"Looks treacherous, doesn't it?" came Clayson's voice as he hopped up on Curly's side of the wagon and held on.

"Plenty," Curly agreed. "What're you gonna do?"

"Use a rope and cross it. The Green, as usual, just north of the fork, where it's narrowest."

"Could be dangerous."

"Not as dangerous as snow in the Sierras. We've got to keep moving."

Curly nodded.

Rip stayed at Curly's side another twenty minutes, which brought them near the Green River about a hundred yards north of where the Big Sandy flowed into the Green in its southward trek toward the sea.

The swift-moving river was a murky brown. Even the foam from the rapids had a tan cast. Ordinarily it was thirty yards from bank to bank at this spot, but now the span was more like forty yards. Tree limbs, bushes, and various other debris bobbed in the water. Curly halted his ox team twenty feet from the water's edge.

Rip hopped down and shouted above the river's roar, "Let's have a meeting. We need to get started right away!"

The wagon master gathered the people about halfway along the line of wagons where the rumble was not so loud. He explained how they would make the crossing. Once the first wagon was on the opposite bank, they would use a rope to keep the others from being swept downstream.

Colonel Wade Moore argued that it would be courting disaster to try to make a crossing with the river that turbulent and deep. Max Rule and D. J. Danco agreed. Rip reminded them they were taking a free ride and had no say.

"Well, *I'm* a paying customer and my opinion does carry weight," Moore said. "I demand that we wait till the river goes down before we attempt to cross."

"Colonel Moore, we're already over a week behind schedule," Rip said. "If we're delayed any more, we're likely to encounter snow in the Sierras, and those mountains are problem enough without that. Besides, we need to get closer to Fort Bridger and the cavalry."

"If Rip feels we can make the crossing, I say we should follow him without reservation," Earl Maxwell said.

The rest of the people agreed, and in spite of the scowl on Wade Moore's face, they made preparation to cross.

Curly and his ox team were well-experienced with river crossings and would go first. Rip would drive the second wagon, with Breanna, Carolyne, and the baby aboard. Jerry Adams would be in the family wagon with his parents.

The wagons were pulled close to the bank, and everybody watched as Curly climbed in the seat of his wagon, popped the reins, shouted "Hyah! Hyah!" at the four oxen, and aimed them toward the swift current.

The experienced oxen did not hesitate, but plunged in, straining into the harness. Suddenly the wheels quit turning and the wagon was afloat. People gasped as it swayed while being carried downstream. The gallant oxen held their heads out of the water and paddled furiously. By the time the wagon had traveled eighty yards downstream, their hooves struck solid footing and the vehicle was soon on dry ground. Curly guided the dripping wagon up the riverbank and stopped slightly downstream from where the rest of the wagons would enter.

Curly slid out of the wagon, went to the tailgate, and lifted out a large coil of rope. He tied one end securely to the axle of the wagon, then walked to the water's edge as he tied a heavy block of wood to the other end. He swung it over his head like a lariat, then slung it across the river. Rip stood on the other bank, ready to grab the rope.

Curly did not get it far enough the first time, but Rip caught it on the second attempt. The block of wood was laid in the seat of wagon number two, and the rope tied securely to the metal brace that held the seat to the bed.

With Breanna and Carolyne seated in the back of the wagon and the baby in her box, Rip snapped the reins and drove the ox team into the water. It was afloat in seconds. The slack rope quickly tightened. Curly's wagon quivered slightly. Within minutes, the second wagon was safe on the opposite bank.

One by one, the wagons were floated across the river, sometimes being assaulted by debris, but without damage.

This changed when the Dean Zimmer wagon was being taken across. In midstream, the load in the wagon shifted, tilting it dangerously. A box of ammunition came loose and crashed into the tailgate. The gate flew open, and the box slid over the edge into the murky river. When the wagon finally reached the opposite bank, Rip asked Dean to inventory the remaining ammunition.

The last vehicle to cross was the Chuck Fallon wagon. Everyone else stood on the far bank and watched. Chuck and Louise were on the seat, and Rhonda rode in the back, near the tailgate. When the wagon was in midstream, a tree slammed into the side of the wagon. The wagon lurched and almost overturned. Chuck saw Louise start to fall and grabbed her arm just in time. He gripped the seat with one hand and held onto Louise with the other. Neither was aware that Rhonda had tumbled over the tailgate and into the river.

Rip, Curly, and most of the other men were occupied with bringing the listing wagon to solid ground and did not see Rhonda fall in. Jerry Adams was standing beside his mother at the edge of the river, and both of them saw Rhonda spill into the churning, angry water. She surfaced after a few seconds and was swept downstream, bobbing up and down, arms waving.

Sally Adams gasped when she saw her son throw off his hat and start removing his boots. "Jerry, no! You'll drown!"

"I've got to save her, Mom!" he said as he ran like a deer along the bank.

"Jerry!" she screamed after him. "Come back! You can't save her!"

By now most of the women and the men not manning the rope were aware of what was happening. They stared wide-eyed at Jerry as he sprinted along the bank.

Rhonda thrashed about, going under and bobbing again to the surface as the swift current carried her farther and farther away. When Jerry was far enough ahead of her, he plunged into the raging stream.

Seconds later, both heads were seen on the surface. Jerry had reached Rhonda. They bobbed down a few times, swirling around and round, then went down again. This time they did not come up.

Sally threw her hands to her cheeks and screamed, "They're gone! They're gone! We've lost them both!"

20

BREANNA BAYLOR AND CAROLYNE FULFORD were standing together, watching the men at work pulling the Fallon wagon ashore, when they heard Sally Adams scream. Along with the bulk of the travelers, they had not seen Rhonda Fallon fall into the river, nor were they aware that Jerry Adams had plunged in after her.

Breanna hurried to Sally and quickly picked up what had happened. She scanned the river and saw no sign of Rhonda or Jerry. The Green took a bend about eight hundred yards downstream and passed from view.

The moment the Fallon wagon was on dry ground, Chuck and Louise became aware that they had lost Rhonda. Louise began screaming that Rhonda had to have fallen in the river. Rose Donaldson and Effie McFadden rushed up and told the Fallons and Rip Clayson that Jerry had gone after Rhonda. Both had been seen together in the river, but had since disappeared.

Dan Adams hurried to his wife and found her distraught, weeping and mumbling that Jerry and Rhonda were dead. Chuck heard what Sally was saying and raced along the river bank, scanning the swirling, muddy water for some sign of his daughter and her rescuer.

Dan asked Breanna to stay with Sally and ran after Chuck. He found that Rip had gotten the jump on him and was already on Chuck's heels.

Downriver, past the bend, Jerry had an arm around Rhonda's neck, holding her head out of the water. She was limp in his grasp.

When he had first reached her, the force of the river caused them to go under two or three times. Moments later, a cluster of floating bushes pressed down on them, and though their heads stayed above the surface, the bushes had hidden them from Sally's view.

Jerry now worked his way to the south bank and finally was able to get solid ground under his feet and drag Rhonda ashore. She had taken in a great deal of water, and her face was a deathly blue.

He picked her up and carried her to the crest of the bank and laid her face-down. She wasn't breathing. Furiously, he began pressing on her back.

"C'mon, Rhonda, breathe! Breathe!"

He felt movement in her back, then she coughed.

"Yes! Breathe!" he shouted, working harder.

Rhonda coughed again and moaned. Water ran from her nose and mouth. She sucked in a breath, choked, and coughed some more.

Chuck, Dan, and Rip drew up, breathing hard. At the same time, Rhonda opened her eyes and coughed up more water. Chuck fell to his knees beside her and gasped, "She's all right! She's all right!"

As he wept for Joy, Chuck Fallon raised his daughter's head and shoulders into his arms and held her close.

Rhonda looked up at Jerry and said weakly, "Jerry...you could have drowned."

Water dripped from Jerry's hair. He ran a palm over his face and nodded. "I love you, Rhonda. I'd risk my life a million times to save you."

Tears welled up in the girl's eyes. She struggled to sit up, and her father helped her. She opened her arms toward Jerry and they embraced, holding each other for a long moment. Chuck looked on and smiled. He liked Jerry very much and hoped he would become his son-in-law.

Rhonda received a tearful welcome into her mother's arms when they returned to the wagons. Chuck told the travelers how Jerry had saved his daughter's life, and they gave him a hero's ovation.

Rip Clayson guided the wagon train a mile south of the river and called for them to form a circle. They would make camp early, since everyone was worn out. They were now just twenty-two miles from Granger. If they could keep up a normal pace when they pulled out in the morning, they could be in Granger by noon day after tomorrow.

Everyone knew about the box of ammunition that was lost in the river. Rip gave the count of how many of what caliber bullets were left, then asked those of each wagon how many they had. The answers were not encouraging.

"If we have one more Snake attack like the last one, we'll be throwing rocks before it's over," Clayson said gravely. "Just makes it that much more important that we get to Granger as soon as we can."

In the morning, the bone-weary travelers had their breakfast and discussed their low ammunition supply. All had hopes of reaching Granger before being assaulted again by the Snakes.

Rip Clayson ate with Carolyne Fulford, Breanna Baylor, and Curly Wesson. Carolyne was holding baby Breanna in one arm while she ate. The infant had already been fed and was drowsy.

Rip chewed on a biscuit and held a tin cup of steaming coffee. "Carolyne, what do you plan to do with the baby when you get to San Francisco?"

Carolyne eyed the little bundle lovingly and replied, "It looks like the Lord has put her in my care, Rip. I plan to keep her and raise her."

"Well, that's commendable. But what if things work out between you and Randall? Maybe he won't want someone else's child in his home."

"I guess I might as well tell you, Rip...and Breanna. Both of you told me, in essence, that Randall has made a fool of me. You've helped me to realize that if he really loved me and wanted me, I wouldn't have to be chasing after him. So...all I'm going to do when I get to San Francisco is find a way to take my little adopted daughter and go back to St. Louis."

Curly chuckled and said, "Well, Carolyne, maybe you'll meet some handsome knight in shining armor who'll sweep you offa your feet and whisk you off to some preacher for a weddin'."

Carolyne looked at Breanna, and Breanna could tell she was

wondering if she had told Curly of their conversation. Breanna shook her head and shrugged her shoulders. Carolyne smiled and said, "Sounds good, Curly, but what do you suppose this knight in shining armor will say when I tell him I've got a little daughter?"

"Well, honey, if'n he loves you like he oughtta, he'll wanna adopt little Breanna, too!"

Breanna's gaze swept casually across Rip's face. He was smiling broadly.

Thirty minutes later, the wagon train broke its circle and headed south. Breanna sat next to Curly, and Rip drove the second wagon with Carolyne and little Breanna at his side.

"Ya know what, honey?" Curly said.

"What?"

"I think Carolyne an' Rip is fixin' to fall head over heels fer each other."

Breanna smiled. "I don't think it's future tense, Curly. Unless I'm blind, they already have. They both belong to the Lord, and He's brought them together and given that precious little baby a home. You watch. It'll all work out."

Curly lifted his hat and scratched his bald head. "You mean God cares that much about people?"

"He does *His* people. Only those who have been born again and washed in the blood of Jesus are His children, Curly. Those, like yourself, who don't know Jesus, God loves…but to be His child and have Him work out a beautiful plan for your life, you have to be saved."

"I guess I need ya to explain this whole thing to me some more."

"I'd love to. Let me get my Bible and—"

"Wait a minute!" Curly said.

Breanna noted that he was looking straight ahead on the trail, eyes wide in astonishment. She followed his line of sight, and what she saw paralyzed her. She sat immobile, her eyes riveted on the three Snake Indians riding toward them. The one in the middle, on the white albino, was Red Claw. The warrior to Red Claw's left carried a white flag on a tree limb. They were holding their horses to a walk and were about a hundred yards away.

Curly drew rein and shouted, "Rip! Rip! We got comp'ny!"

Clayson hauled his wagon to a stop, and the others followed suit. Men who walked beside their vehicles hurried forward when they saw the wagon master leave the seat of the second wagon and run ahead. Others left the wagons to join them, including Max Rule and D. J. Danco.

"Red Claw!" Rip exclaimed as he drew up next to the lead wagon on Curly's side.

"What do ya s'pose he wants?" Wesson asked, chewing furiously on his tobacco wad.

"I don't know, but we'll soon find out."

Every man in the wagon train was assembled at the lead wagon as the three savages closed in. The white flag flapped in the morning breeze.

Breanna watched as Rip hitched up his gunbelt and stepped forward a few feet ahead of Curly's ox team. He raised his right hand palm-forward in a sign of peace.

Red Claw nudged his horse a step or two ahead of his companions and made the same sign. The albino halted, tossing its magnificent head, pink nostrils flared. Red Claw sat rigidly, headdress bowing to the breeze. There were white streaks of clay on his cheekbones. The bear paw with claws painted red dangled on his neck. Red clay was crisscrossed on his chest in heavy stripes. A yellow streak encircled his naked belly, just above the loin cloth. Solid muscles were evident in his arms and shoulders. His eyes were cold and mysterious, hard as polished marble.

Breanna judged that he was no more than thirty years of age. She felt a chill dance down her back as he set his black gaze on her. He held it there for a few seconds, then looked down at Rip and broke the silence with his deep, resonant voice. "I am Red Claw, chief of Snake people. You are Rip Clayson, chief of wagon train."

"Yes, but how do you know my name?" Rip said.

"Little Wolf. We find him with our dead that you and your people kill."

"We wouldn't have killed any of your warriors if we had not been attacked."

The chieftain sent another glance to Breanna, then looked back at Clayson. "Little Wolf tell of woman with sunshine hair he call Medicine Hands. She save his life. This her?" He was pointing at Breanna.

"Yes," Rip replied. "Little Wolf would have died if she had not removed the bullet and cared for him."

Red Claw nodded, gazing at Breanna and drinking in her exquisite beauty. There was unmistakable desire in those black eyes. Breanna saw it, as did most of the men who had gathered. A shudder of revulsion swept through her. She avoided eye contact with him, looking at Rip Clayson's back instead.

"Red Claw did not come with the white flag to ask about Medicine Hands," Clayson said.

"No. When we talk with Little Wolf, he tell us of two men in wagon train who not belong. They not like other men in wagon train."

"What about them?" Rip asked.

The chief then told the story of the two white men who molested the young Snake girl and beat her to death.

"Yes, I know about that," Clayson said. "Little Wolf told me."

"Red Claw come under flag of peace to see if two men who not belong to wagon train ones who rape and kill Sparrow Wing."

"How would you know who the men are?" he asked. "The girl is not alive to identify who did it."

"One of white men who attack and kill maiden lose heel of boot." As he spoke, the chief reached into a leather pouch on his waist. From the pouch he produced the worn right heel of a riding boot. He held it so Rip could see it clearly and said, "One of men in wagon train have heel missing from boot?"

"Yes," Clayson said.

"See if fit," the chief demanded.

Clayson turned and said, "Danco, come here."

Danco limped forward and stood beside the wagon master, but said nothing.

"Take off both boots," Clayson said.

There was hesitation in Danco's eyes.

"Now!"

Danco balanced on one foot, then the other, removing both boots. He handed them to Clayson, who in turn handed them to Red Claw. While every eye watched, the chief put the loose heel in place on the right boot and held both boots side by side. The loose heel fit perfectly, matching the heel on the left boot.

Anger showed in Clayson's face as he snapped at Danco, "You

two told me you knew nothing about that Indian girl!"

Danco was trembling and did not respond.

Red Claw's mouth drew into a thin hard line. Eyes fiery, he threw the boots into Danco's face. "You must turn them over to me, Rip Clayson! They must die!"

Rule tried to run for one of the wagons, but several men grabbed him and wrestled him to the ground. Danco began pleading for his life.

"Red Claw, I can't let you have them," Rip said. "But I assure you, they will be punished by white man's law. Give me the heel. We're on our way to Granger, and I'll turn these men over to the marshal there. They'll face charges of rape and murder, and will be hanged. With that heel, I'll have the evidence to convict them."

Anger darkened Red Claw's features. "No! These men violate and kill Snake girl! They must be punished by Snake law!"

"I can't let you have them, Red Claw," Clayson repeated.

"You find these wicked men worth dying for?" Red Claw said. "Medicine Hands save life of Little Wolf. Because of this, we no more attack...if we ride away with guilty men. If not, we attack. Kill all in wagons."

Even as Red Claw spoke, Clayson's line of sight shifted to the long row of mounted warriors on a distant ridge behind the three Indians. Outlined against the Wyoming sky, they waited like the ageless hills they inhabited, motionless, expectant.

Clayson met Red Claw's fierce stare and said, "I will see that these men pay with their lives under white man's law, Red Claw. But I cannot turn them over to you. I will not."

"You die! *All* die!" Red Claw hissed. He wheeled the albino and galloped toward the ridge where his warriors waited, followed by the two braves.

The wagon train crowd stood in numb fear.

Rip whipped out his gun, pointed it at Danco, and said through clenched teeth, "Tie the killers up. And I mean, tie them good!"

Several men converged on Danco, disarmed him, and took him in hand. As Danco and Rule were being led away, Colonel Wade Moore stomped up to the wagon master, his face blotched with rage.

Moore was so angry, he was breathing raggedly. "Clayson! You're out of your mind! Why should all of us die because of those two scum? I'm tellin' you, call after Red Claw and tell him to come and do what he wants with 'em!"

Breanna was now standing on the ground and stepped up to Moore. "Colonel, Rip is only doing what any decent man would do! He knows the kind of torture Rule and Danco would suffer if he let Red Claw have them."

"So what? They committed the crime…let 'em pay for it!"

"I agree they should pay for it," Breanna said, "but civilized people do not condone torture! Rip is doing the right and humane thing."

"Right and humane?" Moore roared. "Is it right and humane to be so stubbornly stupid that you let innocent men, women, and children die at the hands of these vile savages?"

"That's enough, Colonel!" Darrel Day said. "Rip is not stupid, and he's only stubborn about doing what's right. If we do what you're yelling about, we're no more than savages, just like those Snakes!"

"Don't you people know we're almost out of ammunition? If those Injuns come at us again, we'll run out of bullets. Then what? Y'all gonna do like Clayson said and throw rocks at 'em?"

"Colonel," Clayson said, standing almost nose to nose with him, "since we are not barbarians, we'll do right in this situation. And the God of heaven will bless us and take care of us for so doing. Right now, we need to keep moving toward Granger and the cavalry. So let's go."

A cheer went up from the people, showing their leader that they agreed with his decision.

"All right, let's get the wheels turning!" Rip said.

Wade Moore jerked his revolver out of its holster and lined it on Rip Clayson. "I ain't gonna stand by and let you put us on a suicide mission, Clayson! I'm takin' those two to Red Claw before he comes with blood in his eye!"

"Now look, Colonel, this isn't getting us anywhere," Clayson said. "Put that gun away."

Face flushed beet-red, Moore raised the gun, aimed it between Clayson's eyes, and growled, "You heard me. Tell the men who took Rule and Danco to the wagons to bring 'em back. I'm takin' 'em to Red Claw so I can save the lives of ever'body in this train."

Darrel Day slipped up behind Moore, swung the barrel of his Colt .44 in an arc over his head, and struck the colonel's skull with a heavy, sodden sound. Moore went down, unconscious, and two men picked him up and carried him toward his wagon.

Rule and Danco were bound securely and made to walk behind Earl Maxwell's wagon, tied with lead ropes. They were so relieved not to be handed over to Red Claw that they did not complain.

Just before the wagons were to pull out, Carolyne Fulford approached Rip and said, "I really appreciate a man with good sense, convictions, and the fortitude to stand by them."

A grin spread across the wagon master's face. "Thank you, Miss Carolyne," he said.

"Rip, couldn't you drop the Miss?" she said, moving closer to him. "Just call me Carolyne."

I'd rather call you sweetheart, he thought, but said, "All right, Carolyne. That suits me fine."

She touched his arm tenderly and walked away, heading for her wagon. He watched her go, and said under his breath, "Lord, please let her be the one for me."

When Breanna climbed into the seat beside Curly, she could see that he was shaken.

"What's the matter?" she asked.

"I'm not disagreein' with what Rip's doin', missy, but if'n we don't make it to Granger before Red Claw decides to attack, we're gonna run outta ammunition. When that happens, we're goners."

Rip Clayson moved amongst the wagons, making sure everyone was ready to pull out and that his two prisoners were secured. Breanna and Curly could hear his voice somewhere behind them. He would be coming soon to tell Curly to lead out.

"Curly, I want you to understand something," Breanna said, leaning close to the old man.

"What?"

"We're low on ammunition, yes, but there is something Red Claw doesn't have that the wagon train does."

"And that is?"

"There are some of God's born again children in this train. We have a Father who answers prayer. He'll see us through this."

"But what if God decides it's time for His children in this here wagon train to die, along with those who ain't Christians? Even Christians die, honey."

"Of course they do. But those who are saved would go to heaven. Those who aren't...would go to hell."

"Breanna?"

"Yes?"

"I think it's time I quit fightin' God. You've talked to me so many times about bein' born again, and so has Rip. Can I git born again right now?"

"You sure can!" Breanna said.

She opened her medical bag and pulled out her small Bible. "Let's be sure you understand."

Breanna read Curly several verses, pointing him to the Lord Jesus as the one and only way of salvation. Tears coursed down Curly's leathered old cheeks. He spit his wad of tobacco out and was about to bow his head and call on the Lord to save him when Rip stepped up and said, "Okay, Curly, let's roll 'em out!"

"Just give us a few minutes, Rip," Breanna said. "Curly's about to receive the Lord."

Rip saw the Bible in Breanna's hand and the tears on Curly's cheeks. "By all means! Take your time. I'll be back in a few minutes."

Rip went to the second wagon and told Carolyne what was happening. She rejoiced, and they prayed together for Curly.

After a few minutes had passed, Rip stepped up beside the Wesson wagon and found Curly blowing his nose and wiping tears. "Get it settled, my friend?" he asked.

"He did," Breanna said.

"That's fer sure!" Curly exclaimed. "Now if'n we're killed by them Snakes, I'm ready! Course, if'n the Lord wants to spare us, I wouldn't mind hangin' around this world a little longer!"

"I believe the Lord'll see us through this, Curly," Rip said, extending his hand. "Welcome to the family of God, partner!"

21

John Stranger emerged from Dr. Everett Wall's office, his face grim. He rounded the hitch rail and approached the big black horse, slipped his foot into the stirrup and swung into the saddle. "Well, Ebony ol' boy, I hope you're ready for a good run."

Stranger galloped out of South Pass City, bent low in the saddle, and gave Ebony his head. Top speed was essential, and the horse seemed to know it.

Before leaving Fort Boise, Stranger had wired Dr. Lyle Goodwin in Denver to learn Breanna Baylor's whereabouts. When the return wire told him she was in South Pass City, he headed that direction. He had arrived this very day and had gone to the doctor's office, expecting to secretly look in on Breanna and make sure she was all right. Instead, he found Dr. Everett Wall, who told him that Breanna had been hired to care for a wealthy man's wife in a wagon train headed for California. He also learned from Wall that a man named Frank Miller had escaped from the South Pass jail and stolen a horse. Miller had told the man in the adjacent cell that he was going to break out and go after Nurse Baylor because she had let his wife die. When Stranger heard that, he excused himself and headed out of South Pass City as fast as possible.

Stranger knew the Oregon Trail well. He figured to catch up to the wagon train somewhere near Fort Bridger. Over and over he prayed, asking the Lord to do something, *anything* to stop Frank Miller from getting to Breanna.

As the wagon train moved south toward Granger, Wyoming, the nervous travelers kept their eyes peeled for another attack. Hour after hour, they watched and waited, expecting at any moment to see Red Claw's warriors coming at them from behind the towering rock formations, out of the canyons, or from the top of a ridge.

Max Rule and D. J. Danco walked in fear, lashed to the long ropes tied to the rear of Earl Maxwell's wagon. They were defenseless and vulnerable to Snake bullets as they walked out in the open. When they complained, Rip Clayson told them they would be allowed inside the Maxwell wagon if an attack came.

Colonel Wade Moore, nursing a violent headache, apologized to Clayson for pulling the gun on him and asked if he could have it back. When he gave his solemn oath that he would use the revolver only on Indians, Clayson returned it to him.

As the sun slanted sharply toward the western horizon, Carolyne Fulford, sitting close to Rip on the wagon seat, asked him why Red Claw had not attacked the train. Rip guessed that the crafty Snake chief was playing cat-and-mouse with them, letting their anxiety build as they waited for the attack to come. At least with every turn of the wheels, they were drawing closer to Granger and to the cavalry unit Lieutenant Dodd was bringing from Fort Bridger.

The sun was halfway out of sight behind the mountains

when the Snake war party suddenly came whooping and shooting from behind a giant rock formation. Quickly the wagons were formed into a circle, and the battle was under way.

Rip stayed close to Carolyne and the baby as he fired at the charging Indians from beneath the wagon. Carolyne lay on the floor, holding little Breanna close, and prayed.

Beneath the Wesson wagon, Breanna emptied her revolver, using all the bullets in the gunbelt. When the Indians came in closer, she opened fire with her Derringer.

Surprisingly, after attacking for barely fifteen minutes, the Snakes galloped away.

When Rip learned that not one person in the wagon train had been hit, he praised God and took time to pray with the entire group and offer thanks for His protection. The Snakes had lost five warriors.

Dean Zimmer handed out the last of the ammunition in his wagon. Each person had eight or nine bullets. Breanna had one full load for her Colt .45. Only two .41 caliber bullets could be found. Breanna had one in the Derringer, leaving three bullets for the small gun. The extra two she put in the pocket of her skirt.

Rip Clayson ordered the wagon train to move on. He wanted to get at least another mile in for the day. They had made almost two miles when Rip finally called for a halt. They formed a circle beside a small brook in near total darkness, and the harried people readied for supper. Those who ate near Rip asked why Red Claw had waited so long to attack. He explained that it was part of Red Claw's plan to put a raw edge on their nerves. The Snakes would be back, maybe during the night.

When the sentries were in their places and people were settling in for the night, Breanna and Curly sat next to the big fire.

Curly had countless Bible questions he needed answered, and Breanna was doing her best to answer them.

Rip Clayson was on first watch at the wagon he had been driving. He could hear Carolyne talking softly to the baby as she held her in her arms, patting her to sleep. Little Breanna was cooing contentedly with a full tummy, and soon was asleep.

A quarter moon hung like a small light in the sky. Rip heard motion inside the wagon, then footsteps in the grass. Turning about, he saw Carolyne moving toward him.

"Hello," she whispered.

"Hi. Baby asleep?"

"Mm-hmm."

"You make a wonderful mother, Carolyne," he said.

"Thank you. It came on me sort of suddenly. I didn't have nine months to prepare myself."

"Well, you'll be that much more prepared by the time you have your own first child."

"Yes," Carolyne sighed, "I guess I will. That is...whenever the Lord gives me that special man you talked about. The one who'll treat me right, love me with all his heart, and want me with him no matter where he is or what the circumstances might be." In spite of the Indian danger and the stress that went with it, she was thrilled to be alone with the man she had come to love. She felt so safe in his presence.

"The one who'll marry you, knowing that he'll become an adoptive father the minute he says 'I do'?" Rip said.

"That's the one," she smiled.

"Carolyne..."

"Yes?"

"Do you think little Breanna would…well, would she accept me as her adoptive father if I settled down at ranching as I've been planning on doing sometime soon?" Rip's whole body was trembling.

Carolyne could feel the pulse beating in her temples and throbbing in her ears. "Well…I'm sure she would. I—"

"I really love little Breanna," Rip said. He held Carolyne's gaze with his own and lowered his head till their lips were only inches apart.

"Little Breanna really loves you, too," Carolyne half-whispered.

"I'd really love to kiss little Breanna, but she's asleep. Maybe she wouldn't mind if I kissed her adopted mother instead."

"I'm sure she wouldn't mind."

Rip took Carolyne into his arms as their lips blended in a soft, tender, lingering kiss.

When their lips parted, he held her close and whispered into her ear, "I love you, Carolyne. I realize we haven't known each other very long, but I know…I hope you're the one the Lord has chosen for me."

Carolyne laid her head against his chest. "You know what?"

"What?"

"You've been my knight in shining armor from that first moment you appeared amongst the brush the day you rescued the baby and me. And you know something else? The Lord didn't choose me for you—He chose you for me!"

They kissed again, then Rip said, "It's time for you to get some sleep."

"You're probably right."

"And Carolyne...when little Breanna wakes up in the morning, would you ask her if she and I can consider ourselves 'engaged' to be daddy and daughter?"

"Oh, I already know what she'll say."

"You do?"

"She'll say yes!"

"Well, then it's official," grinned Rip. "And since little Breanna and I are officially engaged to be daddy and daughter, it would only be right that her mommy and I be officially engaged to make it thoroughly official."

Carolyne laughed. "Then so be it," she said, and they kissed again.

When Breanna climbed into the wagon, the lantern burned low. Carolyne stirred on her cot, rolled over, smiled and whispered, "Curly trying to learn everything the first day of his new life?"

Breanna laid her Bible next to the lantern and said, "You know how new converts are. Especially if they get saved late in life."

"Yes. Hungry and eager to make up for lost time."

Carolyne decided to leave it up to Rip to announce their engagement, but she couldn't go to sleep without sharing a bit of the good news with her close friend. "Breanna..."

"Yes?"

"He loves me."

"He loves you? Rip? He told you that?"

"Yes, just a little while ago!"

"Did you tell him—"

"I sure did!"

Breanna bent down and hugged her. "Oh, Carolyne, that's wonderful! I'm so glad for you."

"Yes! Isn't the Lord good?"

"Yes, He is, honey. He sure is."

The two women prayed, thanking the Lord for bringing Carolyne and Rip together. Then Breanna kissed Carolyne's cheek, doused the lantern, and stretched out on her cot. Lying in the dark, she silently thanked the Lord again for giving Rip and Carolyne to each other. Then her thoughts turned to the man she loved. Where was John Stranger tonight? How long would it be till the Lord brought them together?

Breanna's heart was aflutter. The day she had prayed for had finally come. Now, after all these months, she would meet John face to face and tell him what a horrible mistake she had made in sending him out of her life.

Suddenly there was movement on the rolling hills to the east. It was John, tall in the saddle, on Ebony. The long-awaited moment had finally arrived. Tears filled her eyes and began to spill down her cheeks. "Thank you, Lord," she whispered. "Thank You for bringing John back to me."

Ebony skidded to a halt in front of the cabin and John slid from the saddle. Instantly, they were in each other's arms. She reached up and touched his cheek and said in a half-whisper, "I love you, John. I will always love you."

John leaned down, moving his lips toward hers. Breanna

closed her eyes as his arms tightened around her. Tenderly, he kissed her eyelids, then placed a soft, loving kiss on her lips.

Breanna began to wake up. She struggled against consciousness, trying to hold on to sleep and prevent this moment from fading. She wanted to stay in John's presence, stay in his strong, protective arms.

But the dream was gone, and baby Breanna was crying.

Vague gray light filtered into the wagon. Breanna blinked, rubbed her eyes, and saw Carolyne sitting up, holding the baby. "I'm sorry she awakened you."

"That's all right," Breanna sighed. "Nobody can regulate when babies wake up crying."

The dream that had come to her once again haunted Breanna as the wagons rolled out. Rip Clayson had told the travelers that they were now just seven miles from Granger. Unless the Snakes detained them with another attack, they would be there by noon. Not only would they be able to stock up on ammunition, but he also expected Lieutenant Dodd and a cavalry unit to be drawing close. Hope ran high in the camp.

Rip and Carolyne sat close together on the wagon seat, happy to have each other's love. He had announced their engagement to the people at breakfast, and warm congratulations were offered.

In the lead wagon, Breanna read Scripture to Curly, at his request. He stopped her often to ask a question. When they had been on the trail for better than two hours, Breanna looked over at him and smiled. "You've been asking questions all morning, Curly. Now I have one."

The old man's pale-blue eyes twinkled. "Honey, there ain't nothin' I can teach you."

"This isn't that type of question. I just noticed something, and I've got to ask about it."

"What's that?"

"You're not chewing that awful tobacco this morning."

"Oh, that! Well, Miss Breanna, since Jesus come into my heart, I don't have no desire for that stuff any more. Besides," said Curly, dipping his chin and looking at her from the tops of his eyes, "you're right. It is a nasty habit."

Breanna laughed, thanking the Lord inwardly for the change already taking place in Curly Wesson's life. Her laugh, however, was cut short. She and Curly saw them at the same instant. Red Claw and his two warriors rode onto the trail out of the dense woods off to the right. As before, the warrior on Red Claw's left was carrying a white flag. Curly called for Rip.

The train was halted, and Rip was on the ground in front of Curly's ox team, ready to meet the Indians as they drew up. Again, the people left their wagons and gathered to watch. Even Eddie Binder was feeling well enough to join them. Max Rule and D. J. Danco were left tied behind the Maxwell wagon. Carolyne Fulford stood next to the Wesson wagon amongst the others, holding the baby.

Rip could see the long line of Snakes sitting their horses on a distant rise as Red Claw looked down at him from the albino and said, "I come to make offer."

"What kind of offer?" Clayson asked.

"Instead you give me men who kill Sparrow Wing, you give me Medicine Hands."

Even as he spoke, the chief looked at Breanna, who remained

next to Curly on the wagon seat. Curly reached over and took her hand, squeezing it hard. Fear filled her eyes as she looked back at him.

"Under no circumstances will I let you have her," Clayson said.

Red Claw's features darkened and his voice had an edge to it. "Red Claw offers you and these people your lives, foolish man. You will all die if you remain stubborn. Give me Medicine Hands, or coyotes, cougars, and bears will eat your flesh and birds will pick your dead bones clean. Red Claw and his warriors will kill all but Medicine Hands and take her anyhow!"

"You lost five warriors in that last attack," Clayson said. "You'll lose more if you attack us again."

"We have more than you, white eyes. We *will* wipe out wagon train and take Medicine Hands!"

"You cannot have her now or ever!" Rip snapped.

"Red Claw *will* have her! And rest will die!"

The chief yanked the albino around, gouged its sides with his heels, and galloped away with the other two warriors following. Clayson and the people watched to see if Red Claw would turn right around and attack, but when he reached the rest of the band, they rode around a jumble of boulders and disappeared.

Rip told Breanna to ride inside the wagon he was driving. Carolyne would ride in the seat beside him. Breanna gladly climbed into the back of the wagon, carrying her medical bag and the Colt .45. The Derringer was still under her skirt, the two extra bullets in her skirt pocket. She and Carolyne would trade off taking care of the baby.

Rip asked the travelers to push their animals extra hard for Granger, and it was almost noon when the uneven rooftops of the town appeared on the southern horizon. There was excitement among the people. Granger meant ammunition and safety from Indian attack. Lieutenant Dodd would soon be showing up with the cavalry. A military escort to Fort Bridger would take them out of Snake country and away from Red Claw.

But as they reached the outskirts of town, it was obvious that something was wrong. No people or animals could be seen in the yards or on the streets. The town was deserted.

When they reached the center of the town, Curly spotted a man tied to a tree in front of the town hall. He called for Rip, and it took them only a few seconds to recognize Lieutenant Dodd.

Rip and Curly halted the wagons and ran to the tree. Dodd was alive but bloody. As before, they could find no wounds. They cut Dodd loose and helped him to a nearby bench. The people gathered around, stunned by what they were seeing. Dodd told them that the residents of Granger had been repeatedly attacked by the Snakes, and had gone to Fort Bridger for protection. Red Claw had more warriors than Dodd had ever realized. Subchiefs led other war parties to punish the whites for what the two men had done to the Snake girl.

When Dodd had ridden into Granger, Red Claw himself was there to meet him. The Snakes tied him to the tree, killed a dog, and smeared him with its blood. Fortunately no wild animals had come into the town, and by yesterday the blood had dried. Red Claw had cleaned out the town's gun shop, taking all the guns and ammunition, and ridden away.

While Breanna gave Dodd water, Rip looked around at the weary travelers and saw the disappointment and fear on their faces. *There was no ammunition...and no cavalry coming.*

"Mr. Clayson, I'm sorry," Dodd said. "I would have had

troopers here to escort you by now."

"No fault of yours," Rip replied. "We have no choice but to push on to the fort. We should make it in two days."

"Rip, for some reason the Indians didn't take your horse with them," Dodd said. "He's around here somewhere."

"My bay is here?"

"Yes, sir. Ever since I've been tied to the tree, he's shown up from time to time, then moved on. He can't be very far away. I saw him not more than twenty minutes ago."

Clayson asked everyone to spread through the town and find his horse. Hardly had he spoken when Jerry Adams spotted the animal as it came around the side of a building across the street.

"There he is, Mr. Clayson!" Jerry shouted.

The bay nickered when it saw Rip moving toward it. He took hold of the reins, spoke softly to the animal as he stroked its face, then led it to where the people were gathered. He asked Jerry to take the horse and find some grain for it in one of the nearby barns. He was to feed it well, make sure it had a good drink of water, and bring it back as soon as possible. Someone would be riding it to Fort Bridger to bring the cavalry.

Lieutenant Dodd volunteered to make the ride, but Clayson told him he was too weak. Dodd had had no food or water for three days. Clayson then turned and looked at Colonel Wade Moore. The man had become an outcast after pulling his gun on the wagon master. No one had spoken to him, not even Marian.

Clayson moved up to Moore and said, "Colonel, would you like to redeem yourself in the eyes of these people?"

Moore scrubbed a beefy hand over his mouth, nodded, and said, "Yessir, I would."

"All right. I want you to get on my horse as soon as Jerry

brings him back. You can be to Fort Bridger in an hour if you ride hard. Just stay on the trail. Bring the cavalry to us as soon as possible. How about it?"

Moore's back straightened and he smiled. "I'll do it!"

Within a half hour, the bay was ready to go. Wade Moore received the first smile from Marian since Jason's death as he kissed her cheek and strode to the horse. Mounting up, he waved at her and galloped away.

The wagon train moved out of Granger.

Frank Miller rode up to the burned-out wagons and noted the grave mounds nearby. He checked the two wagons that had not been burned. Finding no sign that Breanna Baylor had been part of the train, he followed the wheel tracks that led south, hoping she was still alive.

Miller was almost to the fork of the muddy, swollen Green and Big Sandy Rivers when his eye caught movement in the shadows at the edge of the nearby woods. A dozen war-painted Indians charged out of the woods on horseback and quickly formed a circle around him.

22

RED CLAW HAD SENT most of his warriors into other parts of Wyoming to wreak havoc among the whites, and had run a bluff with Rip Clayson to try to convince him he had large numbers with which he could attack the wagon train.

The chieftain had been surprised at how well the people in Clayson's train fought back. Until he could muster reinforcements, Red Claw was in no position to carry out his threat to wipe out the wagon train and take Medicine Hands for himself. He was down to barely more than thirty warriors. By the time he could gather reinforcements, the wagon train would reach Fort Bridger or beyond, and the woman with sunshine hair would be gone.

He called his braves together and devised a plan. They would launch another attack. While guns were blazing, two of his warriors would move in on the lead wagon, kill the small white man who fought beside Medicine Hands, seize her, and bring her to Red Claw.

The chief had also taken notice of the wagon that Rule and Danco were tied to. He figured they would be placed inside the same wagon during an attack. He ordered his warriors to shoot into the canvas and bed of that wagon, hoping to kill both men.

The wagon train was some three miles out of Granger, the hot summer sun glaring down from the afternoon sky, when Red Claw sent his warriors against it again. Once more the people fought back gallantly.

Two warriors left their pintos and made their way amid blazing guns, smoke, and dust to the lead wagon. They were surprised to see Curly Wesson fighting alone beneath it. When Curly saw the pair on foot, he swung his buffalo gun on them and fired. One of the Snakes went down dead, and the other one quickly disappeared.

Breanna kept herself concealed as much as possible, but still managed to take a shot now and then at the Snakes as they rode around the circle of wagons. When she fired the last .41 caliber bullet, she pulled the canvas shut and laid low next to Carolyne Fulford, who was clutching the baby girl in her arms.

"That's it," Breanna said. "I'm all out."

"I think most everybody else is, too. Only two or three guns are still firing."

Even as Carolyne spoke, all firing stopped. The whooping of the Snakes and the pounding of their ponies' hooves was dying out.

"They're leaving!" Carolyne said.

Breanna sat up. "Maybe they ran out of ammunition, too."

When the warriors drew up where Red Claw was waiting, they had two wounded men and reported that three others had been killed. The surviving brave sent to capture the woman with sunshine hair told Red Claw she was nowhere in sight. Red Claw retorted angrily that she was somewhere among the wagons. They were hiding her, but he would still have her.

Rip Clayson found three men dead after the attack: Darrel Day, Max Rule, and D. J. Danco. Darrel had taken a bullet through the heart while fighting alongside his wife and daughter. An unusual number of Snake bullets had blasted the canvas and wooden sides of the wagon where the two prisoners were huddled.

The travelers joined in sympathy with Molly and Donna Day in their loss. Breanna patched up some minor wounds while graves were being dug for the three dead men.

When the burial was over, the people gathered around their leader in the center of the circle. Rip solemnly announced that the ammunition was gone. All they had now were knives and some broken tree limbs they could use as clubs. He led them in prayer, asking the Lord to help them as they moved on and to bring Colonel Moore with the cavalry before another attack came.

Clara Farnsworth and Jane Maxwell rode in the Day wagon to comfort Molly and Donna. Lieutenant Emery Dodd drove the wagon. Breanna stayed hidden in the wagon driven by Rip Clayson.

When the sun was nearing the mountains to the west, Rip directed the wagons into a wooded area where there were high hills and towering rock formations. The wagons were placed in the usual circle in a small open area. Rip reminded the people that the Snakes had attacked about that time the day before and told them to be ready with their knives and clubs. The women were to take shelter in the wagons if an attack came. Only the men would battle the Indians hand-to-hand. Rip tried to encourage the people, saying Colonel Moore and the cavalry could show up any time.

With Carolyne at his side carrying the baby, Rip went to Breanna, who remained in the wagon, out of sight. Since they were in the forest, Rip said she could come out, and helped her to the ground.

"I hate to make you sit in there," he told her, "but I believe Red Claw will stop at nothing to capture you."

"I'm afraid you're right," she sighed. "I'll be so glad when the cavalry gets here."

"Well, until they do, I'm going to take extra precaution."

"What do you mean?"

"See that tall rock?" Rip said, pointing to a lofty rock formation some two hundred yards to the east. The rock was about four hundred feet in circumference at its base, surrounded by a dirt mound. The mound sloped upward to a point two hundred feet above ground level. From there it was a cone-shaped rock with a cave near the top, some fifty to sixty feet from the base of the mound.

"I climbed that thing once a couple of years ago, Breanna," Rip said. "Had some time on my hands while a midwife was delivering a baby, so I went up there to see how big the cave is."

"Some little boys never grow up," Carolyne said.

Rip gave her a mock frown, then said, "On the east side of the rock, nature has provided a crude staircase all the way to the cave. It winds around to this side just a bit before it gets to the top. You can't see the stairs from here, but they're up there."

Breanna eyed him speculatively. "That's where I'm going?"

"Yes. You'll be safe up there. I don't want Red Claw's warriors to have a chance at grabbing you. From what Curly told me, a couple of them looked like they were aiming to find you under his wagon during the attack. He shot one, but the other one got away. I guarantee you, they'll be back with the same thing in mind. So let's get you up there...now. We'll take water and some jerky and hardtack along so you don't get thirsty or hungry."

"Whatever you say," Breanna said. "For sure, I don't want to get in Red Claw's clutches."

To Carolyne, Rip said, "I won't be gone long. The men are on lookout for any sign of attack. You and baby Breanna stay inside the wagon, all right?"

"Whatever you say," Carolyne smiled.

Rip escorted Breanna into the dense woods, then stopped. "Do you still have the Derringer on you?"

"Yes, but I don't know why. Just got so used to carrying it under my waist band, I stuck it in here after I fired the last bullet."

"Let's have it," he said, reaching into his pants pocket.

Breanna pulled the gun out and placed it in his hand, a questioning look on her face.

Rip showed her a single .41 caliber bullet and said, "I had one left in my saddlebag. Took it out before the colonel rode away. I kept it for a very special reason." He slipped the bullet into the chamber of the small weapon and handed it back to her.

"And what's that?"

"Breanna...if the Snakes should come and overwhelm the wagon train before Colonel Moore and the cavalry get here, you'll be on your own. If Red Claw kills the rest of us and cannot find you, he'll know you're around somewhere. You can't stay up there indefinitely. You'll have to come down for food and water. Should Red Claw find you, you…" Rip took a deep breath, looked away, then back at Breanna. "Breanna, you must use this bullet on yourself before that savage gets his filthy hands on you."

A look of horror filled Breanna's eyes. Her face went pale. "Rip, how could I? I can't believe the Lord would have me do such a thing!"

"Breanna, I hate the thought of it too. But believe me, you don't want to fall into Red Claw's hands. You'd die anyway, but what you'd suffer before you died is beyond anything you can imagine. Promise me. If you see that you're going to fall into his hands, promise me you'll use the bullet. The alternative is just too horrible."

Breanna's hands trembled as she held the Derringer. She said nothing for a long time, struggling with whether it could ever be right for her to take her own life. Finally she said, "I promise." Even then, she wasn't sure she could do it if it ever came to that.

The climb up the crude staircase was slow and difficult. When they reached the cave, Rip laid the canteen and cloth containing the jerky and hardtack on a rock shelf, embraced Breanna, and hurried back to the wagon train.

The cave was shallow, only twelve feet deep and about sixteen feet wide. From her lofty position, Breanna could make out the wagons in the open area. The lowering sun cast long shadows over the camp.

Breanna felt so all alone. Her hand lowered to the Derringer tucked under her waistband. "Oh, Lord," she prayed, "spare me the horror of taking my own life."

✤

Frank Miller watched the Snake Indians ride away, taking the horse he had stolen in South Pass City. He was soaked with the blood of an antelope and tied to a towering pine tree. The Indians had taken him toward the forest that edged up to the Big Sandy River just north of where they captured him. The tree that held him was at the east fringe of the woods, some two hundred yards from the river.

Miller had seen some cougars, wolves, and bears on distant rock shelves and mountainsides while riding after the wagon train. He knew, as did the Snakes, that wild beasts were close by. Terror lurked at the edge of his tormented mind at the thought of being clawed to death.

The smell of blood was awful. What chance did he have of living through this? Frank Miller was going to die, and die an unthinkable death. And then there was eternity. What did that hold? Judgment? Were the Bible fanatics right?

Suddenly it was as though his whole life passed before him, leaving the wicked deeds on the surface. The worst seemed to be his desire to kill Breanna Baylor. Jagged thoughts stabbed his mind. *Did Breanna really let Lorraine die to get back at them for what they had done to her?*

He remembered the words of the stage driver and shotgunner that morning at the Bluebird Café, telling others around them what bad shape the man from the wagon train had been in when they brought him into South Pass City the previous afternoon.

"That pretty young nurse must have mighty skillful hands to operate on a man gutshot like he was and still bring him through," one of them had said.

"I was in the Civil War and saw a lot of men gutshot," one of

311

the townsmen replied. "Most of 'em didn't make it no matter how hard the surgeons tried. Bein' gutshot like this Jay Wyatt was usually means sure death. Miss Breanna is some kind of nurse, all right. A real angel of mercy, she is."

The words burned into Miller's mind. *I saw a lot of men gutshot. Most of 'em didn't make it no matter how hard the surgeons tried...Most of 'em didn't make it...A real angel of mercy.*

Miller felt sick all over. He'd never known Breanna to be anything but kind, compassionate, and merciful. Of course most gutshot people die of their wounds! It wasn't Breanna's fault. Of course she did her best to save Lorraine! *Most gutshot people don't make it no matter how hard the surgeons try.* Breanna did try! Frank had been foolish to believe anything else.

"Oh, Breanna, I'm sorry! So sorry! How could I have been such a fool. Please forgive me, Breanna. Forgive—"

Miller's cry of remorse was cut off by a deep-throated growl. The sound had come from the thick woods off toward the river. He twisted his head in that direction and saw a dark shape among the dappled shadows of the forest, slinking through the trees.

Then it came out into the open at the edge of the woods—a huge male mountain lion. Eyes bulging, Miller tried to scream, but his throat closed around the sound like a fist. He couldn't breathe. The beast growled once more, set its yellow eyes on him, and charged.

John Stranger had seen the fresh graves along the Oregon Trail and could tell that most, if not all, the deaths were caused by Indian attack. The Indians were definitely on the warpath.

Stranger would not let himself believe Breanna's body was in one of those graves.

He had come upon the burned-out wagon train with the fresh graves nearby. Signs on the ground told him that a second wagon train—he hoped the one Breanna was traveling with— had stopped at the site. Whatever survivors there were had been picked up.

Stranger kept Ebony moving at a fast pace. The horse was strong and durable and could run for hours.

Horse and rider neared the fork of the Green and Big Sandy River in late afternoon. Suddenly Ebony nickered and tossed his head, fighting the bit. Stranger knew his horse well. There was danger near, and Ebony sensed it.

"Okay, boy, what is it?"

Stranger's question was answered by the wild scream of a cougar. Ebony's eyes bulged as he danced nervously, looking straight ahead. Stranger sat astride the frightened horse, peering down the trail. The scream came again, high-pitched, then sliding low. Then he saw it. There was a man bound to a pine, and the lion was clawing him!

Stranger whipped his Winchester .44 repeater out of its saddleboot, worked the lever, and forced Ebony forward. The gelding was fearful, but obeyed his master. The cougar's attack continued as Stranger galloped toward the spot.

When he was within fifty yards, Stranger halted the horse, drew a bead, and fired. The big cat ejected a shrill cry and went down, writhing in pain. Stranger was out of the saddle, working the lever again. The cougar swished its tail, raised its head, and was struggling to rise when Stranger took careful aim and fired again. The slug killed the cat instantly.

Stranger ran to the tree and found the man still alive. It took him only seconds to see that it was Frank Miller. Miller's eyes were closed and he was moaning in anguish. His clothing was shredded and crimson-soaked. He had already lost a great deal of blood.

"Miller, can you hear me? It's John Stranger."

Frank Miller opened his eyes and blinked against the blood that flowed into them from his lacerated scalp and forehead. "Stranger? John Stranger?"

"Yes. I'll get a knife from my saddlebag and cut you loose. You hold on."

"No! Wait! There...there isn't time. Stranger, when you...when you see Breanna, tell her...tell her I was wrong. I know she tried to save Lorraine. Tell her, please."

"Yes, I'll tell her."

Miller licked his lips. "And please...tell her I'm sorry. For everything."

"I will," Stranger assured him.

Frank's eyes closed and his head fell forward, never to move again. Stranger cut the body loose and, for lack of a shovel, piled rocks on the body for a grave.

Then he mounted his horse and put it to a gallop. With the wind in his face, he breathed a prayer for Breanna's safety.

23

↑

The last fiery rays of the sun were turning the rugged land a golden purple as Rip Clayson and the people of the wagon train waited among the trees for the cavalry. Clayson had stationed Bud Harbison near the trail to flag them down and guide them to the wagons when they came along.

The dread of another Snake attack was on everyone. Their chances of survival were plenty slim. The Indians would have guns. They would have only knives and clubs. Surely Colonel Wade Moore had made it to Fort Bridger. The cavalry *must* come.

Rip and Carolyne stayed close to each other, with little Breanna in Carolyne's arms. As the sun dropped lower, Rip said, "I know of some rich ranch land over in Jackson Hole. When the Lord sees us through this and we make it to California, we'll get married, then come back to Wyoming and go to ranching. How's that sound?"

"Sounds wonderful to me," she smiled. "And I can tell by the look in little Breanna's eyes that it sounds wonderful to her, too."

"Good! It's settled then. We'll—"

"Rip!" Curly Wesson yelled. "We got trouble! Look!"

Clayson followed Curly's crooked finger as it pointed to the rock formation where Breanna Baylor was hiding. Two dozen Snake Indians were slowly climbing the mound on the south side of the rock, heading for the natural staircase on its east side. In the lead was Red Claw.

Rip's blood ran cold. Somehow the Indians had seen him take Breanna up there!

"What can we do, Rip?" Chuck Fallon asked.

The wagon master turned, face white. "I can't ask any of you men to go with me, but I've got to do what I can to stop Red Claw from—"

Rip's words were cut off by the thunder of hooves as a lone rider rode into camp on a big black gelding.

"John Stranger!" Curly gasped. "What's *he* doin' here?"

Stranger slid quickly from the saddle. "Hello, Rip. The young man you have posted out by the trail told me you have Breanna Baylor in your train, and he told me about Red Claw's threat to take her. He said you've got her in a cave somewhere, and you're out of ammunition."

"Yes!" Clayson said, then pointed to the rock where Breanna was hiding and said, "Red Claw knows she's up there, and he's after her right now!"

Stranger took one look, then whirled and dashed for his horse. While he was mounting, Clayson quickly told him about the staircase and the single bullet Breanna had promised Rip she would use on herself rather than be taken by Red Claw.

Stranger's face blanched at Clayson's last words, and he gouged Ebony's sides, sending him into a gallop. Rip called after Stranger, offering to go with him, but Stranger was already into the forest and out of sight.

✦

Stranger peered upward through the treetops and saw the Indians rounding the base of the big rock, heading for the staircase. The one in the lead was in full headdress. *Red Claw.* Stranger's blood boiled at the thought of the Snake chieftain getting his hands on the woman he loved.

Through the trees, Stranger could see the Indian ponies clustered in a small open area, waiting for their riders to return. He drew rein, slid from the saddle, and pulled the Winchester from its boot. Just as he was about to bolt toward the staircase himself, he looked up and saw Breanna standing at the mouth of the cave. She was watching the Indians climb toward her. Stranger knew there was no way she could see him for the trees. Then she suddenly ducked out of sight.

Just as suddenly, the sound of a bugle cut the air. The cavalry was here!

John Stranger did not know they were coming a hundred strong, but the Snakes took one look at the unit thundering in and made a quick pivot. They bounded down the staircase, heading for their horses as fast as they could run. Some stumbled and fell, picked themselves up, and hurried on.

Stranger looked again toward the cave. Breanna was still not in sight, but Red Claw's desire for her drove him upward. The sound of the bugle did not slow him.

Stranger bolted for the staircase even though the painted warriors were still coming down it. He was within fifty feet of it when the last of the Snakes bounded down the sod base, racing for their pintos. Some were already mounted and galloping away.

John Stranger's heart was in his throat as he reached the staircase and started climbing. He caught a glimpse of Red Claw above him as the chief reached the top and ran toward the cave. A breathless "No-o-o!" escaped his lips. He took the crude stone steps two and three at a time, his heart hammering in his chest.

And then it came.

The loud report of the Derringer slapped the air and echoed like thunder out of the cave and across the rocky, wooded land.

John Stranger stopped. He went cold inside. Breathing the name of the woman he loved, he resumed his charge upward. When he reached the top of the rock stairs, his eyes widened and his scalp tingled at what he beheld near the mouth of the cave.

Red Claw lay flat on his back, his sightless eyes staring vacantly into space. The feathers of his headdress were twisted and crumpled under his lifeless form. A blue hole centered his chest, fringed with blood.

Quickly Stranger's eyes lifted to the face of Breanna Baylor, who was leaning against the back wall of the cave, her cheeks shining with tears. She held the Derringer loosely in her right hand.

At the sight of the tall man silhouetted against the purple sky, she let the weapon slip through her fingers and clatter onto the rock floor.

Breanna found her voice and gasped, "John! Oh, John!"

John Stranger gathered Breanna in his arms, his own eyes swimming with tears. The sound of pounding hooves and barking rifles filtered into the cave, broken by another shrill blast of a bugle. The cavalry had the Snakes on the run.

"Sorry I was late this time," John said, blinking against his tears and smiling into Breanna's eyes.

"I saw the other Indians heading back down the side of the rock," Breanna said. "There was nothing I could do but put my bullet in him."

John cupped one hand under her graceful chin and said, "The Lord's timing is always perfect. That never was *your* bullet. It was meant for Red Claw all the time."

Suddenly it was as though they were in front of the cabin porch in the foothills of the Rockies. Gone was the terror she had known only moments before. Gone was the sound of thundering hooves, barking rifles, and a blasting bugle. This moment seemed to be happening in a silent, far-away world out of the realm of time.

Words long pent-up burst from Breanna's lips, tumbling one on top of the other. "Oh, John! I love you, I love you! I made such a horrible mistake that day in Wichita when I sent you out of my life. I knew it before you were even out of sight, but it was too late. Please forgive me, John! Oh, I've prayed so long and so hard that the Lord would bring you to me so I could tell you how sorry I am and how very much I love you! I've been so—"

John's forefinger was on her lips. "Hush, darling. You don't have to do this. All that matters is that I know you love me as I love you...that we can have each other. There's nothing to forgive."

John lowered his face toward hers. Breanna closed her eyes as his arms tightened around her. Tenderly he kissed her eyelids, then placed a soft, loving kiss on her lips. When their lips parted, John held her close.

This time, it was no dream.

OTHER COMPELLING STORIES BY
AL LACY

Books in the Battles of Destiny series:

☛ *A Promise Unbroken*

Two couples battle jealousy and racial hatred amidst a war that would cripple America. From a prosperous Virginia plantation to a grim jail cell outside Lynchburg, follow the dramatic story of a love that could not be destroyed.

☛ *A Heart Divided*

Ryan McGraw—leader of the Confederate Sharpshooters—is nursed back to health by beautiful army nurse Dixie Quade. Their romance would survive the perils of war, but can it withstand the reappearance of a past love?

☛ *Beloved Enemy*

Young Jenny Jordan covers for her father's Confederate spy missions. But as she grows closer to Union soldier Buck Brownell, Jenny finds herself torn between devotion to the South and her feelings for the man she is forbidden to love.

☛ *Shadowed Memories*

Critically wounded on the field of battle and haunted by amnesia, one man struggles to regain his strength and the memories that have slipped away from him.

☛ *Joy from Ashes*

Major Layne Dalton made it through the horrors of the battle of Fredericksburg, but can he rise above his hatred toward the Heglund brothers who brutalized his wife and killed his unborn son?

Books in the Journeys of the Stranger series:

☞ *Legacy*

Can John Stranger, a mysterious hero who brings truth, honor, and justice to the Old West, bring Clay Austin back to the right side of the law...and restore the code of honor shared by the woman he loves?

☞ *Silent Abduction*

The mysterious man in black fights to defend a small town targeted by cattle rustlers and to rescue a young woman and child held captive by a local Indian tribe.

☞ *Blizzard*

When three murderers slated for hanging escape from the Colorado Territorial Prison, young U.S. Marshal Ridge Holloway and the mysterious John Stranger join together to track down the infamous convicts.

Available at your local Christian bookstore